AGRICULTURAL DEVELOPMENT AND EMPLOYMENT PATTERNS IN INDIA

ABOUT THE AUTHOR

DR. M.R. KHURANA (*b.* 1951) is on the faculty of the Department of Economics, Panjab University, Chandigarh. He holds a Master's Degree from the Panjab University and a Ph.D. in Economics from the Jawaharlal Nehru University, New Delhi. A specialist in the Human Resources Development, he is currently engaged in research in the area of Rural Development.

Agricultural Development AND Employment Patterns IN India

A Comparative Analysis of Punjab and Bihar

M.R. KHURANA
Department of Economics, Panjab University
Chandigarh

Foreword by

G.K. CHADHA
Visiting Fellow, IDS, University of Sussex
Brighton, England

CONCEPT PUBLISHING COMPANY, NEW DELHI 110059

The Indian Council of Social Science Research gave the financial support towards the publication of this work. However, the responsibility for the contents of the book — facts, opinions, conclusions, etc. — is entirely that of the author and not of the ICSSR.

ICSSR Consultant : **Dr. R.P. Sinha**

ISBN 81-7022-439-X

First Published 1992

Published and Printed by
Ashok Kumar Mittal
Concept Publishing Company
A/15-16, Commercial Block, Mohan Garden
NEW DELHI 110059 (India)

Lasertypeset by
Microtech Advance Printing Systems (Pvt.) Ltd.
H-13, Bali Nagar
NEW DELHI 110015

To

The millions of poor

in

India

FOREWORD

The impact of the green revolution technology on employment and earning capabilities of the rural labour households has been shared unevenly by different States of India. The present study examines the changing structure of employment, earnings and consumption of such households between two sharply contrasting economic situations. These are the States of Punjab and Bihar. The spectacular growth profile of Punjab agriculture and a sluggish-cum-fluctuating performance of the same in Bihar are, by now, too well known facts of the agrarian reality in India. The Punjab model clearly shows that rising agricultural production and productivity not only make a far-reaching impact on-farm and off-farm employment and income levels but also strengthens further the inter-sectoral linkages. To the rural labour households in Bihar, such employment and income gains are still a distant dream. In terms of sheer human labour, the Bihar households may be working equally hard yet in the final reckoning, their earning levels are deplorably low.

The study commends itself both for its systematic sample design as well as for the numerous findings emerging from a careful analysis of sample data. The sample consists of 600 households, 300 each from Punjab and Bihar, extending over 8 villages in either case. In addition, 150 migrant labourers were also surveyed in Punjab. The sample villages were carefully selected at varying distances from a designated focal town so that a number of hypotheses bearing on rural-urban interactions could be meaningfully tested, both quantitatively and qualitatively.

The Punjab-Bihar contrasts come up quite succinctly. The author has taken great pains to cover all possible aspects of employment and earnings besides looking deep into the living standards and consumption patterns of sample households in the two States. The findings on farm: non-farm earning gaps, widely differing saving potentials, contrasting behaviour of consumption elasticities, especially for consumer durables and human capital-promoting items, need to be underlined for their policy significance. The woeful inadequacy of earning levels in the interior of Bihar countryside stands out in bold relief. The contrasting poverty scenario follow in natural course. The division of sample households into two categories – predominantly agricultural labour households and predominantly non-agricultural labour households – throw up clear signals about strong farm: non-farm linkages in the Punjab and a distress pursuit of non-farm activities in Bihar. Again, the contrasting position between attached versus daily-wage earning hands is brought out quite convincingly. Yet another useful set of insights comes through comparing the migrant labour with resident labour, especially in the matter of agricultural wage rate for comparable field-crop operations. In brief, the study throws up a rich crop of useful insights on the economic conditions of non-cultivating rural labour households in the two contrasting areas. It is a good study that brings out the interplay between technology and agrarian institutions into bold relief. The structural weaknesses of the Bihar situation are pointed out quite boldly and an equally bold package of policy recommendations is handed over to the policy administrator. The author readily convinces the reader of his conscientious research efforts: meticulous care in handling field data, full understanding of concepts and variables used, intelligent interpretation of contrasting results including the use of a few statistical techniques, and so on. He deserves a pat for all this.

The book is recommended to all those who are interested in India's rural development in general and in economic conditions of the landless labour households in particular.

January 14, 1992

G.K. CHADHA
Visiting Fellow
IDS, University of Sussex
Brighton, England

PREFACE

The present study attempts to examine the changing structure of employment of the non-cultivating labour households in rural India. More specifically, it seeks to examine the employment pattern and the corresponding levels of income and consumption of such labour households in the selected areas of Punjab and Bihar. The basic objective is to understand, on the one hand, the internal dynamics of rural transformation, and the impact of newly cropping up interaction between this internal dynamics and the growing rural-urban linkages on the employment structure of the rural labour households, on the other.

During the past 15-20 years, remarkable changes have occurred in the production technology in Indian agriculture. It is now widely believed that under the spurt of this technological breakthrough, not only that agricultural production and productivity have registered fairly sizeable increases, but the structure of rural employment has also so changed that the relative importance of non-farm activities has steadily grown over the years. Consequently, the quantum of total yearly employment and its components as also the earnings accruing to the non-cultivating rural labour households from various employment avenues are believed to have changed substantially.

Depending upon the irrigation base, infrastructural facilities and institutional framework, the new farm technology has been adopted by different areas in varying proportions. Consequently, the impact of the new farm technology on agricultural production and productivity as also on the rural employment structure has differed from one area to another. It is now widely acknowledged that States such as the Punjab and Haryana have experienced the most profound impact of the new technology, whereas States such as Bihar and Orissa have generally lagged behind. This, however, should not be construed to mean that the whole of Punjab has experienced the same degree of the impact and the whole of Bihar has remained devoid of it. There are some pockets of Punjab such as the sub-mountainous terrain in districts of Hoshiarpur, Ropar and Gurdaspur which are still far behind while in Bihar, districts such as Bhojpur, Rohtas and Nalanda are substantially ahead of others, in the matter of their respective agricultural development.

Another important feature connected with the changing agrarian conditions in India has been the emergence of strong rural-urban linkages over the years due to the expanding inter-sectoral exchanges both on demand and supply sides. These linkages are increasingly facilitated by a growing network of village link roads. Although the physical distance from a nearby marketing and/or industrial town still remains an important constraint on the mobility of men and material, yet the rural-urban linkages have grown substantially over the years and with them have changed the employment pattern and the corresponding levels of income and consumption of the rural population. For example, while some of the old activities have tended to disappear gradually over the years, some others have expanded fast and some new ones have emerged as important sources of employment and earnings for the rural labour households. Further, some of the rural households are getting increasingly linked with the nearby sub-urban and urban towns for the purpose of their employment and earnings, depending upon the level of general development of the area and the availability of infrastructural facilities. In brief, the structure of total yearly employment/earnings of the rural labour households has undergone sizeable changes. The degree of change has varied with the rate of growth of agricultural output on the one hand, and, the possibilities of non-farm employments opening up in rural as well as nearby urban areas, on the other. The extent to which the rural labour households have been able to avail themselves of the non-farm avenues of employment in the nearby urban marketing and/or industrial town has, in turn, depended upon the availability of such employment opportunities on the one hand, and, daily commutability of the working people from their native villages to urban centres of employment, on the other. The prime mover has undoubtedly been the sheer availability of highly lucrative non-farm employment.

It needs to be pointed out that in the wake of the Green Revolution in India, many studies have been conducted by various researchers. In most such studies, an attempt has been made to examine the impact of new farm technology or its specific components on input-output relationship for technology adopters and non-adopters, possibilities of capital formation, employment levels and wage rates, levels of living of different strata of the rural population etc. Some scholars have also sought to investigate farm size-wise gains of the new agricultural technology. In brief, most studies on the impact of the Green Revolution have focused on the production performance, distribution of production gains between different strata of farmers, between surplus and deficit regions, and so on. But if viewed carefully, most of such studies not only pertain to the early years of the Green Revolution but also have had a limited scope of enquiry. For example, those dealing with production effects did not attempt to go into the question of income distribution and those concerned with the later did not generally examine the closely related but crucial aspects of household consumption, savings and so on. Similarly, the scholars dealing with the problem of rural employment have not gone far enough to examine adequately the consumption pattern of those who constitute the lowest rung of the rural society's socio-economic ladder. This implies that these households have continuously been neglected not only by the policy-makers but also by the academicians, a few exceptions notwithstanding. For instance, the institutional and technological changes have almost exclusively been directed towards the farming sector. Concentration of attention towards the farming sector may have its own justification in that the increased agricultural production has been one of the most urgent and major concerns for the country. However, keeping in view the fact that the non-cultivating rural labour households form an integral part of the rural community, both in terms of the size of their population and their involvement in socio-economic activities they should not have been bypassed by researchers. Again, with repeated stress on production and productivity breakthroughs in policy pronouncements and piles of research material thrown up since the arrival of the new production technology, one may be led to believe that an expansion of employment opportunities for these households has not been a prime objective of the Green Revolution. Consequently, one does not know much about the impact of the internal dynamics of rural transformation on the structure of rural employment and the corresponding levels of income and consumption of such households. It can, therefore, be maintained that even though the studies conducted so far do provide a very useful insight into some special aspects, yet they can at best be regarded as disjointed bits. And, as such they do not adequately analyse the changing agrarian reality in areas of high agricultural growth contrasted with that in areas of low growth. Besides, the issues pertaining to the employment pattern of the migrant labour, an important phenomenon of Punjab agriculture, have not attracted much serious research.

From the above, one may easily presume that a systematic and coherent empirical attempt to examine simultaneously the employment-income-consumption nexus of the non-cultivating rural labour households as also the employment pattern of labour seasonally migrating to Punjab is still wanting. It points to a research gap. Based upon a survey of a cross-section of 300 such households from each of the two States of Punjab and Bihar and another 150 migrant agricultural labourers from the sample villages of the former, the present study seeks to fill a part of this research gap. A concrete claim that the present study can make is that with a fairly large sample information gathered over quite a few months, it is the first major attempt by an individual research worker to capture the impact of the newly growing above-mentioned interaction on the employment-income-consumption nexus of the rural labour households of Punjab and Bihar. More specifically, among other things, the questions to which we address ourselves are:

What is the incidence of occupational diversification, its inception as also the factors accounting for it? What are the variations in the overall as well as village-wise pattern of on, non- and total yearly employment/earnings of the rural labour households between Punjab and Bihar? Does the composition of different sources of on-, non- and total yearly employment/earnings in Punjab reveal a pattern distinct than that in Bihar? If so, the nature and extent of these differences? Do labour households in Punjab earn more in terms of per household and per day of employment? Does the differential pattern of total yearly earnings/income between Punjab and Bihar also transmit itself in the consumption pattern or the levels of living of the rural labour households? Have the gains of rapid economic growth in general and agricultural transformation in particular percolated more in Punjab than in Bihar? What are the socio- economic characteristics as also the areas of outmigration of the migrant agricultural labourers in Punjab? What proportion of the year-round employment/earnings in agriculture is enjoyed separately by the resident labour and the migrant labour in rural Punjab? And finally, what are the pull and push factors responsible for inmigration/outmigration?

Concrete empirical answers to the numerous questions posed above should throw adequate light on as to how rural labour households have fared in the total process of socio-economic development witnessed in recent years in varying form and content in different areas of India.

The study is based on the results of my doctoral thesis submitted earlier to Jawaharlal Nehru University, New Delhi. The publication of the study has taken a rather long time due to several personal factors and procedural difficulties. The delay is earnestly regretted.

For whatever academic merit the present study may possess in answering the aforementioned and other related questions, I am indebted beyond measure to my most esteemed Supervisor, Professor G.K. Chadha for his scholastic and inspiring directional guidance, searching criticisms, competent suggestions, constant inspiration and above all for acceding to my request for writing and mailing the Foreword to this book from the IDS, University of Sussex, Brighton, England. Mrs Suneeta Chadha, like an elder sister, has been helping me time and again in meeting various domestic exigencies. I gratefully acknowledge my deep sense of obligation to both of them knowing fully well that mere words of gratitude are by no means the appropriate coins to repay the greatest debt I owe to them.

My personal appreciation and acknowledgments are also due to many people who have helped me in completing this study at one stage or the other. In this regard, I gratefully acknowledge my deep sense of obligation to Prof. G.S. Bhalla, Prof. Ashok Mathur, Prof. Kusum Chopra, Dr. M.H. Qureshi, Dr. R.K. Sharma and other faculty members of the Centre for the Study of Regional Development for their co-operation and invaluable advice in several ways. I would like to record a special debt of gratitude to Mr. V. Muralidhar for his generous and willing help in data processing. My occasional discussions with Mr. P.N. Dhar, Formerly Deputy Director, N.S.S.O., New Delhi and Dr. Gopal Krishan, Prof. of Geography at the Panjab University, Chandigarh, have been extremely stimulating and highly useful. I pay my sincere tributes to both of them.

I shall be failing in my duty if I don't gratefully acknowledge the affectionate encouraging, I have always been receiving from Prof. V.K. Gupta Prof. H.S. Shergill and Sh. S.N. Ahuja of the

Department of Economics, Panjab University, Chandigarh and also from Sh. R.P. Sharma, Sh. R.D. Sharma, Sh. T.R. Bahia, S. Darshan Singh and Dr. A.S. Mann of A.S. College, Khanna. However, no words are enough to express my gratitude to my most reverred teacher late Principal J.N. Sharma of A.S. College, Khanna for helping me to reach this stage in my academic life. I must at the same time place on record the considerable help rendered by a large number of my students in the listing as well as identification of the selected sample households in the study area of Punjab. In Bihar, I was assisted by a number of new friends in this process. Although, it is not possible to name each and every individual in this regard, yet I would always remember the help and co-operation extended to me by Mr. Bhogendra Jha, the then B.D.O., Itarhi, Mr. Lal Bihari Singh of B.D.O. Office, Buxar, Mr. Ram Singhasan Singh, Mr. Avadhesh Singh, Mr. Anil Kumar, Mr. Surender Singh, Mr. Doodh Nath Harijan and Mr. Ramraj Singh in the process of data collection. Over and above, I would like to thank my sample households in the two study areas for their meticulous patience in parting with the information used for this study.

I am especially indebted to my friends Dr. Kulwant Singh, Joint Director, ISTM, New Delhi, Dr. H.S. Sidhu, Reader in Economics at the Guru Nanak Dev University, Amritsar, Dr. D.M. Diwakar currently at the Centre for Water Resources Studies, Patna University, Patna and Mr. S.D. Saha of A.S. College, Khanna whose useful suggestions have been of immense help at many a time. I feel obliged to the members of the staff of the libraries of Jawaharlal Nehru University, Planning Commission, Indian Council of Social Science Research, Central Statistical Organisation, National Sample Survey Organisation and Krishi Bhawan, New Delhi, for their readiness to meet my frequent requests for research material.

Finally, I wish to express my appreciation for my wife, Swarn, who with her formidable fortitude and matchless tolerance, not only rode out the frequent pockets of turbulence of domestic upheavals but also did not let my sons Ajay, Amit and Anjan feel my absence.

Though, I deem it a privilege to acknowledge the assistance I have received from all the above-mentioned quarters, yet needless to say, the responsibilities for errors of fact and judgement are mine alone.

M.R. KHURANA

CONTENTS

LIST OF TABLES AND FIGURES

APPENDIX TABLES

FIGURE

1

THE OBJECTIVE AND THE SCOPE

Although a vigorous clamour for the development of non-farm sector as a policy alternative has been witnessed in India in the recent years, yet the Indian economy continues to be predominantly an agricultural economy. And despite rapid strides observed in the growth of secondary and tertiary sectors, agriculture still seems to be ruling the roost in India. It continues to occupy a place of prime importance in the overall economy in several of its important manifestations. Firstly, not only that around two-thirds[1] of the country's existing workforce ekes out its subsistence in this sector directly, but also a vast majority of the would-be entrants to the labour force to be brought about by the persisting demographic pressures in the decades to come, will continue to gain their livelihood in this sector. Furthermore, in view of its exceedingly slow pace in the matter of employment generation in the rural as well as in the urban areas, the non-agricultural sector in India has not much to commend itself, as yet. As such, there does not seem to be any escape from agricultural employment for the vast majority of our rural population in the near future. In sum, contrary to our policy objectives, larger and larger number of people are expected to fall back upon the agricultural sector for want of adequate alternative employment opportunities. Secondly, although the relative share of agriculture and other allied activities in Gross Domestic Product as well as in our annual export earnings has considerably declined over the past couple of years, yet the observed behaviour is not in any way inconsistent with the pattern of a growing economy. Moreover, in absolute terms, while Gross Domestic Product at Factor Cost (at 1980-81 prices) as originating from the above mentioned activities, has more than doubled[2] between 1960-61 and 1989-90; our annual export earnings from the same have got multiplied by as many as 17 times[3] during this period. This testifies to the fact that in both these respects, agriculture still plays an important role. Finally, and even more importantly, there is a very intimate connection and interaction between agricultural growth and overall economic development. This is due to the fact that in the course of its own growth process, it tends to forge highly significant inter-sectoral linkages[4] with the non-farm sector, which, in turn, have an important bearing for overall economic development. For instance, besides supplying raw material for quite a number of industries in the non-farm sector, it creates demand for the products of the latter. Moreover, it has been held in some academic circles that it is in this sector that the battle for long-term economic development in South Asia (including India) will be won or lost.[5] As such, quite expectedly, any change taking place in this sector is bound to influence the life of a large number of people as well as the economy as a whole. It is not surprising therefore that the programmes of agricultural development have been emphasized through various Five Year Plans during the post-independence planning era.

British Regime and the Indian Economy

In passing, it is important to note that on the morrow of independence, India economy was in shambles. The economic consequences of the British rule in India were, in fact, quite disastrous. This was mainly due to the rapacious colonial exploitation which the British imperialists carried out clandestinely by pursuing various measures since the dawn of the East India Company in 1599 A.D. The 'suction mechanism' as perpetuated by the then British masters due to their ingrained vested interest, virtually led to overall economic ruin of the Indian economy. The agricultural sector was the worst hit in this regard. It was in a precarious state and exhibited an amalgum of acute backwardness and stagnation. It was characterised by low land and labour productivity, growing rural proletarinisation and pauperisation of the peasantry due to skewed distribution of land, underutilisation of labour and other resources, huge food deficits, etc. The natural fall out of the Britishers' callous attitude towards Indian agriculture was that during the entire period of first-half of the twentieth century, the recorded annual growth of the agricultural sector was as meagre as 0.8 per cent[6] only. Moreover, the foodgrains output remained stagnant during this period. In sum, the Indian economy on the eve of independence presented a spectacle of abject economic deprivation and untold sufferings of the masses with few contemporary parallels.[7] And in partition of the country in 1947, the already slogging Indian economy received yet another severe blow from its erstwhile British masters.

New Farm Technology in Rural India

Needless to say that confronted with socio-economic conditions of precarious existence for a vast majority of the Indian people, the pressing concern of the planners and policy-makers in India was, therefore, to embark upon such strategies of development as could help the country in attaining economic growth with social justice. Thus, awakened by political resurgence that swept many contemporary Asian and African countries during the post-Second World War period, guided solely by the objective of national regeneration and emboldened by the now defunct Russian experience, the planning process got initiated in India in 1951 with the launching of the First Five Year Plan. Since then, the country has experienced nearly four decades of planning. Consequently, contrary to what has been observed regarding the shocking immiserisation of the Indian masses before independence as also judged against the innate complexities of the process of economic development, the progress of the Indian economy, ever since the inception of planning, has been, by no means, a mean achievement. During the period of planned economic development in general, and since the mid-sixties in particular, thanks to the onset of the Green Revolution in Indian agriculture, the rural economy in India has experienced remarkable changes. Such spectacular changes in the farm sector in India have taken place mainly because of the introduction of the new production technology. The new production technology consists of a highly complementary package of biochemical as well as mechanical innovations.[8] While the former comprises irrigation-seed-fertilizer package, pest and disease control measures, etc., tractor, thresher, harvester, tubewell and other mechanical equipments and the like are included in the latter. Available evidence suggests that with a given land base, the said two components of the new farm technology have a differential impact on the timeliness and scale of field crop operations, soil structure, plants, animals, labour-absorption,[9] composition of costs on different farm sizes,[10] and so forth.

Under the spurt of this technological breakthrough, while on the one hand, agricultural production and productivity have registered fairly big increases, on the other, factor proportions and their relative shares have also undergone a tremendous change.[11] A characteristic feature of the Indian agricultural growth experience since the mid-sixties has been that depending upon the irrigation base, infrastructural facilities and institutional framework, the new technology has been adopted by different areas in varying proportions. Consequently, the impact of the new farm technology on agricultural production and productivity as also on the rural employment structure has differed from area to area.

It is now widely acknowledged that States such as the Punjab and Haryana have experienced the most profound impact of the new farm technology, whereas States such as Bihar and Orissa have generally lagged behind. This, however, should not be construed to mean that the whole of Punjab has experienced the same degree of the impact and the whole of Bihar has remained devoid of it. There are pockets of Punjab such as the sub-mountainous terrain of districts Gurdaspur, Hoshiarpur and Ropar which are relatively much less developed than others, while in Bihar, Districts such as Nalanda, Bhojpur and Rohtas are substantially ahead of others in the matter of agricultural development.

The induction of the new farm technology has initiated a process of qualitative rural transformation. This is characterised by changes in the socio-economic outlook and attitudes of the different sections of the rural community. These changes have occurred in a manner that economic values are becoming increasingly dominant over social values. In the areas of the Green Revolution, caste which once used to be the most dominant institution of the rural society is losing its influence, and caste-based obligations are now given relatively less recognition in the economic life of the rural people compared to the pre-Green Revolution era. Caste rigidities are breaking. The traditional 'Jajmani' system, which had been regulating the socio-economic life of the rural people since long, is gradually being replaced by formal contractual relations.[12] Consequently, caste-based occupational classification is gradually disappearing. Low caste people are moving out of their ancestral occupations in search of better economic professions. Inter-generational and intra-generational occupational mobility seems to be increasing at a faster rate.[13] The people in the countryside are becoming more and more receptive to new ideas, attitudes and values. In brief, the economic, social and institutional set-up of the village economy is undergoing important changes.

Under the impact of the technological change, the factor proportions in agriculture have changed substantially. So have changed the structure and the level of employment. While on the one hand, the relative importance of the non-farm activities partially inspired by the agricultural expansion itself, seems to have grown steadily over the years; the locale of some of these activities has also shifted from the rural to the nearby urban and sub-urban areas, on the other. Consequently, lots of non-farm activities are gradually disappearing from the villages. However, simultaneously some other activities are expanding fast. Besides, some new activities are also emerging as the important sources of employment and income to the non-cultivating rural labour households. Still further, some of these households are gaining employment in the nearby sub-urban and urban towns. In brief, in areas of the Green Revolution, these households have started enjoying multiple sources of employment and income. In the changing conditions, some working members of such households are employed as wage labourers inside agriculture; some others are also employed in non-agricultural activities in the rural as well as in the nearby urban areas. Employment in the nearby urban centres has been opened up to them because of expanding industrial and commercial activities and facilitated by an expanding network of village link roads. Although physical distance from the town still remains an important constraint, yet the growing network of village link roads and consequently the increasing urban contact, coupled with the internal dynamics of rural transformation, have an important bearing on the changing employment structure of the rural labour households.

Empirical Evidence on New Farm Technology

Recent years have witnessed a spate of research contributions by the Indian as well as foreign research workers to the study of the new technology. It is, however, a pity that very few studies regarding the impact of agricultural growth and rural transformation on rural labour households have appeared so far.[14] Most studies on the impact of the Green Revolution have focused on production performance, distribution of production gains between small and large farms, between surplus and deficit regions, and so on. At best, the category of the landless labour households has figured only marginally, say, in terms of the impact of tractorisation on labour employment, real wage behaviour, cropwise labour use, etc. Comprehensive studies on the total household economy of this category of rural workers have been rather exceptional. Perhaps, the preoccupation of researchers and policy administrators with agricultural production and problems connected with the Green Revolution was due to the fact that in the wake of the introduction of the new farm technology, a large number of economic issues have come up. These issues are of diverse variety. As the process of technological transformation of Indian agriculture was initiated with the introduction of the IADP in the early sixties, some researchers examined critically the achievements of the programme in terms of its objectives of increase in yield levels and the volume of foodgrains production. The broad finding about the programme was that it did not succeed much either as a 'path finder' or as a 'pace setter'. It did not make an immediate impact on output at the national level. It was found that the production increase in IADP districts was non-significant and this experiment did not virtually make any perceptible dent on India's agricultural economy.[15]

Next, while a fiercer controversy has centred around the farm-size productivity relationship,[16] some studies have explored extensively the input-output relationship under the old and the new technology for different strata of farmers.[17] Some research workers while attempting to investigate the input cost and the composition of cost for adopters and the non-adopters of the new technology have highlighted its social and economic implications.[18] Still others have sought to look into the possibilities of capital formation in agriculture under the impact of the new farm technology.[19] Some studies also deal with the institutional finance and co-operative credit in the light of the rising requirements of the new agricultural technology.[20] Some researchers have also attempted to highlight the role of 'semi-feudal' production relations and other institutional bottlenecks as a barrier to agricultural development.[21] A lively debate on the emergence of capitalism and the mode of production in Indian agriculture has also ensued following the onset of the Green Revolution.[22] It is, however, a different matter that it has enmeshed itself only into an abstract conceptual controversy.

Further, empirical studies on the pattern of distribution of gains of the improved farm technology have also swelled in number. Some Indian scholars have found that the distribution of production gains of the new agricultural technology has been highly skewed. In particular, the production gains accruing from new investments following the adoption of the new agricultural technology, especially for tubewell installations and irrigation channels, the distribution of seeds and fertilizers, etc. have tilted heavily in favour of the big land operators. Consequently, the weaker sections of the society of which the small farmers and the landless labourers constitute a fairly large multitude, have generally remained devoid of such gains.[23] In a sense, they have viewed the perpetuation of rural poverty and economic destitution as an off-shoot of the Green Revolution. Such views have gained further support from some foreign observers of India's Green Revolution who maintain that a host of social and political problems such as social polarisation, class conflict and social tensions due to growing inequality have emerged much more quickly than anticipated in the areas of the Green Revolution. On the basis of impressions gathered hastily via their talks with officials and non-officials and also during short trips to some areas of the Green Revolution, some foreign scholars feared the 'Green Revolution' turning into 'Red'.[24] Their pessimism is based upon apprehensions arising out of deteriorating employment prospects of the weaker sections under the impact of rising mechanisation, growing regional disparities with irrigated areas progressing steadily and the unirrigated areas lagging behind and the strengthening of socio-economic and political power of the rich peasants in the rural areas, and so on. Some scholars of this genre have anticipated the emergence of the 'generations of problems' consequent upon the arrival of the Green Revolution, perhaps basing their analyses in the vein of historical consequences of all major technological changes occurring from time to time.[25]

The other set of studies strike an optimistic note. Such studies concede that although the gains have been unevenly distributed, yet in absolute terms, all groups have registered some gains from the introduction of the new agricultural technology.[26] Consequently the view that the gains of the new farm technology have tilted in favour of the big farmers alone does not either exist or has been exaggerated by the critics. Their main conclusion is that the advent of the new farm technology has made a perceptible dent both on the absolute poverty as well as is intensity. By implication, these studies refute the impression that the new farm technology tends to accentuate poverty and leads to immiserization of peasantry. It is held in many quarters that the new farm technology has helped on reduce the relative income inequality among the adopting sub-sets.[27] However, some scholars while not ruling out altogether the possibility of future agricultural unrest, conclude that symptoms of the rise of dual economy were not discernible in the areas.[28] And moreover, there is not enough empirical substance either for the growing rural tensions or to the view that such tensions have mainly originated from the introduction of the new agricultural technology.[29] Some scholars mildly concede these problems which according to them are of minor nature only. While accepting growth as the main objective, they have advocated that resources must be placed at the disposal of the large farmers to secure maximum growth. Widening inequalities in the same region can be taken care of later by appropriate fiscal and redistribution measures.[30]

The pattern of spatial distribution of production gains of the new farm technology also forms the subject matter of recent research. In such works, it has been observed that the pattern and the intensity of adoption of the new technology and the resultant gains are unevenly distributed among different regions[31] of the country and also between different districts within a state. Besides, the impact of the new technology on the levels of living of adopters and non-adopters, wage rates,[32] levels of living and poverty of agricultural labourers,[33] the participation of female labour,[34] the employment opportunities outside agriculture, tenancy and changes in land relations,[35] etc. has also been explored by a number of researchers. A few research workers have also investigated the impact of the new farm technology on farm employment[36] as also productivity levels of major crops.

It needs to be pointed out here that most such studies relate to the early years of the Green Revolution. Moreover, each individual study has had only a limited scope of inquiry. For example, studies dealing with the production effects did not attempt to go into the question of income distribution and those concerned with the later did not generally examine the closely related but crucial aspects of household consumption, savings and so on. Similarly, the scholars dealing with the problem of rural unemployment have not gone farther to examine adequately the consumption patterns of those who belong to the lower strata of the rural hierarchy. In plain words, most literature dealing with the Green Revolution and the consequent agricultural development does not attempt specification of the household economy in terms of the employment — income — consumption nexus of the rural labour households. Not only this, in some of the studies, the conclusions have been derived just by referring to historical parallels (as in the case of Byres). Consequently, in the absence of enough empirical substance, the conclusions reached in such studies tend to be borne out of casual observations. Further, some other studies are based on unduly small sample coverage, and some of them suffer from technical inadequacies as well.

The foregoing discussion shows that most studies on the impact of Green Revolution have generally bypassed the rural labour households in a manner as if most of them constitute only a fractional cost of a farm operation and not an integral part of the rural economy. This neglect might have been based on the presumption that since rural agricultural sector continues to provide employment opportunities to ensure a minimum subsistence level, most such households seek employment somewhere within the agricultural sector itself. In a sense, these households have continuously been neglected not only by the policy makers but also by the academicians, a few exceptions notwithstanding. For instance, the institutional and technological changes have been directed largely towards the cultivating households. The exclusive pre-occupation of researchers as well as policy administrators with the cultivating households may have its own justification, presumably because increased agricultural production has been one of the most urgent and major concerns for the country. But keeping in view the fact that the rural labour households form an integral part of the rural community both in terms of the size of their population as well as their participation in various socio-economic activities, they should not have been ignored. Though some reforms are claimed to have been exclusively designed for the economic betterment of such households, yet their half-hearted implementation has rendered them almost a paper exercise only. Furthermore, the expansion in employment opportunities of these households has not been a prime objective of the Green Revolution. Consequently, one does not know much about the impact of the internal dynamics of rural transformation on the household economy of such households. It is, nevertheless, important to note that the role of employment generation as a policy instrument in the strategy of development planning in the times to come, is being increasingly recognised. In fact, there has been a growing realisation that proper utilisation of the vast mass of unemployed and underemployed labour is the "only effective way for the fulfilment of the major objectives of development planning, namely, elimination of poverty, reduction in equality and sustenance of a reasonable rate of economic growth".[37]

Further, over the past 15-20 years, a new phenomenon of great significance has emerged inside the Punjab agriculture. In seasons of wheat harvesting, rice transplantation and rice harvesting, a large number of agricultural labourers migrate into Punjab from other states. This is mainly due to certain pull and push factors, operating simultaneously in the inmigrating as well as in the outmigrating states. Moreover, during the past 8-10 years, in terms of the number of migrants, a shift has taken place heavily in favour of Bihar against eastern Uttar Pradesh. Further, regardless of the reasons for this migration and its related aspects, it needs to be pointed out that the employment of this labour force has certainly many socio-economic implications for the inmigrating as well as outmigrating areas. Unluckily, this important phenomenon has not attracted adequate attention of researchers.[38] Consequently, issues pertaining to employment pattern of the migrant *vis-a-vis* local labour remain by and large unexplored.

The Present Study

The preceding discussion implies that a single systematic empirical attempt to examine the position of the rural labour households in the matter of employment, income and consumption as also the employment/earning pattern of the migrant labour in rural Punjab has yet to appear. Thus, there is a big research gap. The present study is a modest attempt to fill this gap. The study compares employment, income and consumption status of such households in Punjab with their counterparts in Bihar. Besides, an attempt is made to study the pattern of employment and earnings of the migrant labour in rural Punjab. The basic idea is to understand, on the one hand, the internal dynamics of the agricultural transformation, and the impact of the newly emerging interaction between this internal dynamics and the growing rural-urban linkages on the employment and earning structure of the rural labour households, on the other. The States of Punjab and Bihar, and the specific areas within the two States, have been chosen to provide both contrast and similarity. The sampling details are set out in Chapter 2.

The Study Seeks to Examine

1. The variations in the nature, composition and extent of on-farm as well as non-farm activities, in which rural labour households are engaged in the two states and to account for the factors that underlie such variations;
2. The quantitative significance of these activities as the source of employment and income to the households engaged in them;
3. The consumption pattern of such households in the selected areas;
4. The extent and intensity of poverty among the sample households in the two study areas;
5. Out of the year-round wage-paid on-farm employment/earnings in Punjab, the proportion that is enjoyed separately by the local labour and the migrant labour; and
6. If the migrant agricultural labour into rural Punjab outflows from the agriculturally developed/backward areas of Bihar.

The criterion adopted for the selection of the sample areas in the two States, a comparative profile of these areas, sample procedure as also the size of the sample are set out in Chapter 2. Chapter 3 describes the concepts and the variables used in the present study. Issues pertaining to the structure of on-farm employment/earnings between the resident labour of the two study areas are examined in Chapter 4. Chapter 5 compares the pattern of non-farm employment/earnings between the labour households of Punjab and Bihar. While Chapter 6 examines the pattern of total yearly employment/earnings, an attempt is also made here to look into the levels of net household income as also in the levels of poverty prevalent in the two study areas on the basis of per capita net household income. Chapter 7 examines some issues pertaining to the migrant labour as also its employment and earnings. Chapter 8 describes, in reasonable detail, the consumption pattern of the sample households in the two states. Finally, the main conclusions and a few policy recommendations are given in Chapter 9.

NOTES

1. Planning Commission (1990), *Employment : Past Trends and Prospects for 1990s,* Working Paper, Government of India, New Delhi, May, p. 3.
2. Ministry of Finance (1991), *Economic Survey 1990-91*, Economic Division, Government of India, p. S-5.
3. Ministry of Finance (1991), *Ibid.* pp. S-81 — S-83.
4. G.K. Chadha (1985), *Agricultural Growth and Rural Non-Farm Activities : An Analysis of Indian Experience,* Paper presented at the International Seminar on the Role of Rural Industries for National Development in the Asian Region, held at Korea Rural Economics Institute, Seoul, from April 22 to 25, 1985, p. 3.
5. Gunnar Myrdal (1968), *Asian Drama : An Enquiry Into the Poverty of Nations.* Vol. II, Allen Lane, The Penguin Press, London, See especially Ch. 26, p. 1241.
6. Raj Luxmi (1987), A Districtwise Analysis of Growth of Agricultural Production, Productivity and Area in Bihar. Paper presented in Alakh N. Sharma and Shaibal Gupta (ed.), *Bihar : Stagnation or Growth*, Spectrum Publishing House, Patna, Delhi, p. 139.
7. For a detailed discussion on the subject under consideration see R. Palme Dutt (1979 Rep) *India Today,* Manisha Granthalaya (P) Ltd., Calcutta. Also see A.I. Medovoy (1988), *The Indian Economy*, Progress Publishers, Moscow, see especially Ch. I — III, pp. 5-95.
8. C.H. Hanumantha Rao (1975), *Technological Change and Distribution of Gains in Indian Agriculture,* The Macmillan Company of India Limited, Delhi; G.K. Chadha (1979), *Production Gains of New Agricultural Technology,* Publication Bureau, Panjab University, Chandigarh, 1979, p. I; Master Hari Singh (1980), *Agricultural Workers' Struggle in Punjab,* People's Publishing House, New Delhi, p. 2; and L.N. Dutta (1982), "Relative Efficiency, Farm Size and Peasant Proprietorship : A Case Study of Ranchi District (Bihar)", *Indian Journal of Agricultural Economics,* Vol. XXXVII, No. 1, January-March, pp. 76-82.
9. Don, Kanel (1967), "Size of Farm and Economic Development", *Indian Journal of Agricultural Economics,* Vol. XXII, No. 2, April-June, pp. 26-44.
10. C.H. Hanumantha Rao (1975); *op. cit.* pp. 77-79.
11. For some important recent studies on the subject, see, The Indian Society of Agricultural Economics (1983); *Indian Journal of Agricultural Economics,* Vol. XXXVIII, No. 4, October-December, pp. 391-434.
12. B.K. Agarwala and P.C. Deb (1971), *Inter-generational Occupational Mobility in Ludhiana,* Punjab Agricultural University, Ludhiana.
13. M.P. Kaushal (1969), *Mechanisation of Agriculture and Community Relations*, Paper read at 10th All India Sociological Conference, Delhi.
14. One such study is, Harbans Singh (1991), *Agricultural Development and Rural Labour*, Concept Publishing Company, New Delhi.
15. D.K. Desai (1969), "Intensive Agricultural District Programme : Analysis of Results", *Economic and Political Weekly,* Vol. IV, No. 26, Review of Agriculture, June 28, pp. A83-A90. Also see Dorris D. Brown (1971), *Agricultural Development in India's Districts,* Harvard University Press, Massachusetts, Cambridge, p. 33.
16. The issue of 'farm-size and productivity relationship' has been extensively explored in the context of Indian agriculture by a large number of scholars.

A.K. Sen, Dipak Mazumdar, Morton Paglin, Ashok Rudra and G.S. Sahota are among the earlier batch of researchers examining the above mentioned issue. For more upto date discussion in this regard, please see, Krishna Bhardwaj (1974), "Notes on Farm Size and Productivity", *Economic and Political Weekly,* Vol. IX, No. 13, Review of Agriculture, March 30, pp. A11-A24; G.K. Chadha (1978), "Farm Size and Productivity Revisited : Some Notes from Recent Experience of Punjab", *Economic and Political Weekly,* Vol. XIII, No. 39, Review of Agriculture, September 30, pp. A87-A96; and Pol Barbier (1984), "Inverse Relationship between Farm Size and Land Productivity : A Product of Science or Imagination?", *Economic and Political Weekly,* Vol. XIX, Nos. 51-52, December 22-29, pp. A189 — A198.

17. Some important studies on the subject are J.Q. Harrison (1972), *Agricultural Modernisation and Income Distribution,* Ph.D. Thesis, Princeton University; S.S. Sidhu (1972), *Economics of Technical Change in Wheat Production in Punjab, India,* Ph.D. Thesis, University of Minnesota; Pranab Bhattacharya and Abdul Majid (Jr.) (1976), "Impact of Green Revolution on Output, Cost and Income of Small and Big Farmers", *Economic and Political Weekly,* Vol. XI, No. 52, Review of Agriculture, December 25, pp. A147-A150; and Surendra Singh (1977) *Transformation of Agriculture in Ganganagar District of Rajasthan,* Ph.D. Thesis (Unpublished) Panjab University, Chandigarh.
18. G. Parthasarthy (1973), *Changes in Rice Farming and Their Social and Economic Impact : A Case Study of a Delta Village in Andhra,* (Mimeo); A.S. Kahlon and Gurbachan Singh (1973), *Social and Economic Implications of Large Scale Introduction of H.Y.Vs. of Rice with special reference to Gurdaspur District",* also see their study on Wheat in Ferozepur District, Punjab Agricultural University, Ludhiana; and G.S. Bhalla (1974), *Changing Agrarian Structure of India — A Study of the Impact of Green Revolution in Haryana,* Meenakshi Prakashan, Meerut-Delhi.
19. Baldev Singh (1973), *Capital Formation in Haryana Agriculture,* Ph.D Thesis, Kurukshetra University, Kurukshetra.
20. Harwant Singh and A.S. Kahlon (1971) "A Study of Credit Requirements and advances to Farmers in Patiala District", *Indian Journal of Agricultural Economics* Vol. XXVI, No. 4, October-December, pp. 496-503.
21. For the pioneering field studies undertaken by individual scholars on the subject, see; Pradhan H. Prasad (1973), "Production Relations; Achilles' Heel of Indian Planning", *Economic and Political Weekly,* Vol. VIII, No. 19, Special Article, May 12, pp. 869-872; ——— (1974), "Reactionary Role of Usurer's Capital in Rural India", *Economic and Political Weekly,* Vol.IX, Nos. 32-34, Special Number, August, pp. 1305-1308; ——— (1975), "Agrarian Unrest and Economic Change in Rural Bihar : Three Case Studies", *Economic and Political Weekly,* Vol. X, No. 24, Special Article, June 14, pp. 931-937; ——— (1976), "Poverty and Bondage", *Economic and Political Weekly,* Vol. XI, Nos. 31-33, Special Number, August, pp. 1269-1272; ——— (1980), "Rising Middle Peasantry in North India", *Economic and Political Weekly,* Vol. XV, Nos. 5-7, Annual Number, February, pp. 215-219, ——— (1987), "Agrarian Violence in Bihar", *Economic and Political Weekly,* Vol. XXII, No. 22, Special Article, May 30, pp. 847-857; and ——— (1987), "Towards a Theory of Transformation of Semi-Feudal Agriculture", *Economic and Political Weekly,* Vol. XXII, No. 31,

Special Article, August 1, pp. 1287-1290; also see, A. Bhaduri (1973), "A Study in Agricultural Backwardness under Semi-Feudalism", *The Economic Journal,* Vol. 83, March, pp. 120-137.

22. Ashok Rudra (1970), "In Search of the Capitalist Farmer", *Economic and Political Weekly,* Vol. V, No. 26, Review of Agriculture, June 27, pp. A85-A87; —— (1971), "Capitalist Development in Agriculture — Reply", *Economic and Political Weekly,* Vol. VI, November 6, pp. 2291-2292; Utsa Patnaik (1971), "Capitalist Development in Agriculture: A Note", *Economic and Political Weekly,* Vol. VI, No. 39, Review of Agriculture, September 25, pp. A123-A130; ——— (1986), "The Agrarian Question and Development of Capitalism in India", *Economic and Political Weekly,* Vol. XXI, No. 18, Special Article, May 3, pp. 781-793; Paresh Chattopadhyay (1972), "Mode of Production in Indian Agriculture : An Anti-Kritik", *Economic and Political Weekly,* Vol. VII, No. 53, Review of Agriculture, December 30, pp. A185-A192; and Ranjit Sau (1973), "On the Essence and Manifestation of Capitalism in Indian Agriculture", *Economic and Political Weekly,* Vol. VIII, No. 13, Review of Agriculture, March 31, pp. A27-A30.

23. Pranab Bardhan (1970), "Green Revolution and Agricultural Labourers in India", *Economic and Political Weekly,* Vol. V, Nos. 29-31, Special Number, July, pp. 1239-1246; ——— (1970), "Green Revolution and Agricultural Labourers : A Correction", *Economic and Political Weekly,* Vol. V, No. 46, November 14, p. 1861; G. Parthasarathy (1971), *"Green Revolution and the Weaker Sections",* Thacker and Co, Bombay; V.M. Dandekar and N. Rath (1971), "Poverty in India — 1: Dimension and Trends", *Economic and Political Weekly,* Vol. VI, No. 1, January 2, pp. 25-48; ——— (1971), "Poverty in India-II : Policies and Programmes", *Economic and Political Weekly,* Vol. VI, Nos. 2, January 9, pp. 106-146; and A.V. Jose (1974), "Trends in Real Wage Rates of Agricultural Labourers", *Economic and Political Weekly,* Vol. IX, No. 13, Review of Agriculture, March 30, pp. A25-A30.

24. Wolf Ladejinsky (1969a), "The Green Revolution in Punjab : A Field Trip", *Economic and Political Weekly,* Vol. IV, No. 26, Review of Agriculture, June 28, pp. A73-A82; ——— (1969b), "Green Revolution in Bihar — The Kosi Area : A Field Trip", *Economic and Political Weekly,* Vol. IV, No. 39, Review of Agriculture, September 27, pp. A147-A162; ——— (1970), "Ironies of India's Green Revolution", *Foreign Affairs,* Vol. 48, No. 4, July, pp. 758-768; Clifton R. Wharton (1969), "The Green Revolution : Cornucopia or Pandora's Box", *Foreign Affairs,* Vol. 47, No. 3, April, pp. 464-476; Francine R. Frankel (1971), *"India's Green Revolution : Economic Gains and Political Costs",* Oxford University Press, Bombay; T.J. Byres (1972), "The Dialects of India's Green Revolution", *South Asian Review,* Vol. 5, No. 2, January, pp. 99-116; Andre Gunder Frank (1973), "Reflections on Green, Red and White Revolutions in India", *Economic and Political Weekly,* Vol. VIII, No. 3, January 20, pp. 119-124; and also see, Yujiro Hayami (1981), "Agrarian Problem of India : An East and Southeast Asian Perspective", *Economic and Political Weekly,* Vol. XVI, No. 16, Special Article, April 18, pp. 707-712.

25. Walter P. Falcon (1972), "The Green Revolution : Generation of Problems" in *Comparative Experience of Agricultural Development in Developing Countries of Asia and the South East Since World War II,* The Indian Society of Agricultural

Economics, Bombay, pp. 295-315.

26. For a penetrating discussion on this subject, please see B.Sen (1969), "Regional Dispersion of Agricultural Income Implications of the New Technology", *Economic and Political Weekly,* Vol. IV, No. 52, Review of Agriculture, December 27, pp A190-A196; —— (1970), "Opportunities in Green Revolution", *Economic and Political Weekly,* Vol. V, No. 13, Review of Agriculture, March 28, pp. A33-A40; R.W. Herdit and E.A. Baker (1972), "Agricultural Wages, Production and High Yielding Varieties", *Economic and Political Weekly,* Vol. VII, No. 13, Review of Agriculture, March 25, pp. A23-A30; G.S. Bhalla and G.K. Chadha (1983), *"Green Revolution and the Small Peasant : A Study of Income Distribution among Punjab Cultivators",* Concept Publishing Company, New Delhi; C.H. Hanumantha Rao (1975), *Op Cit.* pp. 135, 150 and 178; and Deepak Lal (1976), "Agricultural Growth, Real Wages and the Rural Poor in India", *Economic and Political Weekly",* Vol. XI, No. 26, Review of Agriculture, June 26, pp. A47-A61.
27. G.S. Bhalla (1974), *op. cit.* p. 48.
28. Peter von Blanckenburg (1972), "Who Leads Agricultural Modernisation? — A Study of Some Progressive Farmers in Mysore and Punjab", *Economic and Political Weekly,* Vol. VII, No. 40, Review of Agriculture, September 30, pp. A94-A112.
29. C.H. Hanumantha Rao (1975), *op. cit.* pp. 179-180.
30. N.A. Majumdar (1970), "Intra-sectoral Dualism and Agricultural Growth", *Economic and Political Weekly,* Vol. V, 13, Review of Agriculture, March 28, pp. A2-A5; and Dharma Kumar (1970), "Technical Change and Dualism within Agriculture in India", *Journal of Development Studies,* No. 1, October, pp. 50-59.
31. C.H. Hanumantha Rao (1975), *op. cit,* Chapter 8, pp. 91-104.
32. Some of the important studies on the theme of the impact of the new technology on the wage rates of agricultural labourers are by P.K. Bardhan (1970, 1973), N. Krishnaji (1971), A.V. Jose (1974), Deepak Lal (1976), Sheila Bhalla (1979), G. Parthasarthy and K. Adiseshu (1982), Rakesh Basant (1984). For further details, please see, Appendix-I A.
33. The impact of new technology on rural poverty has been studied by quite a number of researchers. In particular, see, P.K. Bardhan (1973), "On the Incidence of Poverty in Rural India of the Sixties", *Economic and Political Weekly,* Vol. VIII, Nos. 4-6, Annual Number, February, pp. 245-254, Indira Rajaraman (1975), "Poverty, Inequality and Economic Growth : Rural Punjab, 1960-61 — 1970-71", *Journal of Development Studies,* Vol. XI, No. 4, pp. 278-290; M.S. Ahluwalia (1978), "Rural Poverty and Agricultural Performance in India", *Journal of Development Studies,* Vol. XIV, No. III, April, pp. 298-323; and J.N. Sinha (1981), "Full Employment and Anti-Poverty Plan : The Missing Link", *Economic and Political Weekly,* Vol. XVI, No. 50, December 12, pp. 2043-2052; also see Pradhan H. Prasad (1985), "Poverty and Agricultural Development", *Economic and Political Weekly,* Vol. XX, No. 50, December 14, pp. 2221-2224.
34. Martin, H. Billings and Arjan Singh (1970), "Mechanisation and the Wheat Revolution : Effect on Female Labour in Punjab", *Economic and Political Weekly,* Vol. V, No. 52, Punjab", *Economic and Political Weekly,* Vol. V, No. 52,

Review of Agriculture, December 26, pp. A169-A174.

35. Sheila Bhalla (1977), "Changes in Acreage and Tenure Structure of Land Holdings in Haryana, 1962-72", *Economic and Political Weekly,* Vol. XII, No. 13, Review of Agriculture, March 26, 1977, pp. A2-A15.
36. Some important micro-and macro level studies on the effect of different types of mechanisation on farm employment of labour have been conducted in India. In particular, see Martin H. Billings and Arjan Singh (1970), "Mechanisation and Rural Employment with Some Implications for Rural Income Distribution", *Economic and Political Weekly,* Vol. V, No. 26, Review of Agriculture, June 27, pp. A61-A72; ——— (1972), "The Effect of Technology on Farm Employment in India", in *Comparative Experience of Agricultural Development in Developing Countries of Asia and the South East Since World War II,* The Indian Society of Agricultural Economics, Bombay, pp. 332-342; A. Rudra (1971), "Employment Patterns in Large Farms of Punjab", *Economic and Political Weekly,* Vol. VI, No. 26, Review of Agriculture, June 26, pp. A89-A94; S.S. Acharya (1973), "Green Revolution and Farm Employment", *Indian Journal of Agricultural Economics,* Vol. XXVIII, No. 3, pp. 30-45; Raj Krishna (1974), "Measurement of Direct and Indirect Employment Effect of Agricultural Growth with Technical Change", in E.O. Edwards (ed), *Employment in Developing Nations : Report on a Ford Foundation Study,* Columbia University Press; C.H. Hanumantha Rao (1975), *Op. Cit.* Chapter 9, pp. 105-122, and A.S. Oberai and Iftikhar Ahmed (1981), "Labour Use in Dynamic Agriculture : Evidence from Punjab", *Economic and Political Weekly,* Vol. XVI, No. 13, March 28, pp. A2-A4. Besides, attempts have been made to study the problem of rural unemployment/under employment. For a detailed discussion on the subject, please see, Appendix-I B.
37. Planning Commission (1990), *op. cit.*
38. So far, only two studies have appeared on the theme of migrant labour in rural Punjab. See Bipin Chandra (1982), *A Study of Migrant Agricultural Labour in Punjab* (mimeo), August; and Manmohan Sharma (1982), "Impact of Migratory Labour on the Rural Economy of Punjab State", *Man and Development,* Vol. IV, No. 3, pp. 66-130.

2

STUDY AREAS AND SAMPLE HOUSEHOLDS

In Chapter 1, the major issues posed by research work on the effects of the Green Revolution, were taken note of. It was pointed out that enough work has not been done on the economic well-being of the non-cultivating rural labour households whose number has been increasing over time. The present study, dealing with these types of rural households, is based on field sample data gathered from nearly six hundred households from eight villages of Punjab and Bihar. In the present chapter, it is proposed to introduce the study areas, the sample design and give some introductory information on the sample households.

The Choice of States

The data for the present study were gathered from a few selected villages of Punjab and Bihar. Our choice of these States is based on many considerations. Since the mid-seventies. Bihar has commanded a preponderantly big share of migrant labour coming into Punjab like eastern Uttar Pradesh did in the earlier years. This was due to the fact that with the arrival of the 'second' Green Revolution in Punjab (i.e. rice revolution on the lines of wheat revolution of the late sixties), the demand for labour increased substantially intensifying further the process of seasonal migration of labour into Punjab agriculture. The Bihar labour is said to be comparatively better skilled in rice cultivation and also cheaper than the resident rural labour in Punjab. The reasons for this important shift notwithstanding, even otherwise, it might be very interesting to ascertain the economic base of the non-cultivating rural labour households in the State which sends out many thousand labourers annually for gainful seasonal employment and the State which has considerably expanded its absorptive capacity for seasonal migrant labour. It might as well be very useful to ascertain whether the migrant labour comes to Punjab from relatively less developed agricultural areas of Bihar. In particular, to assess the relative operation of the 'pull' and the 'push' factors in causing the seasonal exodus from rural Bihar.

Further, since the fundamental objective of the present study is to spell out the variations in the employment pattern and the corresponding income and consumption levels of the non-cultivating rural labour households in the two States, it is reasonably fair to choose one State which is comparatively developed and another which is relatively backward in general, and agricultural development in particular. The choice of Punjab and Bihar meets this objective fairly adequately.

It needs to be stressed here that in as much as the dynamics of agricultural transformation is the outcome of the interplay of technology, institutions and environment, the States of Punjab and Bihar reveal distinct matrices of these factors. Table 2.1. offers some striking differences between Punjab and Bihar.

TABLE 2.1: Levels of Agricultural Development in Punjab and Bihar: 1983-84

Sl. No.	Indicator	Punjab	Bihar
1	2	3	4
1.	Yield Rate of Rice (kg/ha)	3063	1016
2.	Yield Rate of Wheat (kg/ha)	3015	1554
3.	Yield Rate of Foodgrains (kg/ha)	2837	1062
4.	Cropping Intensity	1.66	1.35
5.	Percentage oı Net Irrigated Area to Net Sown Area	85.68	33.21
6.	Percentage of H.Y.V. Area under Wheat and Rice to their Total Cropped Area	98.18	58.44
7.	Fertilizer Consumption (kg/ha) of Gross Cropped Area	143.20	27.40

Source: 1. Statistical Abstract of Punjab for different years, E.S.O., Punjab.
2. Fertilizer Statistics for different years, F.A.I., New Delhi

To begin with, it is evident that the yield rates of paddy, wheat and foodgrains are much higher in Punjab compared with those in Bihar. In the matter of irrigation, which is the most important ingredient for the adoption of the new farm technology. Bihar is trailing far behind Punjab. It is obvious from the fact that in 1983-84, the percentage of net irrigated area to net sown area was between 2-3 times higher in Punjab compared with that in Bihar. Further, the proportion of area under H.Y.V. seeds for the two major crops of wheat and paddy to the total cropped area under these two crops in Bihar was nearly 1.7 times less than that in Punjab. Similarly, in the matter of fertilizer consumption, Bihar's intake is extremely low in comparison to that of Punjab.

As regards the rainfall, whereas Punjab receives an average annual normal rainfall of nearly 593.0 millimetres, the average figure for Bihar ranges between 1205.0 millimetres to 1362.0 millimetres.[1] Thus being a predominantly rainfed State and also the one with a large number of unharnessed rivers such as the Ganga, the Gandak, the Ghaghar, the Kosi and the Mahananda, the State of Bihar is more vulnerable to natural disasters like droughts and floods.

A Profile of Punjab and Bihar Economies

It is worthwhile to look broadly into the economic structure of the States selected with special reference to their agricultural and infra-structural base. Tables 2.2 and 2.3 provide the essential details in this regard.

Table 2.2 shows that as per 1981 Census, Punjab with 2.45 per cent of nation's total population and 1.53 per cent of total area has a density of population of 333. On the other hand, Bihar with 10.20 per cent of nation's population and 5.29 per cent of total area, has a density of population of 402. Further sex-ratio is considerably higher in Bihar than in Punjab. Not only thus, the percentage of rural population to total population was lower in Punjab (72.0%) compared with that in Bihar (88.0%). Again, the percentage of workforce engaged in agriculture is higher in Bihar (79.0%) compared with that in Punjab (58.0%). This shows that in terms of the rural-urban distribution of population and the relative strength of agricultural workforce, the economy of Punjab is relatively more diversified than that of Bihar, with agriculture continuing to be the mainstay of a much higher proportion of total population in rural Bihar, compared with rural Punjab.

TABLE 2.2: Demographic Features of Punjab and Bihar: 1981 Census

Sl. No.	Indicator	Punjab	Bihar
1	2	3	4
1.	Percentage Share in Country's Total Area	1.53	5.29
2.	Percentage Share in National Population	2.45	10.20
3.	Density of Population	333	402
4.	Sex-ratio (females/'000 males)	879	946
5.	Percentage of		
	(i) Literate Population to Total Population	40.86	26.20
	(ii) Rural Population to Total Population	72.32	87.53
	(iii) Workers to Total Population	29.35	29.68
	(iv) Workforce in Agriculture (Cultivators and Agricultural Labourers) to Total Workers	58.03	79.07
	(v) Agricultural Labourers to Total Workforce in Agriculture	38.20	44.90

Source: 1. Statistical Abstract of Punjab for different years, E.S.O., Punjab.
2. Statistical Abstract of India for different years, C.S.O., New Delhi.

Table 2.3 read with Table 2.1 reveals that irrespective of the level of per capita income at 1970-71 constant prices being over three times higher in Punjab than in Bihar, the economics of both the States are predominantly agricultural in character. This is substantiated by the fact that in 1983-84, the contribution of agricultural sector in the net State domestic product of Punjab and Bihar was nearly 35.0 per cent and 46.0 per cent respectively at 1970-71 constant prices. It is further clear that the net sown area as a percentage of total cultivable area constitutes nearly 98.0 per cent in Punjab compared with just 66.0 per cent in Bihar. Further, food crops account for as high as 89.0 per cent of gross cropped area in Bihar against 75.0 per cent in Punjab.

It is important to note that because of relatively assured means of irrigation, Punjab is much ahead Bihar in the adoption of high yielding seed varieties. The percentage of area under H.Y.V. of rice and wheat to total cropped area of these two crops is much higher (98.0%) in Punjab, compared with only about 58.0 per cent in Bihar. Since, the success of H.Y.V. seeds depends critically on the use of chemical fertilizers, the consumption of fertilizers in Punjab stood at 143.0 kg/ha of gross cropped area, while it was as low as 27.0 kg/ha of gross cropped area in Bihar. Although the number of fertilizer sale

TABLE 2.3: Selected Indicators of Punjab and Bihar Economies: 1983-84

Sl. No.	Indicator	Punjab	Bihar
1	2	3	4
1.	Per Capita Income at 1970-71 Constant Prices (Rs.)	1497	468
2.	Percentage Contribution of Agriculture in Net State Income at 1970-71 Prices	35.16	45.80
3.	Proportion of Net Sown Area to Total Cultivable Area	98.25	65.70
4.	Percentage of Area under Foodgrains to Gross Cropped Area (1983-84)	74.57	89.43
5.	Number of Tractors/'000 ha of Net Sown area (1980-81)	29	1.84
6.	Number of Energised Pumpsets and Tubewells/'000 ha of Net Sown Area	90.41	24.71
7.	Number of Operational Holdings in 1980-81 (000)	1020	11030
8.	Average Size of Holding in 1980-81 (hectares)	3.82	1.00
9.	Percentage Share of Small, Marginal and Sub-marginal Farmers (i.e. those operating below 2 hectares) in the Total No. of Operational Holdings (1980-81)	38.92	86.48
10.	Percentage of Villages Connected with All Weather Roads (as on 31.3.1985)	99.00	33.00
11.	Percentage of Electrified Villages (on 30.6.1984)	100.00	48.53
12.	Number of Fertilizer Sale Points/'000 ha of Net Sown Area (on 31.3.1984)	1.44	1.02
13.	Percentage of Fertilizer Sale Points (as in 12 above) of Co-operative Societies and other Institutional Agencies	52.33	7.93
14.	Percentage of Rural Population Covered by Active Agricultural Credit societies	13.64	8.84

Source: 1. Statistical Abstract of Punjab for different years, E.S.O., Punjab, Chandigarh.

2. Bihar Through Figures 1981, The Directorate of Statistics and Evaluation, July 1984, Bihar, Patna.
3. Fertilizer Statistics for different years, FAI, New Delhi.
4. All India Report on Agricultural Census 1980-81, Govt. of India, New Delhi, p. 191.
5. Seventh Five Year Plan: Mid Term Appraisal, Annexure IV, Transport Sector (Roads), Transport, division, Planning Commission, Government of India, August, 1987.

points per thousand hectares of net sown area in 1983-84 did not differ much between the two States, yet there are important differences between the two in the matter of institutional control of such fertilizer sale points. It is obvious from the fact that while in Punjab, the co-operative and other institutional agencies managed more than half of such sale points, the corresponding figure in Bihar was as low as nearly 8.0 per cent. Also, in Punjab, while active agricultural credit societies covered nearly 14.0 per cent of the rural population, this coverage was only about 9.0 per cent in Bihar.

In the matter of the adoption of mechanical innovations also, Bihar is way behind Punjab. For instance, on 30-6-1981, against 29 tractors per thousand hectares of net sown area in Punjab, Bihar had hardly two tractors for an equivalent figure of net sown area. Again in 1983-84, while Punjab had about 90 energised pumpsets and tubewells per thousand hectares of net sown area, the corresponding figure for Bihar was roughly 25 pumpsets and tubewells. Further, in terms of the development and the adequacy of various institutions catering to the requirements of agriculture, the Punjab is relatively much better placed than Bihar. Though land reforms in Punjab are not qualitatively much different from those in most other Indian States, yet in the matter of abolition of intermediaries, the Punjab has a relatively better record of performance. In Bihar, on the other hand, the powerful farmers' lobby in the State politics has always stood firmly in the way of effective implementation of land reforms. Consequently, in spite of much publicity about the land reforms, the bulk of the cultivable land still remains concentrated in the hands of big land owners relatively much more in Bihar compared with Punjab. Further, the problem of fragmentation of land holdings is nearly non-existent in Punjab, while it is still in an acute shape in Bihar. For instance, as brought out by All India Report on Agricultural Census (1980-81), the number of operational holdings was approximately 11 times larger in Bihar than in Punjab. Further, the average size of operational holding in Bihar is roughly 4 times smaller than that of Punjab. Also, the number of small, marginal and sub-marginal farmers (i.e. those cultivating below 2 hectares) is very large in Bihar nearly 87.0 per cent than in Punjab, where they account for nearly 39.0 per cent.

In the matter of infrastructural facilities also, Bihar is lagging far behind Punjab. This is due to the fact that the pattern of railway development in Bihar is tremendously constrained by its economic and physical geography. The Ganga poses one of the biggest hurdles in the development of railways in Bihar since it is bridged only at two or three points. The dissected and forested terrain of Chota Nagpur areas poses yet another problem in the development of the means of transportation. Similarly, the flood prone Kosi basin is acutely deficient both in railway and road transport facilities. Such transport disadvantages are not operating in Punjab. Consequently in 1985, while in Punjab 99.0 per cent of the villages were connected with all weather roads, Bihar could not make much headway in this respect. Further, against cent per cent rural electrification in Punjab, the corresponding figure for Bihar was only 49.0 per cent.

From the foregoing discussion it is evident that in the matter of technological factors, institutional set-up and infra-structural facilities, Punjab is much better placed than Bihar. Thanks to the relatively more conducive institutional and infra-structural set-up, speedy and up to date farm practices emerging from research at Punjab Agricultural University, Ludhiana, and better extension services, the State enjoys a conspicuous advantage in the adoption of H.Y.V. seeds, improved and up to date farm practices, use of chemical fertilizers, tubewell irrigation, mechanisation of agriculture and a very high degree of agricultural commercialisation. On the other hand, because of relatively adverse position of Bihar in the matter of all these factors, the State has experienced a lopsided development. This, in turn, has perpetuated the general backwardness of the State economy. Not only this, there are acute disparities in the levels of development of various sub-regions of the State. In the matter of agricultural development, the position is more desperate. Unlike Punjab, some districts of Bihar are extremely backward while some others are doing fairly well. District Bhojpur belongs to the latter category.

The Chosen Districts: Similarities and Contrasts

With the objective of locating districts with a comparable agricultural base, district Ludhiana in Punjab and district Bhojpur in Bihar, have been selected as the areas of the present study. While Ludhiana is universally acknowledged as the best agricultural district in Punjab, Bhojpur is one of the best agricultural districts of Bihar. And the impact of the Green Revolution, although of differing intensity, is quite substantial in both. Before settling on these two districts, a small districtwise exercise based on a few indicators of agricultural development was carried out for all the districts of Punjab and Bihar, on the basis of 1975-76 data, available in published reports and documents of the two States. Although data for Punjab were available for later years as well, yet non-availability of comparable data for Bihar restricted our choice to the year 1975-76 for carrying out this exercise. Besides existence of a focal town of almost comparable dimension in each selected district, the indicators chosen for this exercise were: (X_1) proportion of net sown area to the total cultivable area; (X_2) cropping intensity; (X_3) proportion of net irrigated area to the net sown area;.(X_4) proportion of H.Y.V. area of wheat and rice to the total cropped area under these two crops; (X_5) per hectare intake of chemical fertilizers; (X_6) yield rate of rice; and, (X_7) yield rate of wheat.

On the basis of these seven indicators, composite index was worked out for all the districts in the two States. The results of this exercise are set out in Table 2.4. On the said scale, district Ludhiana ranked first in Punjab. In Bihar, Nalanda had a slightly higher score than Bhojpur. However, since it did not have a focal town of comparable dimension, our choice fell on Bhojpur district. Further, it is interesting to note that because of their high potential of agricultural development both Ludhiana and Sahabad (now divided into Bhojpur and Rohtas districts) were selected among the first batch of 7 districts under the I.A.D.P. programme. Though district Rohtas could also stake its claim on this ground and despite the fact, Dalmia Nagar of Rohtas district is comparable to the Khanna town of district Ludhiana in terms of industrial activity, but it had to be dropped in favour of Bhojpur for the following reason:

Two towns of Dalmia Nagar and Dehri-on-Sone are separated from each other just by a metalled road. Under such circumstances, the comparability of two situations in the two States does not seem to be reasonable and unbiased; and, moreover on the basis of 1971 Census. Buxar town of Bhojpur district, and Khanna town of district Ludhiana, were more or less comparable in terms of their respective population size.

Thus with the objective of ensuring a comparable rural-urban situation Khanna in Ludhiana and Buxar in Bhojpur have been chosen as the focal towns. The present study, in a way, attempts to capture the impact of these two towns on the rural areas in their respective hinterlands. Around each of these two towns, a sample of

TABLE 2.4: Districtwise Composite Index of Agricultural Development in Punjab and Bihar: 1975-76

Sl. No.	District	Standardised value of indicator							Composite	Rank Index
		X_1	X_2	X_3	X_4	X_5	X_6	X_7		
1	2	3	4	5	6	7	8	9	10	11
PUNJAB										
1.	Gurdaspur	1.03	1.07	0.87	0.77	0.80	0.88	0.88	6.30	9
2.	Amritsar	0.97	1.03	1.25	1.05	1.00	0.90	1.02	7.22	6
3.	Kapurthala	1.03	0.86	1.08	0.96	1.31	1.08	0.91	7.23	5
4.	Jallandhar	1.02	1.02	1.15	1.09	1.41	1.06	1.03	7.78	2
5.	Hoshiarpur	0.98	1.00	0.57	0.70	0.64	0.78	0.89	5.56	11
6.	Roopnagar	0.93	1.07	0.53	0.77	0.61	0.66	0.86	5.43	12
7.	Ludhiana	1.01	1.11	1.16	1.11	1.54	1.33	1.19	8.45	1
8.	Ferozepore	0.94	0.98	1.02	1.05	0.82	1.13	0.98	6.92	8
9.	Faridkot	1.03	0.91	1.10	0.99	0.99	1.32	0.99	7.33	4
10.	Bhatinda	1.03	0.94	0.88	0.99	0.38	1.00	0.88	6.10	10
11.	Sangrur	1.01	1.05	1.09	1.10	0.81	1.19	1.10	7.35	3
12.	Patiala	1.01	1.05	0.97	1.04	0.87	1.00	0.99	6.93	7
BIHAR										
1.	Patna	1.22	1.07	1.94	0.76	2.19	1.52	0.98	9.68	5
2.	Nalanda	1.32	1.15	2.95	0.98	1.87	1.26	1.13	10.66	1
3.	Gaya	0.97	1.00	2.31	0.65	1.11	0.84	0.84	7.72	13
4.	Nawada	1.08	1.00	2.85	1.11	1.24	0.80	1.12	9.20	8
5.	Aurangabad	1.01	0.98	2.57	1.06	0.99	1.12	0.75	8.48	10
6.	Bhojpur	1.29	1.14	2.49	1.72	1.62	1.39	0.96	10.61	2

Contd.

TABLE 2.4 *Contd.*

1	2	3	4	5	6	7	8	9	10	11
7.	Rohtas	1.26	1.11	2.43	1.51	1.63	1.44	0.96	10.34	3
8.	Saran	1.18	1.17	1.73	1.97	1.60	0.96	1.28	9.89	4
9.	Siwan	1.26	1.12	1.76	1.70	1.31	0.85	1.04	9.04	9
10.	Gopalganj	1.18	1.18	1.96	1.89	1.25	0.92	1.18	9.56	6
11.	Champaran (East)	1.30	0.95	0.83	1.15	0.98	0.73	0.99	6.93	19
12.	Champaran (West)	1.17	1.14	1.05	0.83	0.86	0.99	1.05	7.09	18
13.	Muzaffarpur	1.28	1.05	0.81	1.33	1.67	0.88	0.90	7.92	12
14.	Vaishali	1.20	1.08	0.80	1.36	1.14	0.80	0.73	7.11	17
15.	Sitamarhi	1.24	1.11	0.65	0.92	0.73	0.71	0.89	6.25	21
16.	Darbhanga	1.05	1.02	0.77	1.44	1.02	0.73	1.23	7.26	16
17.	Samastipur	1.15	1.10	1.11	1.54	1.14	1.27	0.98	8.29	11
18.	Madhubani	1.21	1.03	0.44	0.87	0.40	0.96	0.96	5,87	22
19.	Begusarai	1.25	1.07	1.00	2.30	1.74	0.70	1.32	9.38	7
20.	Monghyr	0.93	1.04	1.41	1.11	1.02	0.93	0.93	7.37	15
21.	Bhagalpur	1.07	1.02	1.63	0.71	0.85	1.20	0.93	7.41	14
22.	Santhal Parganas	0.83	0.82	0.25	0.83	0.33	1.18	0.99	4.93	28
23.	Saharsa	1.03	1.13	1.17	1.45	0.38	0.90	0.77	6.83	20
24.	Purnea	1.07	1.11	0.38	0.73	0.41	0.77	1.01	5.48	23.5
25.	Katihar	1.04	1.05	0.40	0.91	0.47	0.67	0.94	5.48	23.5
26.	Hazaribag	0.69	0.88	0.25	0.40	0.21	0.91	0.97	4.31	30
27.	Giridih	0.72	0.82	0.24	0.52	0.21	1.15	1.32	4.98	27
28.	Dhanbad	0.73	0.82	0.25	0.28	0.19	1.34	1.11	4.72	29
29.	Ranchi	0.89	0.85	0.25	0.65	0.29	0.90	1.43	5.26	25
30.	Palamau	0.73	0.90	0.74	0.49	0.22	0.91	1.13	5.12	26
31.	Singhbhum	0.71	0.82	0.18	0.15	0.17	0.99	1.05	4.07	31

Note: 1. Standardisation has been done by dividing the figures for the respective districts with the State figure for each indicator.
2. An explanation of the indicators $X_1, X_2, X_3 \ldots X_7$ is given in the text.

8 villages has been selected. Villages located unidirectionally from the town, have been so chosen that the effect of the distance itself is captured in rural-urban employment nexus. It shall be worthwhile to present some broad features of the areas under study which have an important bearing on the employment pattern and the corresponding levels of income and consumption of the population of these areas.

Physical Features

Located centrally in the State of Punjab, district Ludhiana — the harbinger of the Green Revolution in India, forms a part of Punjab Malwa in the Punjab-Plain-North of the great Indo-Gangetic plain. Compared with the centrally located district Ludhiana of Punjab, Bhojpur in Bihar is located on the Western border of the State. It is a new district which was formed in November 1972 by splitting the old district of Sahabad into two districts-Bhojpur and Rohtas.

More or less rectangular in appearance, the total area of district Ludhiana is about 3793 square kilometres.[2] In comparison, district Bhojpur with a total area of about 4077 square kilometres[3] is relatively bigger in size. Even though physical diversities[4] are not completely ruled out from the microscopic viewpoint in the two districts, yet on the whole the topography of the two districts appears to be flat, and as such, both can admit extensive use of farm machinery and other farm practices. Further, while the soils in Ludhiana, supported by a strong irrigation base, have responded well to the use of high yielding varieties of improved seeds and chemical fertilizers, the alluvium soils of Bhojpur, although endowed with a matching level of fertility, have not so far come under high yielding seeds in a big way. It needs to be stressed that soils of Bhojpur, if properly harnessed, do have adequate potential for considerable expansion of crop yield rates and total agricultural output.[5]

With respect to the environmental factors, both the districts experience extreme variations in climate. And finally, in both the districts, summer rains (accounting for nearly three-fourths of the average annual rainfall) are more important from the point of view of agriculture.

In spite of these above-mentioned similarities, a very significant difference between the two districts is in terms of rural-urban link roads. Because of thick network of rural link roads in Ludhiana, the agricultural sector of the district has received a great fillip which has further strengthened the rural-urban linkages bearing important implications for the employment-income-consumption nexus of the rural population. These facilities in the case of Bhojpur are available on a much lower scale.

Demographic Features

Table 2.5 brings out a few demographic features of the two districts.

TABLE 2.5: Demographic Features of Ludhiana and Bhojpur Districts: 1971-81

Sl. No.	Indicator	Ludhiana		Bhojpur	
		1971	1981	1971	1981
1	2	3	4	5	6
1.	Percentage of Respective State Population	10.47	10.83	3.54	3.44
2.	Percentage of Respective State Area	7.51	7.66	2.36	2.36
3.	Density of Population (persons/sq.km)	374	472	496	588
4.	Sex-ratio (Females/'000 males)	846	859	967	944
5.	Percentage of:				
	(a) Literate Population to Total Population	42.63	50.60	25.38	31.35
	(b) Rural Population to Total Population	65.19	57.99	91.48	89.28
	(c) Main Workers to Total Population	29.57	30.39	28.10	25.21
	(d) Workforce in Agriculture (Cultivators and Agricultural Labourers) to Total Workforce	50.80	43.84	81.50	79.08
	(e) Agricultural Labourers to Total Workforce in Agriculture	35.32	40.08	50.76	47.08

Source: (i) Statistical Abstract of India 1985, C.S.O., New Delhi.
(ii) Bihar Through Figures 1981, Directorate of Statistics and Evaluation, July 1984, Bihar, Patna.

It may be noticed that even though the percentage shares of State population as well as area have been higher in Ludhiana than in Bhojpur during 1971-81, yet on account of relatively higher pressure of population in Bhojpur, density of population has been much lower in the former compared with the latter. The opposite has been noticed with respect to sex-ratio. While sex-ratio in Ludhiana has registered an increase from 846 females per thousand males in 1971 to 859 females per thousand males in 1981, in Bhojpur the corresponding figure has come down from 967 in 1971 to 944 in 1981. Further, with respect to the literacy, Ludhiana continues to be far ahead than Bhojpur. Similarly, the lower proportion of rural population to total population in district Ludhiana indicates that over the period, the dependence on agriculture in this district has been lower compared to its Bihar counterpart. This is corroborated by the fact that as per 1981 Census, the percentage of agricultural workforce in Ludhiana is roughly half to that of Bhojpur. In other words, it implies that the pace of urbanisation, because of setting-up of agro-based industries and other industrial activities and the consequent expansion of the tertiary sector, has been faster in Ludhiana than in Bhojpur during the decade of 1971-81. But this type of trend has not appeared as yet on a comparable scale in Bhojpur. Consequently, nearly 80.0 per cent of the workforce still continues to be dependent upon agriculture for its livelihood during 1971-81. Further, while the percentage of agricultural labourers to total agricultural workforce has increased from nearly 35.0 per cent in 1971 to about 40.0 per cent in 1981 in Ludhiana, the corresponding figure has recorded decline in Bhojpur from 51.0 per cent in 1971 to 47.0 per cent in 1981. However, the percentage of agricultural labourers to total agricultural workforce continues to be lower in Ludhiana as against Bhojpur over the said period. This implies that relatively higher proportion of agricultural workforce is engaged as cultivators in Ludhiana than Bhojpur. This, in turn, means that the proportion of agricultural labourers to total agricultural workforce being higher in Bhojpur than in Ludhiana, agricultural wage rates are bound to be lower in the former compared with the latter.

Agricultural Development

With respect to the level of agricultural development in Ludhiana and Bhojpur districts, it can be seen from Table 2.6 that even though the level of extensive cultivation is sufficiently high in both, yet the yield rates of wheat and paddy are considerably higher in the former compared to the latter. These differences are explained largely in terms of differences in irrigation facilities, rural electrification, use of chemical fertilizers, adoption of H.Y.V. seeds, and so on.

Table 2.6, when compared to Tables 2.1 and 2.3, indicates that practically in all the indicators. the two are the best agricultural districts of their respective States. It is obvious that the proportion of net sown area to the total cultivable area, cropping intensity, per hectare use of chemical fertilizer stood higher both in Bhojpur and Ludhiana districts than their respective State figures. It is in spite of the fact that such data for the State relate to the later years. This is presumably because of relatively stronger irrigation base of these two districts compared to their respective States. Though many factors have contributed in their conspicuous position in the matter of agricultural development, yet, it may be worthwhile to mention in passing that it might be their early selection under the Intensive Agricultural District Programme which has played a pivotal role in helping them to achieve the distinction of one of the best agricultural districts in the two States of Punjab and Bihar.

An important common feature of the two districts is that the economy of both is mainly agricultural in character and both are surplus in food. Further, since both are lacking in mineral resources, there is limited scope for establishing mineral based industries. Again both being among the first seven districts selected under Intensive Agricultural District Programme (I.A.D.P.), they pioneered the adoption of H.Y.V. seeds in their respective States. While paddy, wheat, cotton, sugarcane, vegetables and some pulses are the major crops of district Ludhiana; paddy, wheat, *khesari* and same other pulses such as *'masoor'* and *'arhar'* are grown in district Bhojpur. Ludhiana has been lucky to have the well known Punjab Agricultural University located at the district headquarters. This ensured an effective availability of the extension services to the local farmers as also the quick flow of knowledge about modern techniques of production developed in the University from time to time. This is perhaps an important factor to put Ludhiana at the top in the matter of agricultural modernization. Bhojpur, in comparison, was not fortunate to have such an effective liaison with any Agricultural University or research institute. The nearest Agricultural University is in district Ranchi, located nearly 400 km away from Bhojpur.

Industrial Situation

Apart from its impressive performance in the agricultural sector, district Ludhiana enjoys the distinction of being the industrial hub of

Punjab. The hosiery and engineering goods, bicycles and bicycle parts, two wheelers, electric goods including sewing machines, fans, etc. Manufactured in district Ludhiana are well known all over the world. A number of agro-based industries have also come up recently in the wake of the Green Revolution. Dispersal of industrial activity outside the city limits of Ludhiana is another important development of the recent times. Smaller towns such as Khanna, Jagraon and Samrala are also emerging as important industrial and commercial centres. During the seventies, the industrial expansion of Khanna town has been extremely fast.[6]

TABLE 2.6: Levels of Agricultural Development in Ludhiana and Bhojpur: 1982-83

Sl. No.	Indicator	Ludhiana	Bhojpur
1	2	3	4
1.	Proportion of Net Sown Area to the Total Cultivable Area	99.70	89.54
2.	Cropping Intensity	1.78	1.37
3.	Yield Rate of Wheat (kg/ha)	3521	1349
4.	Yield Rate of Rice (kg/ha)	3940	1211
5.	Percentage of Area under H.Y.V. of Wheat and Paddy to their Total Cropped Area	100.00	544.33#
6.	Fertilizer Consumption (kg/ha of GCA)	174.61	33.72
7.	Percentage of Net Irrigated Area to Net Sown Area	95.26	62.69
8.	Number of Energised Pumpsets and Tubewells/'000 ha of Net Sown Area#	91.79	18.20
9.	Number of Tractors/'000 ha of Net Sown Area	544.00	1.78$
10.	Percentage of Electrified Villages@	100.00	30.23

Notes: #. Relates to the year 1978-79
@. Relates to the year 1980
$. Relates to the year 1980-81

Source: 1. Statistical Abstract of Punjab for various years, E.S.O., Punjab Chandigarh.
2. Bihar Through Figures 1981, The Directorate of Statistics and Evaluation, July 1984, Bihar, Patna.
3. Fertilizer Statistics 1982-83, F.A.I., New Delhi.
4. Agricultural Situation in India for different years, Directorate of Economics and Statistics, Ministry of Agriculture, Government of India, New Delhi.

In comparison to Ludhiana, Bhojpur is not as much developed in terms of industrial activities. Nevertheless, the district has been expanding its industrial base. Some small scale industries of general type such as rice hulling, leather tanning, powerlooms, hurricane lanterns, agricultural implements, printing, furniture making etc. have come up mostly in the urban centres and block headquarters in the district. Further, the pace of agro-industrial activities has gone up. In recent years, district Bhojpur has witnessed tremendous increase in its rice output as a consequence of which the rural landscape of the district is now punctuated by rising rice shelling activity. Some villages have become important food processing and marketing centres. For example, even a small village, named Akhauripur Gola has as many as six rice shellers, one oil mill, catering to a fast expanding food marketing centre. Industrial complexes are coming up at Buxar, Dumraon and Jagdishpur. Of course, there are many such agro-industrial villages in Ludhiana also.

Sample Villages

The present study is based on primary data collected from a number of villages from Punjab and Bihar. It is perhaps in the fitness of things to have a synoptic view of the socio-economic milieu operating in these villages. This should assist a proper analysis of the issues relating to employment, income and consumption levels of the rural labour households. As explained later in this chapter, 8 villages were purposively selected at fairly comparable distances from the respective focal towns of the two States. Table 2.7 provides a locational profile of the sample villages of Punjab and Bihar respectively. It is evident that Majri in Punjab and Mathia Gurdas in Bihar are the nearest sample villages (2 km each) from the respective focal towns. Similarly Jalajan (17 km) in Punjab and Unwans (18 km) in Bihar are the farthest sample villages from the said towns. The remaining six villages in the two States are located in between at varying distances.

All the villages in Punjab are located mostly on the main road by and large. The locational picture of Bihar, villages is also the same. None of the sample villages is more than one km away from the main road. The condition of link roads between the village inhabitations and the main road is much better in Punjab than in Bihar. Further, both the focal towns have a railway station and a sub-divisional tehsil headquarters.

TABLE 2.7: A Locational Profile of Punjab and Bihar Sample Villages

Sl. No.	Village		Distance (in km) from						
			Focal Town	Main Road	Railway Station	Block Hqrs.	Tehsil/ Sub. Divi-sion Hqrs.	District Hqrs.	Canal/ Canal Distri-butary
1	2		3	4	5	6	7	8	9
A. PUNJAB									
1.	Majri	(V1)	2.00	0.00	2.00	18.00	2.00	41.00	0.00
2.	Rasulra	(V2)	3.00	0.50	3.00	19.00	3.00	42.00	0.00
3.	Ikolaha	(V3)	5.00	0.00	5.00	21.00	5.00	44.00	0.00
4.	Kotla Dhak	(V4)	8.00	0.00	8.00	24.00	8.00	47.00	0.00
5.	Faizgarh	(V5)	9.00	0.75	9.00	25.00	9.00	48.00	2.00
6.	Isru	(V6)	12.00	0.00	12.00	28.00	12.00	48.00	0.00
7.	Nasrali	(V7)	15.00	1.00	15.00	31.00	15.00	45.00	0.00
8.	Jalajan	(V8)	17.00	0.00	17.00	33.00	17.00	48.00	3.00
B. BIHAR									
1.	Mathia Gurdas	(V1)	2.00	0.75	2.00	2.00	2.00	71.00	0.00
2.	Lalganj	(V2)	3.00	0.75	3.00	3.00	3.00	72.00	0.00
3.	Hukaha	(V3)	4.00	0.30	4.00	4.00	4.00	73.00	0.00
4.	Nathpur	(V4)	7.00	0.00	7.00	4.00	7.00	76.00	0.00
5.	Sarasti	(V5)	10.00	1.00*	10.00	1.00*	10.00	79.00	0.00
6.	Itarhi	(V6)	11.00	0.00	11.00	1.00	11.00	80.00	0.00
7.	Konch	(V7)	15.00	0.50	15.00	4.00	15.00	84.00	0.00
8.	Unwans	(V8)	18.00	0.00	18.00	7.00	18.00	87.00	0.00

* Though some houses are located on the main road itself, but the main village is about one km from the main road and block headquarters.

Table 2.7 further reveals that in terms of distance from the district headquarters, the sample villages of Punjab are favourably placed than Bihar villages. However, with respect to the distance from the block headquarters. Bihar villages enjoy an edge over their Punjab counterparts. In as much as nearness to block headquarters is more important from the point of view of agricultural development, the Bihar villages enjoy a slight locational edge over the Punjab villages. It is, however, a different matter that a nearby block office may not be administered as effectively as the one slightly away. Perhaps, the Bihar position conforms to this pattern.

Table 2.8 gives an account of the size and demographic characteristics of the sample villages in the two study areas. There are considerable inter-village variations in the geographical area, number of households and their population size, density of population, sex-ratios and average household size in both the States. Further, with respect to the castewise distribution of population, the percentage share of scheduled caste and backward class population is relatively much lower in the Punjab villages compared with their Bihar counterparts.

It may also be observed from Table 2.8 that the pressure of population in terms of density of population is much higher in Bihar compared to Punjab villages. This is further, corroborated by the land-man ratio (i.e. land available per man) which is significantly higher in Punjab than in Bihar. By looking at the land-man ratio figures, one finds that the land availability is as low as .15 in village Itarhi in Bihar and as high as .82 in village Nasrali in Punjab. Although there is not a significant difference in the sex-ratio between Punjab and Bihar all village figures, yet the corresponding figure for average size of household is higher in Bihar compared with Punjab.

It is important to note that agricultural labourers in Punjab are drawn basically from the scheduled castes, and artisans from the backward classes. Compared with it in Bihar, both scheduled castes and backward classes are the main source of labour supply in the farm sector. While scheduled castes and backward classes account for nearly 38.0 per cent and 11.0 per cent respectively of the population of all the Punjab villages taken together; their share in Bihar is nearly 16.0 per cent and 70.0 per cent respectively. In other words, around 49.0 per cent of the overall population in Punjab villages is earning its livelihood from agricultural labour or artisans. But in case of Bihar, the glaringly high figure of about 86.0 per cent of scheduled castes and backward classes, depending mainly on agricultural labour, can explain the low wage rate and the consequent economic plight of the agricultural labour there.

Table 2.9 shows that although the level of extensive cultivation (percentage of net sown are to total cultivable area), is almost the same in the sample villages of the two States, yet wide variations can be found in the level of their agricultural development. For example, cropping intensity (the ratio of gross cropped area to net sown area)

TABLE 2.8: Size and Demographic Characteristics of Punjab and Bihar Sample Villages: 1980-81

Sl. No.	Village/s		Indicator									
			Size of Sample Village (Acres)	Total House-holds (No.)	Total Popu-lation (No.)	Density of Popu-lation (persons/ Sq. km.)	Sex-ratio (Females/ 000' males)	Average House-hold size	Landman ratio	Castewise Percentage Distribution of Population		
										Scheduled Castes and Scheduled Tribes	Backward Castes	Other Castes
1	2		3	4	5	6	7	8	9	10	11	12
A. PUNJAB												
1.	Majri	(V1)	269	109	604	554	836	5.54	0.39	55.80	·8.11	36.09
2:	Rasulra	(V2)	1048	267	1811	427	844	6.78	0.50	35.12	13.69	51.19
3.	Ikolaha	(V3)	1694	516	3260	475	853	6.32	0.46	42.24	7.33	50.43
4.	Kotla Dhak	(V4)	298	69	423	350	808	6.13	0.63	33.33	13.48	53.19
5.	Faizgarh	(V5)	444	145	979	544	890	6.75	0.42	41.16	9.50	49.34
6.	Isru	(V6)	1546	463	2791	446	881	6.03	0.48	31.45	14.73	53.82
7.	Nasrali	(V7)	1833	315	2009	271	904	6.38	0.82	34.10	11.80	54.10
8.	Jalajan	(V8)	805	157	954	293	842	6.08	0.79	50.42	7.02	42.56
	All		7937	2041	12831	399	865	6.29	0.55	38.48	10.92	50.60

Contd.

TABLE 2.8: *Contd.*

1	2		3	4	5	6	7	8	9	10	11	12
B. BIHAR												
1.	Mathia Gurdas	(V1)	122	59	355	724	811	6.02	0.34	53.24	29.30	17.46
2.	Lalganj	(V2)	305	146	1068	862	921	7.32	0.26	3.56	95.13	1.31
3.	Hukaha	(V3)	586	129	904	381	872	7.01	0.57	21.35	41.59	37.06
4.	Nathpur	(V4)	241	69	427	436	802	6.19	0.49	63.23	36.77	0.00
5.	Sarasti	(V5)	714	103	831	288	746	8.07	0.74	5.78	91.58	2.64
6.	Itarhi	(V6)	895	695	4939	1364	837	7.11	0.15	9.64	79.49	10.87
7.	Koneh	(V7)	329	122	752	565	889	6.16	0.40	40.29	36.17	23.54
8.	Unwans	(V8)	991	278	2150	536	903	7.73	0.44	15.26	62.51	22.23
	All		4183	1601	11426	675	854	7.14	0.33	16.15	69.63	14.22

Source: 1. Revenue Records of the respective Punjab and Bihar Sample Villages.
2. Door to door listing of the Sample Villages in Punjab and Bihar.

TABLE 2.9: Important Indicators of Agricultural Development of Punjab and Bihar Sample village: 1980-81

Sl. No.	Village		Indicator					
			Level of Extensive Cultivation	Cropping Intensity	Proportion of Net Irrigated Area to Net Sown Area	Net Sown Area (Acres) Per		
						Pumpset (including Diesel Engines)	Tractor	Thresher
1	2		3	4	5	6	7	8
A. PUNJAB								
1.	Majri	(V1)	100.00	1.80	100.00	7.38	33.71	39.33
2.	Rasulra	(V2)	100.00	1.84	100.00	9.00	34.96	30.30
3.	Ikolaha	(V3)	100.00	1.94	100.00	9.19	36.76	30.14
4.	Kotla Dhak	(V4)	100.00	1.95	100.00	5.43	29.56	17.73
5.	Faizgarh	(V5)	100.00	1.91	100,00	4.66	33.75	16.20
6.	Isru	(V6)	100.00	2.00	100.00	5.36	27.92	10.55
7.	Nasrali	(V7)	100.00	1.88	100.00	7.58	46.97	13.93
8.	Jalajan	(V8)	97.36	1.91	100,00	10.55	104.00	42.82
	All		99.72	1.92	100.00	7.27	38.08	18.16
B. BIHAR								
1.	Mathia Gurdas	(V1)	99.75	1.63	88.33	0.00	0.00	0.00
2.	Lalganj	(V2)	99.86	1.54	93.21	0.00	0.00	93.33
3.	Hukaha	(V3)	99.81	1.53	94.35	46.64	256.50	171.00
4.	Nathpur	(V4)	100.00	1.92	98.10	70.33	0.00	0.00
5.	Sarasti	(V5)	100.00	1.94	92.33	76.63	0.00	0.00
6.	Itarhi	(V6)	100.00	1.48	90.65	18.73	187.25	124.83
7.	Konch	(V7)	100.00	1.82	93.62	74.50	298.00	298.00
8.	Unwans	(V8)	95.17	1.51	67.34	31.82	297.00	127.29
	All		98.74	1.63	86.59	39.10	367.50	183.75

Note: 1. Minor adjustments have been made because the data were gathered from different sources.
2. In the subsequent Tables, notations V1, V2, V3, ... V8 are used for the respective sample villages instead of their names.

Source: 1. Revenue records of the respective Punjab and Bihar sample villages.
2. Door to door listing of the sample villages of Punjab and Bihar.
3. Department of Irrigation in the two States at the block level.

is significantly higher in Punjab compared with Bihar sample villages. However, wide inter-village variations are noticeable in this behalf within the two States. The higher cropping intensity in Punjab villages is mainly because of their large irrigation base compared with that of Bihar villages. Moreover, the Punjab villages enjoy better and more assured sources of irrigation compared with Bihar villages. This is due to the fact that while in the former, huge investments have been made in installing tubewells, Bihar is still largely irrigated by canals. The concerted efforts of the Punjab Government in rural electrification has also tremendously contributed in the strong tubewell irrigation base of the State, while this is generally lacking in Bihar. This is evident from the fact that the net sown area per pump set, is comparatively much lower in Punjab villages compared with Bihar villages.

Table 2.9 further reveals that the level of mechanisation is much higher in Punjab villages compared with that in Bihar villages. For example, net sown area per tractor and thresher is again much lower in Punjab villages than in Bihar villages. Moreover, in some sample villages of Bihar, the tractors are either non-existent or negligibly small in number. The same can be said of threshers.

Irrigation is considered to be the sheet-anchor of agricultural development under the new farm technology. From Table 2.9, it is clear that the entire net sown area in Punjab villages is irrigated. The level of irrigation in Bihar villages is also very high, although some scope still exists for extending the irrigation base further. Further, it is evident that while tubewell (including diesel engines) irrigation is the major source of irrigation in all sample villages of Punjab; canals are the major source of irrigation in Bihar villages. This is due to the fact, that water table in Bihar villages being very deep, the cost of sinking a tubewell is far higher in Bihar than in Punjab. It may be mentioned in passing that no major inter-village differences are discernible in the cropping pattern pursued by the sample villages of Punjab as well as Bihar. Paddy, wheat, vegetables and cotton are the major crops of the Punjab villages while paddy, wheat, and 'khesari; etc. are those of the Bihar villages.

Social and Other Amenities

Table 2.10 provides information on the availability of some social and other amenities to the sample villages in the two States. In Punjab

Isru (i.e. V6.), being a focal point village, enjoys a unique position in that almost all amenities of social well-being are available in the village itself. However, the position of other sample villages is also fairly encouraging since most of these facilities are available at short distances. Some villages are catered to by the focal town since they are much closer to it than the focal point village (Isru). On the whole, irrespective of the source providing various social and other amenities, the Punjab villages are enjoying most items. In Bihar, on the other hand, there is nothing like focal point village. However, Itarhi (again V6 in Bihar) being block headquarters, has access to most amenities of social well-being, their condition and functioning notwithstanding. The position of other Bihar villages is relatively more desperate.

Sample Design

As mentioned in the preceding section, the urban industrial town of Khanna was chosen from Punjab, and, Buxar from Bihar. Eight villages located unidirectionally, at varying distances from each of these focal towns, were purposively selected on the Khanna-Malerkotla road in district Ludhiana and on the Buxar-Itarhi-Unwans road in Bhojpur district. An attempt was made to include only those villages in the two scenarios which were, as far as possible, at comparable distances from the respective focal towns of Khanna and Buxar.

The distance of the focal town has been taken from the habitations of the respective sample villages instead of their outer geographical frontiers. Consequently, the rural-urban proximity also includes the distance of the link road between the main road and the village habitation.

Selection of Households

After selecting the sample villages, a complete enumeration of all households in the 16 villages was prepared. This ensured, *inter alia*, a close look at the village level revenue records as well. We had a total of 3642 households in the two sets of villages (2041 households in the Punjab villages and 1601 in the Bihar villages). To identity the non-cultivating rural labour households from amongst the total rural households. "activity criterion" was applied for every working male

TABLE 2.10: Village-wise Availability of Social and other Amenities in the Sample Villages of Punjab and Bihar

Sl. No.	Social and Other Amenities	State	VILLAGE							
			V1	V2	V3	V4	V5	V6	V7	V8
1	2	3	4	5	6	7	8	9	10	11
	Distance (km) From the Attached/Nearest Located:									
1.	Primary School	PJB	0.00	0.00	0.00	0.00	0.00	0.00	0.00	0.00
		BHR	1.00	0.00	0.00	0.00	0.00	0.00	0.50	0.00
2.	High School	PJB	2.00	2.00	0.00	3.00	3.00	0.00	1.00*	2.00
		BHR	2.00	3.00	4.00	4.00	1.00	0.00	3.00	0.00
3.	Public/Private Library	PJB	2.00	2.00	0.00	3.00	3.00	0.00	0.00	2.00
		BHR	2.00	3.00	4.00	4.00	1.00	0.00	3.00	0.00
4.	General Hospital/Health Centre	PJB	2.00	2.00	0.00	3.00	3.00	0.00	0.00	2.00
		BHR	2.00	3.00	4.00	4.00	1.00	0.00	3.00	0.00
5.	Veterinary Hospital	PJB	2.00	3.00	5.00	4.00	3.00	0.00	3.00	2.00
		BHR	2.00	3.00	4.00	4.00	1.00	0.00	4.00	0.00
6.	Banking Facilities	PJB	2.00	2.00	0.00	3.00	3.00	0.00	3.00	2.00
		BHR	2.00	3.00	4.00	4.00	1.00	0.00	3.00	0.00
7.	Co-operative Society/Bank	PJB	3.00	2.00	0.00	4.00	3.00	0.00	3.00	5.00
		BHR	2.00	3.00	4.00	4.00	1.00	0.00	3.00	0.00
8.	Facilities for Agricultural Marketing	PJB	2.00	3.00	5.00	4.00	3.00	0.00	3.00	5.00
		BHR	2.00	3.00	4.00	4.00	1.00	0.00	4.00	7.00
9.	Fertilizer Depot	PJB	2.00	2.00	0.00	4.00	3.00	0.00	3.00	2.00
		BHR	2.00	3.00	4.00	4.00	1.00	0.00	3.00	0.00
10.	Repair Shop for Agricultural Implements	PJB	2.00	3.00	5.00	4.00	3.00	0.00	1.00*	2.00
		BHR	2.00	3.00	4.00	7.00	10.00	11.00	15.00	18.00
11.	Soil Testing Laboratory	PJB	18.00	19.00	21.00	24.00	25.00	28.00	31.00	33.00
		BHR	71.00	72.00	73.00	76.00	79.00	80.00	84.00	87.00

Contd.

1	2 *	3	4	5	6	7	8	9	10	11
12.	Milk Collection Centre/Dairy	PJB	2.00	3.00	5.00	4.00	3.00	0.00	3.00	5.00
		BHR	2.00	3.00	4.00	7.00	10.00	11.00	15.00	18.00
13.	Government Fair Price Shop/Ration Depot	PJB	3.00	2.00	0.00	4.00	3.00	0.00	3.00	5.00
		BHR	1.00	0.00	1.00	4.00	1.00	0.00	0.00	0.00
14.	Post Office	PJB	3.00	2.00	0.00	4.00	3.00	0.00	0.00	0.00
		BHR	5.00	4.00	3.00	4.00	1.00	0.00	4.00	0.00
15.	Electricity Office	PJB	2.00	3.00	4.00	4.00	3.00	0.00	2.00	2.00
		BHR	2.00	3.00	4.00	4.00	1.00	0.00	4.00	7.00
16.	Petrol Pump	PJB	0.00	1.00	3.00	2.00	1.00	1.00	4.00	5.00
		BHR	2.00	3.00	4.00	7.00	10.00	11.00	15.00	18.00
17.	Telephone Facilities	PJB	1.00	0.00	0.00	3.00	3.00	0.00	0.00	2.00
		BHR	2.00	3.00	4.00	7.00	10.00	11.00	15.00	18.00
18.	Wine Shop	PJB	2.00	3.00	0.00	3.00	3.00	0.00	3.00	2.00
		BHR	2.00	3.00	4.00	4.00	1.00	0.00	4.00	7.00
19.	Recreational Facilities	PJB	2.00	3.00	5.00	8.00	9.00	12.00	15.00	17.00
		BHR	2.00	3.00	4.00	7.00	10.00	11.00	15.00	18.00
20.	Focal Point Village	PJB	10.00	9.00	7.00	4.00	3.00	0.00	3.00	5.00
		BHR	—	—	—	—	—	—	—	—
21.	Electrification	PJB	Yes	Yes	Yes	Yes	Yes	Yes	Yes	Yes
		BHR	No	No	No	No	No	Yes	No	Yes
22.	Drinking Water Facilities	PJB	HP.W	HP.W	HP.W	HP.W	HP.W	HP.W	HP.W	HP.W
		BHR	W.HP	W.HP	W.HP	W.HP	W.HP	W.HP	W.HP	W.HP
23.	Existence of Villages Industries	PJB	No	4 Iron and Steel Mills	No	No	No	No	No	1 Sewing machine Spare parts Factory
		BHR	No	No	No	No	No	2 Rice Shellers	No	No

Note: 1. PJB = Punjab, 2. BHR = Bihar, 3. HP = Hand Pump, 4. W = Wells

* In Punjab, these facilities are located on the Khanna-Malerkotla Road which is about 1 km from the Nasrali village (V7).

member of these 3642 households. "Income criterion" came in only at the stage of classifying the households into PALH and PNLH groups. According to "activity criterion", only those households which derived a major part of their total family income from any form of wage employment were chosen. On the contrary, such households as were deriving a major part of their total family income from self-cultivation or tenancy cultivation or self-employment in secondary and tertiary activities, had to be excluded from the purview of the present study.

As a result of the above exercise, a total of 657 non-cultivating rural labour households emerged in the sample villages of the Punjab and 459 in those of Bihar. We chose 300 such households each from Punjab and Bihar. The choice of the number of households from each of the sample villages was made on the basis of proportionate probability sampling technique. In other words the number of sample households was roughly in proportion to their total number in each sample villages.

After determining the number of households to be selected from each sample village, Tippett's Random Number Table was made use of for the selection of the first sample household in each sample village. An interval was found for the selection of the subsequent sample households in each sample village by dividing the total number of non-cultivating rural labour households with the number of households to be selected from that very sample village. The subsequent households were selected by adding the chosen interval to the random start, and so on.

In the case of migrant agricultural labourers, lottery system was adopted and the sample was roughly 25.0 per cent of the total number of migrants in each group in the sample villages of Punjab.

Data Collection Method

The data for the study were gathered with the help of three schedules: Village Schedule, Resident Labour Household Schedule and Migrant Labour Schedule. The Village schedule was framed for collecting the overall information about the location, land utilisation and other socio-economic characteristics of the sample villages. The household schedule sought detailed information on employment, income and consumption as also other socio-economic and demographic features of the selected households. The schedule on the migrant agricultural labour also contained various socio-economic questions besides other details regarding migration itself. In both the States, a pilot survey covering 24 schedules was undertaken for pretesting the adequacy and the relevance of the questionnaire. This pretesting was quite fruitful in as much as some duplication and some omissions became obvious. Incorporating all these changes, the final questionnaire was canvassed through a personal interview method covering 300 non-cultivating rural labour households from either State, and another 150 migrant agricultural labourers in the Punjab villages. The reference period of the study is the agricultural year 1980-81. The data were gathered between April 25, 1981 to July 24, 1981 from Punjab and between July 27, 1981 to Oct 10, 1981 from Bihar.

Categorisation of Sample Households

In the burgeoning empirical evidence on the issues under consideration, it is a common practice to classify and sub-classify the rural labour force in a variety of ways. Consequently, depending upon the quantum of a particular type of work done, source of income, mode of wage payment, possibilities of alternative job opportunities or job mobility, the interaction between the rural social and economic hierarchy operating at the village level, land status and several other suchlike factors, the rural labour force is generally placed into several categories[8] such as agricultural and non-agricultural, attached farm servants and casual agricultural labourers working on daily or on contractual basis, free and unfree labour, pure wage earners and wage-earners-cum-small farmers and so on and so forth.

As mentioned earlier, in the present study, the "income-criterion" was employed for classifying the sample households in two broad categories. The households deriving a major part of their total annual income from agricultural wage employment were designated as predominantly agricultural labour households (or PALH group) and others as 'predominantly non-agricultural labour households' (or PNLH group). The analysis of consumption pattern has, however, been carried out without adhering to this classification.

Table 2.11 provides villagewise break-up of sample households in Punjab and Bihar. Rows 10 to 12 in the said Table provide similar information for the migrant agricultural labourers in the study area

TABLE 2.11: Overall and Villagewise Break-up of Sample Households in Punjab and Bihar

Sl. No.	Village Description	State	VILLAGE								All Villages
			V1	V2	V3	V4	V5	V6	V7	V8	
1	2	3	4	5	6	7	8	9	10	11	12
1.	Total Households	PJB	109	267	516	69	145	463	315	157	2041
		BHR	59	146	129	69	103	695	122	278	1601
2.	Total Non-cultivating Rural	PJB	47	102	170	16	50	138	76	58	657
	Labour Households	BHR	40	56	40	32	23	130	58	80	459
3.	2 as Percentage to 1 Above	PJB	43.12	38.20	32.95	23.19	34.48	29.31	24.13	16.94	32.19
		BHR	67.80	38.36	31.01	46.38	22.33	18.71	47.54	28.78	28.71
4.	Number of Sample Households	PJB	21	47	78	7	23	63	35	26	300
		BHR	26	37	26	21	15	85	38	52	300
5.	4 as Percentage to 2 Above	PJB	44.68	46.08	45.88	43.75	46.00	45.65	46.05	44.83	45.66
		BHR	65.00	67.07	65.00	65.63	65.62	65.39	65.52	65.00	65.36
6.	Predominantly Agricultural	PJB	4	13	29	3	11	45	33	25	163
	Labour Households (PALH)	BHR	15	12	24	21	14	76	38	52	252
7.	6 as Percentage to 4 Above	PJB	19.05	27.66	37.18	42.86	47.83	71.43	94.29	96.45	54.33
		BHR	57.69	32.43	92.31	100.00	93.33	89.41	100.00	100.00	84.00
8.	Predominantly Non-agricultural	PJB	17	34	49	4	12	18	2	1	137
	Labour Households(PNLH)	BHR	11	25	2	—	1	9	—	—	48
9.	8 as Percentage to 4 Above	PJB	80.95	72.34	62.82	57.14	52.17	28.57	5.71	3.85	45.67
		BHR	42.31	67.57	7.69	—	6.67	10.59	—	—	16.00
10.	Total Number of Migrants	PJB	52	75	142	37	44	108	115	37	610
11.	Migrants in the Sample (No.)	PJB	12	20	35	9	10	27	28	9	150
12.	11 as Percentage to 10 Above	PJB	23.08	26.67	24.65	24.32	22.73	25.00	24.35	24.32	24.59

of Punjab. In particular, a perusal of this table, brings out clearly the contrast between Punjab and Bihar in terms of the classification of the sample households into PALH and PNLH groups. For example, in Punjab, about 54.0 per cent (163 out of 300) of the sample households belong to the PALH group while 46.0 per cent of them draw their incomes predominantly from non-agricultural sources of employment. In sharp contrast, as high as 84.0 per cent of the sample households in Bihar depend primarily on agricultural employment as the major source of their income; non-agricultural activities are the main source of earnings only to 16.0 per cent of them. A village-to-village comparison between Punjab and Bihar further confirms that higher proportion of sample households are seeking employment through non-farm activities in the former than in the latter. It is interesting to note that beyond a certain distance from the focal town, the labour households in Bihar extend their dependence nearly completely on agricultural employment. In Punjab, on the other hand, irrespective of the number of households, non-farm employment is available as the major source of income even in the extremely remote villages from the focal town. It is thus obvious that the fast growing agriculture of Punjab has generated many non-farm avenues of employment, partly in the rural and partly in the urban areas, and a very high proportion of the rural labour households is getting more and more involved in such activities. Such avenues are opening up for the rural labour households of Bihar but only marginally; for an overwhelming majority of them, the dependence on agricultural wage employment continues to be fairly high.

Introductory Information on the Sample Households

It might be useful to give some introductory information about the sample households. In this regard, a few broad characteristics of such households are shown in Table 2.12. It is important to note that the size of the family (average number of members) as well as the average number of earners per family are almost the same between the two States as also between each pair of nearly equally distanced villages from the focal town. Again, the percentage of families having earning women and/or children, as also the percentage of family members recorded as earning women and/or children do not display significant variations either between the two States or between each paid of equally distanced (from the focal town) villages.[7] This indicates that seemingly the board composition of the non-cultivating rural labour households from both the study areas is nearly the same.

TABLE 2.12: Introductory Information on the Sample Households in Punjab and Bihar

Sl. No.	Item	State	Village V1	V2	V3	V4	V5	V6	V7	V8	All Vill-ages	PALH	PNLH
1 2	3	4	5	6	7	8	9	10	11	12	13	14	
1.	Number of Sample Households	PJB	21	47	78	7	23	63	35	26	300	163	137
		BHR	26	37	26	21	15	85	38	52	300	252	48
2.	Average Family Size	PJB	5.81	5.04	5.40	6.57	6.61	5.46	5.66	5.27	5.52	5.72	5.28
		BHR	5.81	5.54	5.62	5.05	6.13	5.86	5.82	5.65	5.71	5.65	6.04
3.	Percentage of Families Having:												
	(a) Earning Men	PJB	100.00	100.00	100.00	100.00	100.00	100.00	100.00	100.00	100.00	100.00	100.00
		BHR	100.00	100.00	100.00	100.00	100.00	100.00	100.00	100.00	100.00	100.00	100.00
	(b) Earning Women	PJB	80.95	61.70	76.92	85.71	78.26	85.71	97.14	88.46	80.33	88.96	70.07
		BHR	61.54	75.68	80.77	85.71	100.00	85.88	92.11	88.46	84.00	89.68	54.17
	(c) Earning Children	PJB	4.76	6.38	6.41	14.29	17.39	12.70	14.29	11.54	10.00	144.11	5.11
		BHR	11.54	5.41	7.69	14.29	26.67	10.59	13.16	—	9.33	9.52	8.33
4.	Percentage of Family Members Recorded As:												
	(a) Earning Men	PJB	26.23	26.58	26.84	26.09	23.68	26.74	25.76	27.74	26.37	27.28	25.39
		BHR	25.83	27.25	30.10	20.80	29.35	26.46	26.65	24.76	26.44	26.37	26.48
	(b) Earning Women	PJB	15.57	13.08	16.63	[illegible]	18.42	19.19	22.73	20.44	17.80	19.91	15.27
		BHR	13.88	15.57	19.85	18.85	20.71	19.94	19.95	19.71	18.83	20.31	11.39
	(c) Earning Children	PJB	0.82	1.69	1.19	2.17	3.29	2.62	3.03	2.19	2.05	2.89	0.96
		BHR	1.99	0.98	1.37	2.83	5.43	2.01	2.26	—	1.75	1.82	1.38
5.	Average Number of Earners Per Family	PJB	2.23	1.88	2.15	2.64	2.59	2.32	2.51	2.33	2.25	2.49	1.96
		BHR	2.16	2.19	2.57	1.83	2.92	2.49	2.49	2.24	2.36	2.40	2.16

In spite of such apparent similarities, it is, however, important to note that within each of the two States of Punjab and Bihar, the percentage of families having earning women and/or children, as also the percentage of family members recorded as earning women and/or children tends to increase as we move away from the focal town into the interior of the countryside. Bearing in mind the fact that the levels of poverty are relatively higher in the remote villages than in the nearby villages from the urban focal town, it can be safely argued that the poor families of the remote areas have a larger number of working women and/or children. Further, assuming that the PALH group is comparatively poorer than the PNLH group, the corresponding high percentages of women and/or children for the former lend further substance to the above view.

Assets and Liabilities of Rural Labour Households

Assets and liabilities of rural labour households are other important aspects which convey very meaningful information about their economic life. We may, therefore, compare the value of assets and liabilities as reported by our respondent households in the two study areas. Table 2.13 provides very useful information in this regard. A perusal of this table reveals that almost in every aspect of economic life, whether it relates to the realm of production or home consumption or standard of living, one discovers that every villages in Punjab is far ahead compared with its counterpart in Bihar. The differential between Punjab and Bihar needs to be underlined, in particular, with respect to livestock and poultry among the productive assets, and residential accommodation, need and/or status based assets, etc. among the household assets category. Further, PALH and PNLH groups of Punjab show marked superiority over their counterparts in Bihar in every respect and from all standpoints. Finally, the higher level of liabilities of Punjab households than those of Bihar are perhaps going in the building of productive assets, especially in livestock and poultry. It can, therefore, be safely argued that areas experiencing rapid agricultural transformation on the one hand, and strong rural-urban ties on the other, are bound to experience the 'trickling down' of development gains even in the matter of assets formation by those who are at the lower ladder of the socio-economic hierarchy. On the other hand, such a phenomenon has yet to occur on any marked scale in Bihar.

TABLE 2.13: Pattern of Assets and Liabilities of Rural Labour Households in Punjab and Bihar

(Mean Value in Rs.)

Sl. No.	Item	State	Village V1	V2	V3	V4	V5	V6	V7	V8	Average	PALH	PNLH	d_i*
1	2	3	4	5	6	7	8	9	10	11	12	13	14	15
Productive Assets														
1.	Land	PJB	—	—	—	—	—	—	—	—	—	—	—	—
		BHR	603.85	437.84	55.77	652.38	—	403.53	52.63	23.08	281.83	221.63	597.92	169.78
			(18.38)	(12.10)	(2.05)	(22.49)	—	(13.60)	(2.31)	(1.15)	(10.10)	(8.45)	(16.33)	
		d_i	—	—	—	—	—	—	—	—	—	—	—	—
2.	Implements and Machinery (Fodder cutter, Sickle, Spade Band, Loudspeaker, etc.)	PJB	52.67	54.91	81.92	92.14	85.87	65.38	201.20	53.27	84.14	84.72	83.46	-1.49
			(0.62)	(0.70)	(1.07)	(1.19)	(1.01)	(0.89)	(3.00)	(0.85)	(1.12)	(1.17)	(1.06)	
		BHR	9.00	11.00	19.00	9.62	8.00	23.01	18.66	7.42	15.03	15.64	11.81	-24.49
			(0.27)	(0.30)	(0.70)	(0.33)	(0.28)	(0.77)	(0.81)	(0.37)	(0.54)	(0.62)	(0.32)	
		d_i	485.22	399.18	331.16	857.80	973.38	184.14	978.24	617.92	459.81	441.69	606.69	
3.	Livestock, Poultry, Piggery, etc.	PJB	1674.32	1169.57	1698.33	1641.43	2857.17	2011.67	1626.00	1672.12	1756.43	1952.55	1523.10	-21.99
			(19.69)	(14.87)	(22.10)	(21.12)	(33.48)	(27.39)	(24.23)	(26.60)	(23.32)	(27.07)	(19.25)	
		BHR	381.08	919.92	666.35	416.67	988.00	767.09	577.03	537.85	666.46	646.17	772.96	19.62
			(11.60)	(25.43)	(24.55)	(14.37)	(34.56)	(25.77)	(25.30)	(26.78)	(23.83)	(24.53)	(21.11)	
		d_i	339.36	27.14	154.87	293.94	189.19	162.25	181.79	210.89	163.55	202.17	97.05	
A.	Total Productive Assets (1+2+3)	PJB	1727.19	1224.49	1780.26	1733.57	2943.04	2077.05	1827.20	1725.38	1840.58	1037.26	1606.56	-21.14
			(20.31)	(15.57)	(23.17)	(22.31)	(34.49)	(28.28)	(27.22)	(27.45)	(24.44)	(28.24)	(20.31)	
		BHR	993.92	1368.76	741.12	1078.67	996.00	1187.16	648.32	568.35	961.49	881.26	1382.69	56.90
			(30.25)	(37.84)	(27.30)	(37.19)	(34.84)	(40.04)	(28.42)	(28.30)	(34.47)	(33.60)	(37.76)	
		d_i	73.78	-10.54	140.21	60.71	195.49	74.96	181.84	203.58	91.43	131.18	16.19	

Contd.

TABLE 2.13: *Contd.*

1 2	3	4	5	6	7	8	9	10	11	12	13	14	15
Household Assets													
4. Residential Accommodation	**PJB**	4197.61	4170.21	3817.53	3335.71	3693.48	3457.94	3270.01	3059.62	3684.78	3437.73	3951.82	14.95
		(49.35)	(53.04)	(49.05)	(49.36)	(43.28)	(47.09)	(48.72)	(48.67)	(48.77)	(47.66)	(49.97)	
	BHR	1765.38	1748.65	1453.85	1371.43	1406.67	1398.82	1247.37	1159.62	1416.33	1351.98	1754.17	29.75
		(53.73)	(48.34)	(53.56)	(47.28)	(49.21)	(47.18)	(54.69)	(57.74)	(50.78)	(51.54)	(47.91)	
	d_i	137.77	138.48	162.58	179.69	162.57	147.20	162.15	163.85	160.16	154.27	125.28	
5. Need Based Assets (Utensils, Cots, Bedding, Charkha, etc.)	**PJB**	510.24	518.51	493.40	487.86	476.09	452.06	405.14	391.15	469.22	438.25	506.06	15.47
		(6.00)	(6.59)	(6.42)	(6.28)	(5.58)	(6.16)	(6.04)	(6.22)	(6.23)	(6.08)	(6.40)	
	BHR	187.50	186.49	179.42	145.48	147.33	137.12	141.71	122.69	150.42	143.87	184.79	28.44
		(5.71)	(5.16)	(6.61)	(5.02)	(5.15)	(4.63)	(6.22)	(6.11)	(5.39)	(5.48)	(5.05)	
	d_i	172.13	178.04	175.01	235.35	223.15	229.68	185.89	218.81	211.94	204.62	173.86	
6. Status Based Assets (Radio/Transistor, Watch/Clock, Fan Sewing machine, Furniture, etc.)	**PJB**	593.81	587.02	530.58	511.43	489.35	438.41	379.86	366.15	489.05	424.20	566.20	33.47
		(6.98)	(7.47)	(6.91)	(6.58)	(5.73)	(5.97)	(5.66)	(5.82)	(6.49)	(5.88)	(7.16)	
	BHR	51.54	48.24	80.77	12.86	20.00	22.45	26.71	17.50	32.09	27.69	55.21	99.39
		(1.57)	(1.33)	(2.98)	(0.44)	(0.70)	(0.76)	(1.17)	(0.87)	(1.15)	(1.06)	(1.51)	
	d_i	1052.13	1116.87	556.90	3876.91	2346.75	1852.83	1322.16	1992.29	1424.01	1431.96	925.54	
7. Gold and Jewellery	**PJB**	1197.62	1152.13	961.54	942.86	767.39	794.44	754.29	676.92	908.67	769.63	1074.09	39.56
		(14.08)	(14.65)	(12.51)	(12.13)	(8.99)	(10.82)	(11.24)	(10.77)	(12.07)	(10.67)	(13.58)	
	BHR	240.38	212.16	240.38	269.05	273.33	193.53	196.05	117.31	200.33	196.23	221.88	13.07
		(7.32)	(5.86)	(8.86)	(9.28)	(9.56)	(6.53)	(8.60)	(5.84)	(7.18)	(7.48)	(6.06)	
	d_i	398.22	443.05	300.01	250.44	180.76	310.50	284.74	477.04	353.59	292.21	384.09	

Contd.

TABLE 2.13: *Contd.*

1 2	3	4	5	6	7	8	9	10	11	12	13	14	15
8. Cash and Other Financial Claims	PJB	278.81	210.60	149.35	260.00	164.65	123.60	75.17	67.00	150.56	106.05	203.53	91.92
		(3.28)	(2.68)	(1.94)	(3.34)	(1.93)	(1.68)	(1.12)	(1.07)	(2.00)	(1.47)	(2.57)	
	BHR	47.00	53.24	19.04	22.95	15.33	25.58	20.79	22.79	28.49	22.00	62.60	184.55
		(1.43)	(1.47)	(0.70)	(0.79)	(0.54)	(0.86)	(0.91)	(1.13)	(1.02)	(0.84)	(1.71)	
	d_i	493.21	295.57	684.40	1032.90	974.04	383.19	261.57	193.99	428.47	382.05	225.13	
B. Total Household Assets (4+5+6+7+8)	PJB	6778.10	6638.47	5903.45	6037.86	5590.96	5266.46	4884.46	4560.85	5690.01	5175.87	6301.70	21.75
		(79.69)	(84.43)	(76.83)	(77.69)	(65.51)	(71.72)	(72.78)	(72.55)	(75.56)	(71.76)	(79.69)	
	BHR	2291.81	2248.78	1973.46	1821.76	1862.67	1777.49	1632.63	1439.90	1827.67	1741.77	2278.65	30.82
		(69.75)	(62.16)	(72.70)	(62.81)	(65.16)	(59.96)	(71.58)	(71.70)	(65.53)	(66.40)	(62.24)	
	d_i	195.75	195.20	199.14	231.43	200.16	196.29	199.18	216.75	211.33	197.16	176.55	
C. Total Assets (A + B)	PJB	8505.29	7862.96	7683.71	7771.43	8534.00	7343.31	6711.66	6286.23	7530.57	7213.13	7908.26	9.64
		(100.00)	(100.00)	(100.00)	(100.00)	(100.00)	(100.00)	(100.00)	(100.00)	(100.00)	(100.00)	(100.00)	
	BHR	3285.73	3617.54	2714.58	2900.43	2858.67	2964.66	2280.95	2008.25	2789.16	2623.03	3661.33	39.58
		(100.00)	(100.00)	(100.00)	(100.00)	(100.00)	(100.00)	(100.00)	(100.00)	(100.00)	(100.00)	(100.00)	
	d_i	158.86	117.36	183.05	167.94	198.53	147.70	194.25	213.02	169.99	174.99	115.99	
D. Total Liabilities (On 30-06-1981)	PJB	468.89	204.55	627.73	733.85	351.96	633.16	395.00	898.87	529.13	705.58	319.20	-54.76
	BHR	616.42	321.14	392.88	305.00	510.79	413.15	433.20	520.87	436.19	446.24	383.38	-14.09
	d_i	-23.93	-36.31	59.78	140.61	-31.09	53.25	-8.82	72.57	21.31	58.12	-16.74	
E. Debt Payments made during 1980-81	PJB	87.94	38.59	52.09	90.99	25.87	41.10	26.43	125.79	52.46	63.25	39.64	-37.33
	BHR	204.88	37.36	58.26	38.33	137.46	117.86	92.41	141.06	106.52	113.90	67.75	-40.52
	di	-57.08	3.29	-10.59	137.39	-81.18	-65.13	-71.40	-10.83	-50.75	-44.47	-41.49	

Note: 1 PJB = Punjab; 2 BHR = Bihar; 3 $di = \frac{PJBi - BHRi}{BHRi}$; $di^* = \frac{PNLHi - PALHi}{PALHi}$

5. *i* is the value of *i*th item. 6. Figures in the parentheses are the percentage of the total value of assets.

Occupational Diversification in Punjab and Bihar

An important outcome of the Green Revolution phenomenon has been the rising occupational diversification in rural India. While a preponderant majority of our sample households reported occupational diversification from farm to non-farm avenues of employment, there were some who reported the other way round. As expected, the occupational diversification has witnessed varying degree of change in different areas depending upon the institutional, social, economic, technological and infra-structural differences. It is, therefore, useful to have a synoptic view of the degree, inception as also the factors responsible for occupational diversification in the two areas which represent contrasting situations. A broad idea of the activities in which rural labour households are engaged is also expected to pave the way for a meaningful analysis of employment-income-consumption nexus in the comparative framework, which we propose to take up later in the subsequent chapters.

Table 2.14 through Table 2.16 present the detailed information on various aspects of occupational diversification in Punjab and Bihar. These tables show that the degree of occupational diversification is much higher in Punjab (nearly 65.0% of our sample) compared with Bihar (only 22.0%). This implies that the percentage of households opting out of agriculture since the mid-sixties has been much higher in Punjab compared with Bihar. The fast expanding economy of Punjab has enabled a large number of these households to move into non-farm occupations, partly in rural areas themselves and partly in urban-industrial centres. Most of the occupational diversification has occurred in the wake of the Green Revolution in Punjab. In other words, the process of Green Revolution has set into motion a chain of related economic activities, and, consequently enhanced the prospects for the rural labour households to get employment from more diverse sources. The diversity of employment opportunities faced by Bihar households remains severely restricted. And finally, the occupational diversification has mainly occurred due to economic factors. The other factors have played only a secondary role.

Before we conclude, it might be in order to have a broad view of the type of activities in which the non-cultivating rural labour households are engaged in both the study areas. As a consequence of the rural economic transformation and growing rural-urban linkages, the avenues of gainful employment seem to be diversified in both the study areas. Landless rural labour households are earning a part of their income by working in small industries and workshops in the focal town or in nearby villages. Some members of such households are engaged in various types of farm as well as non-farm activities. Further, some working members of such households also work as construction workers in the focal towns of the respective States. Some are engaged in self employed labour activities such as barber's work, shoe-repair and cycle repair, etc. For some households, a part of annual household income also accrues from dairying/poultry, etc. Further, driven by their general economic deprivation the involvement of women and child labour in different types of earning activities is quite common both in Punjab and Bihar villages. Although education consciousness is growing among such households, yet the school going children often form an integral part of the labour force, particularly in peak seasons, such as wheat harvesting, rice transplantation and harvesting, etc. Besides, they are engaged to look after the grazing of the livestock.

TABLE 2.14: Incidence of Occupational Diversification in Punjab and Bihar

Sl. No.	Villages/s	Punjab			Bihar		
		Sample House-holds (No.)	Households Reporting Diversifi-cation (No.)	4 as Percen-tage to 3	Sample House-holds (No.)	House-holds Reporting Diversi-fication (No.)	7 as Percen-tage to 6
1	2	3	4	5	6	7	8
1.	V1	21	21	100.00	26	12	46.15
2.	V2	47	40	85.11	37	26	70.27
3.	V3	78	53	67.95	26	3	11.54
4.	V4	7	3	42.86	21	0	0.00
5.	V5	23	17	73.91	15	6	40.00
6.	V6	63	34	53.97	85	11	12.94
7.	V7	35	16	45.71	38	5	13.16
8.	V8	26	12	46.15	52	3	5.77
	All	300	196	65.33	300	66	22.00

TABLE 2.15: Inception of Occupational Diversification in Punjab and Bihar

Sl. No.	Period	Number of Households Reporting Occupational Diversification		Differential (d_i)
		PJBi	BHRi	
1	2	3	4	5
1.	Before 1960-61	25 (8.33)	14 (4.67)	78.57
2.	1960-61 - 1965-66	18 (6.00)	5 (1.67)	260.00
3.	1965-66 - 1970-71	61 (20.33)	21 (7.00)	190.48
4.	1970-71 - 1975-76	61 (20.34)	15 (5.00)	306.67
5.	1975-76 - 1980-81	31 (10.33)	11 (3.66)	181.82
6.	All	196 (65.33)	66 (22.00)	196.97

1. PJB = Punjab. 2. BHR = Bihar 3. $di = \frac{PJBi - BHRi}{BHRi}$
4. *i* is the number of households in each period.
5. Figures in the parentheses represent in percentages of the total sample.

TABLE 2.16: Reasons for Occupational Diversification in Punjab and Bihar

Sl.	Reason Type	Punjab	Bihar
1.	Economic	140 (46.67)	38 (12.67)
2.	Social	23 (7.67)	8 (2.67)
3.	Institutional	10 (3.33)	10 (3.33)
4.	Others	23 (7.66)	10 (3.33)
	All	196 (65.33)	66 (22.00)

Note: 1. Economic reasons include low wage rate, long working hours, problem of getting regular employment, introduction and popularity of new/cheep substitutes, high cost of raw materials, low income in case of sole dependence on traditional services, low profit/income or loss in previous family occupation etc.
2. Social reasons cover quarrel with employer, below social status, disliking for ancestral occupation, marriage, etc.
3. Institutional reasons include disturbances by the Government, redemption from landlord's debt, non-availability of cultivable land, non-availability of common grazing land and lack of capital for purchasing livestock or other productive assets.
4. Other reasons include physical problem like accident with thresher/week eye sight, tough nature of the work, old age, father's death, parents did not teach the ancestral occupation, lockout in the factory, retirement from service, lack of means of transport, dacoity, litigation and illiteracy, etc.

Thus, it is obvious from above discussion that members of such households work in all types of earning activities in and out of the village. Depending upon the locational advantage of a particular village, non-farm activities are becoming increasingly important sources of their employment, as farm activities in and around the village.

Limitations

It would be rather presumptuous to claim that the present study is free from all limitations. One major limitation of the study is that the data were acquired through a single visit survey method. As is well known, the rural labour households generally do not maintain any record of their total yearly employment, income or consumption. They invariably respond to the queries on the basis of their memory. One cannot, therefore, completely rule out the possibility of memory lapses on the part of the respondents, especially because most of them are devoid of even elementary education. Nevertheless, we hope that the error margin created by such memory biases is not big, particularly because many cross-checks were provided for in the questionnaire to straighten out inconsistencies and mental lethargies on the part of the respondents.

Further, the present study is based on one year data alone. Consequently, the generalisations attempted on the basis of the study need to be understood with due caution. Inasmuch as the new farm technology had acquired a fair degree of 'maturity' by the close of the seventies, the 1980-81 picture should be highly meaningful, representing, as it does, a regime of stability and concreteness as regards the effects of technological changeover.

Moreover, the emerging interaction between the internal dynamics of the rural transformation and the growing rural urban linkages on the households economy of the rural labour households should have assumed a concrete shape after the lapse of a full decade. Accordingly, an analysis based on a more recent although single year would be more useful than the one for two or three years in the early or middle seventies. We believe this to be a big advantage.

The conclusions are expected to be helpful to those engaged in policy making. Hopefully, these may help the planners in devising suitable measures to combat the problems of rural unemployment, underemployment and poverty emerging from two parts of Indian economy which have witnessed impressive growth in their agriculture and yet provide their typical peculiarities in the matter of rural proletarinization.

NOTES

1. Central Statistical Organisation (1987): *Statistical Abstract of India 1985*, Monthly and Annual Rainfall 1984 (1) Table 13, Department of Statistics, Ministry of Planning, Government of India, June, New Delhi, p. 41.
2. Central Statistical Organisation (1987): *Ibid.*, Area and Population, Table 2, p. 10.
3. Central Statistical Organisation (1987): *Ibid.*, p. 4.
4. Broadly speaking, district Ludhiana consists of two heterogeneous regions viz., the 'bet' and the 'Non-bet'. But from the microscopic view point, it can be divided into 3 sub-regions namely. Bet (river land frequently flooded), Dhaya Neecha (lower upland) and Dhaya Uncha (higher upland). The latter is the area of the present study in case of district Ludhiana. Similarly, District Bhojpur can be divided into two parts, viz., the low lying Alluvial plain of the North and the Flat region of the South. The former lies between the famous river, the Ganga and main line of Eastern Railway and the latter while stretching from southern embankments of the main line of Eastern Railway extends up to the South Western extremes. The present study was conducted into the latter in case of Bhojpur district.
5. The final report of All India Soil Survey Scheme by the Indian Council of Agricultural Research bears adequate testimony to the high fertility of soils in Bhojpur district. For example, see Indian Council of Agricultural Research (1953), *"Final Report of All India Soil Survey Scheme"*, Bulletin No. 73, Chapter X, pp. 70-80. See especially, p. 78.
6. District Census Handbook Ludhiana District Series 17, Punjab 1971.
7. Hereafter, the expression 'equally distanced', 'more distanced' 'less distanced' villages etc. would refer to distance from the chosen focal town.
8. For a detailed and highly meaningful discussion on the subject of categorisation of the rural labour force, please see, Ministry of Labour (1954), *Report on Intensive Survey of Agricultural Labour : Employment, Underemployment, Wages and Levels of Living*. Vol. 1, Government of India, New Delhi, pp. 91-93; (1960), *Report on the Second Agricultural Labour Enquiry* : (1956-57), Vol. 1, Government of India, New Delhi, p. 148; Ramkrishna Mukerjee, (1961), Rural Class Structure in West Bengal, reprinted in A.R. Desai ed., (1969), *Rural Sociology in India*, Popular Prakashan Pvt. Ltd., Bombay, pp. 281-286; V.S. Vyas, (1964), *Agricultural Labour in Four Indian Villages*, Sardar Patel Agro Economic Research Centre, Vallabh Vidyanagar, Sardar Patel University, Gujarat and Daniel and Alice Thorner (1965), types of Employer-Labour Relationship in Indian Agriculture in, *Indian Journal of Agricultural Economics 1940-64 : Selected Readings*, The Indian Society of Agricultural Economics, Bombay, pp. 287-302.

3

THE CONCEPTS, VARIABLES AND THE METHODOLOGY

In empirical research, it is a convention to set out some essential details about the concepts and the variables as also about the methodology used, since a well devised framework of research usually succeeds in avoiding bias, limiting the scope for subjective conjectures and ambiguities, and putting things in a clear perspective. In tune with the usual practice, an attempt is made to straighten out these preliminaries so that the subsequent analysis lends itself to a proper appreciation.

Concepts and Definitions

We describe below, in reasonable detail, the various concepts used in the study and the procedures followed for computing the variables used.

The basic unit of analysis for the present study is a household. A household as the unit of analysis has been preferred because it constitutes not only a composite unit of consumption, but a composite unit of employment and income as well. In typical rural households in India, economic decisions are generally for the family as a whole; there is a generally no system of decision-making at individual level, although some elderly members do wield more importance in such matters. The basic objective is essentially to increase the feeding capacity of the household as a whole.

The Household

The term 'household' as used in the present study is defined as the unit in which all the members of the family are normally living together and are sharing their meals from the same kitchen. Any person, sharing his principal meals with the household for more than six months during the reference year has been considered as a member of the household. Such a person may be the head of the household, a relation, a protege of the head or a guest. Temporary guests have not been included. The married girls, whose *Muklawa* in Punjab and *Gauna* in Bihar did not take place, have been treated as household members[1]. Further, only those households have been taken into account where the minimum number of members in the family was two irrespective of their age or sex. Due to size variations of different households, per capita estimates have been derived to ensure comparability across categories of households in a given area or across households in different areas. Age of the members refers to the number of completed years preceding the date of inquiry.

Earner

An earner is defined as one who makes a contribution to household income through his/her earning from farm and/or non-farm employment. While the labour contributed by the students has been included in the total mandays of employment in a particular operation, wherever reported, they were not treated as earners since their involvement was only marginal and confined to two or three points of time in the year. The return to their labour was, however, duly included in the total family earnings. In fact, wage payment accrued to the whole family team of which they were marginal partners.

Human Labour

Human labour is measured in terms of adult man-days of work. An adult manday consists of 8 work-hours. Labour quality differentials manifest themselves between regions, age, sex, etc. and the ideal situation would be to take cognizance of such attributes while working out earning differentials. Unluckily, we could not rigorously invoke such measures since any attempt to standardize labour units on the above counts would almost always be based on guess and varying interpretations. The aspect of quality differentials could not, therefore, be pursued in detail. To arrive at standard mandays of human labour, female and child labour days have been converted into manday units taking one woman-day equal to 0.75 man-day and one child-day equal to 0.5 man-day.[2]

Total Yearly Employment/Earnings

The total yearly employment and earnings, as used in the present study, consist of two components, viz. on-farm and non-farm. Each of these two components is further split into three sub-components. The three sub-components of on-farm employment include wage employment, non-wage (self) employment and dairying and poultry; while rural wage employment, urban wage employment and others including self employment are the three sub-components of non-farm employment. Earning per day of employment has been obtained by dividing the total earnings accruing from a particular source with the total mandays of employment in that source. A brief description of each of these items is given below:

(i) *On farm Wage Employment/Earnings*

Wage employment/earnings is the most dominant constituent of the total on-farm employment/earnings. It is contributed by household members while working either as attached farm servants for their respective employers or on daily basis in on-farm activities such as ploughing, sowing and transplantation, weeding, harvesting and threshing and other agricultural operations such as manuring, watering, etc.

The earnings accruing from such sources of employment consist of cash and kind wages (including those from wage-receipt land and other perquisites such as meals, tea, clothes, footwear, etc.) earned by all the working members on attached as well as daily basis during the reference year. The interest on the cash component of wages which is usually paid at the beginning of the year to the attached farm servants in Punjab has been included in wage earnings. The kind wages have been converted into cash by using the farm harvest prices of the relevant commodities prevailing in the sample villages in the two study areas. The money equivalent of other perquisites, wherever reported, has also been duly accounted for.

The concept of wage receipt land, mentioned in the preceding paragraph, is applicable to Bihar only. In Bihar, the dominant mode of wage payment to the attached farm servants is in the form of a tiny, rent free, piece of land. Conceptually, net income derived from the cultivation of such a tiny plot is essentially a wage-earning in kind. We have, therefore, clubbed this income with other constituents of wage income, reported earlier. Net income from this type of crop husbandry has been obtained by deducting the cost of standard inputs such as expenditure on seeds, fertilizers, irrigation, repair and maintenance of farm implements from the gross value of output (including that of by-products). Home produced inputs such as seeds, manures, etc. have been evaluated at the prices prevailing in the villages at the time of their actual usage.

(ii) *On-Farm Non-Wage Employment/Earnings*

This sub-component includes employment on owned-land, leased-in land and mandays spent on gathering the remains of wheat and paddy, etc. The same procedure has been followed for arriving at net income from owned-land and leased-in land, as for the cultivation of wage-receipt land except that an additional element of cost, namely paid-out rent, has now to be accounted for while arriving at net income from crop husbandry.

(iii) *Dairying and Poultry*

Another important segment of total on-farm employment and earnings comes from dairying and poultry activities. This includes mandays of employment in the rearing and maintenance of all variety of cattle and poultry. The cattle stock mainly consists of milch, draught, youngstock, sheep/goat, hen, etc. It needs to be clarified that income from this head is net of intermediate inputs such as green fodder, dry fodder, expenditure on medicine, etc. No costs could be computed for family labour gone into the rearing of dairying and poultry since concrete information on this account could not be conveyed by the respondent households.

Non-Farm Employment/Earnings

All avenues of employment/earnings other than those reported earlier under the three on-farm sub-components are treated items of non-farm employment/earnings. Such employment avenues are open to rural labour households *mostly* through wage employment although in same cases, self-employment is also availed of.

The wage employment in such activities is available both in the rural as well as urban areas. Some working members of these households are engaged as wage-earners in or around their village as construction workers, carpenters, watch-men etc. While some others get wage-employment as industrial or construction workers, porters in the grain market, etc., in the nearby urban town. With the basic objective of studying the impact of growing rural-urban linkages, the employment/earnings arising from such activities have been stratified and studied under two heads, viz. Rural Wage Employment and Urban Wage Employment. While earnings from such activities are mostly in cash, 'other perquisites' wherever reported, have also been taken into account.

Others (Including Self-employment)

This includes mandays of employment/earnings contributed by the following categories of economic enterprises:

(i) artisans and craftsman such as blacksmith and weaver, etc.,
(ii) service personnel such as barber, cobbler, sweeper, dyer, washerman, sweet-maker, cartage, and other traditional services such as dancer, loudspeaker and bandmaster, etc.,
(iii) self-employed tradesman such as rope-making, households enterprises, spinning, butcher, fisherman, rickshaw-puller, petty shopkeeper, wood cutting and selling, vegetable selling, broom selling, goldsmith, engine repair, cycle repair, and tailoring, etc.

Net Household Income

The concept of net household income as used in the present study, emanates mainly from two sources i.e. the wage source and the non-wage source. The 'wage source' of household income covers wage receipts earned by all the earning members of the household in farm (including net earnings from wage-receipt land) and non-farm (both in rural and urban areas) activities. The non-wage source of household income includes net earnings from dairying and poultry, cultivation of owned or small pieces of leased-in land, and others including self employment (non-farm) category of economic enterprises. The latter sources of net household income also includes income received by the household on account of transfer payments such as remittances, pensions and other State assistance in the form of scholarships to its student members. Per capita estimates have been derived by dividing the net household income with the household size.

Consumption Expenditure

In the present study, the consumption expenditure of the sample households consists mainly of two sets of items: namely food-items and non-food items. Expenditure made on cereals (wheat, maize and rice etc.), milk and milk products, meat, fish and eggs, vegetables and fruits, salt and spices, and beverages (including expenditure made in the focal town on petty refreshments, *pan, khaini,* cigarette, tobacco, *bidi* and other intoxicants etc.) has been covered under food-items. On the other hand, expenditure incurred on fuel and light, clothing and bedding, footwear, education, conveyance, medicine and health, consumer durables (consisting of domestic utensils, furnitures, radios/transistors, watches, bicycles, sewing machines, electric fans, etc.) and miscellaneous goods and services (covering expenditure on cinema and other amusements, barber charges, laundry and toiletry, etc.) has been treated as expenditure on non-food items. Further, the expenditure made on marriage and other social ceremonies, though studies separately as well, has been treated as part of the non-food expenditure.

The total consumption expenditure of the sample households is made of cash and non-cash (or kind) components. For cash component, while the sample households have to rely upon market purchases, the non-cash component is largely wage receipt in the form of kind earnings and other perquisites (tea, meals, etc.) although home-grown production also makes a marginal contribution. The value of such non-cash component items are valued at village level prices. It is worthwhile pointing out that 'other perquisites' are consumed only by the working members at their place of work, and, as such, are not shared by other members of the household. In the present study, however, the money equivalent of these 'other perquisites has been added to the household expenditure under the relevant commodity heading. For a more meaningful analysis, per capita estimates have been derived to take note of the variations in household size.

Poverty

One of the central issues in research on poverty is that of defining a poverty line i.e. determination of a cut-off point for separating the poor from the non-poor. As a result of the intense debate that has revolved around this issue, two main approaches have come into the limelight. While the first approach defines the poverty line in terms of income level or some minimum expenditure level required to purchase a socially accepted minimum bundle of goods;[3] the other proceeds in terms of nutritional norms such as the intake of calories and proteins to keep a person fit in the working condition[4].

While adhering to either of these two approaches, cut-off points for estimating the incidence of poverty have been variously suggested by a number of researchers. Almost all such cut-off points are essentially arbitrary in nature due to the fact that if two or more such points are used for estimating poverty from the same data, these may reveal glaring differences in the extent of poverty and may pose challenges of far reaching consequences for the policy-makers.

Out of the various cut-off points available for poverty measurement, those suggested by Bardhan are based on careful scrutiny of expenditure data for various parts of India, for a few points of time. For the head-count method of measuring poverty, Bardhan's norms have been very extensively made use of. We also borrow Bardhan's norms.[5] Accordingly, a per capita monthly expenditure of Rs. 15.00 at 1960-61 all-India rural prices has been taken as the cut-off point for the present study. Further, while taking note of inter-State and rural-urban prices differentials, the equivalents of Rs. 15.00 at all-India rural prices for rural Punjab and Bihar have been worked out at Rs. 15.90 and Rs. 15.80 respectively at 1960-61 prices.[6] The corresponding yearly figures for rural Punjab and rural Bihar are Rs. 190.80 and Rs. 189.60 respectively.

To arrive at the cut-off points for the year of the study, a suitable price index is needed. The most suitable index is Consumer Price Index for Agricultural Labourers which is constructed by the Ministry of Labour, for various parts of the country, on a regular basis. Moreover, luckily for us, these index numbers have 1960-61 as their base and the problems of working out the 1980-81 norms for poverty measurement is easily resolved. The average annual figures of Rs. 833.80 and Rs. 811.49 are finally worked out[7] as the minimum per capita income for measuring poverty in rural Punjab and rural Bihar, respectively. The problem of poverty in the present study is studied on the basis of these cut-off points.

Methodological Frame

In the present study, a comparative analysis of the employment pattern and the corresponding levels of income and consumption of the non-cultivating rural labour households of Punjab and Bihar, has been carried out in terms of seeking empirical answers to various hypotheses. These hypotheses are mainly tested by comparing the averages. For this purpose, mean values have been estimated for all variables included in the present study. It needs to be mentioned here that mean values for such components where the percentage of positive responses is very high are comparatively more reliable than those mean values where the percentage of such responses is low. Further, in addition to the mean values, percentages have also been presented side by side to make the analysis more meaningful. Still further, to lend statistical concreteness to our findings, for most of the variables used in the study, the effect of distance from the respective focal towns of Punjab and Bihar is worked out through linear statistical relations such as

$$Y_i = \alpha + \beta D_j$$

Where Y_i is the value of the *i*th variable observed cross-sectionally among the eight sample villages, D_j is the distance between the *j*th village and the focal town, β measures the effect of the distance, α is the intercept indicating the value of *Y* when the effect of the distance is neutralised or is zero.

To study the consumption pattern, mean values for different items of consumption expenditure have been estimated and compared on per capita basis. Further, with the objective of examining a well received proposition in the existing literature that 'higher income households generally consume smaller proportion of their income than do lower income households', we have estimated the average propensity to consume between equally distanced pair of Punjab and Bihar villages. Further, we have analysed the distribution of consumption expenditure in terms of decile groups formed on the basis of net household income. The percentage share of each such decile group in the total as well as individual commodity expenditure has also been worked out. Besides, for each commodity group. Gini's[8] Concentration ratio co-efficient has also been estimated.

Further, to complete the discussion on the consumption pattern of Punjab-Bihar labour households, expenditure elasticities have been estimated for different items of consumption. Conventionally, such elasticities are considered to be highly useful for looking into the significance of different components of consumption in the family-budgets of any set of households. It needs to be pointed out that in a *ceteris paribus* framework, almost all theories of consumer behaviour treat consumption to be a function of income. In most empirical studies conducted so far in the field of consumer behaviour, while many non-economic factors have been placed in the *ceteris paribus* framework possibly due to their being unimportant in affecting the consumption of a particular commodity in a significant way; efforts have, however, been made to isolate the impact of important economic determinants such as prices, income, assets, etc. on its consumption. Assuming that the numerous non-economic factors determining the consumption of a particular commodity are unimportant and individually generate an error term, which, in turn, confirms to some probability distribution with zero mean and constant variance, the demand Q_{ik} for the *i*th commodity by the *k*th households can be written in a mathematical form. Symbolically.

$$Q_{ik} = f_1 (Y_k, P_1 P_2, P_3, \ldots P_n, R_{ik})$$

Where Y_k stands for the income of the *k*th household.

$P_1, P_2, P_3, \ldots P_n$ denote the prices of the *n* commodities
R_{ik} is a random variable; and
f_1 shows the functional relationship.

Again, if it is assumed that on the one hand, $P_1, P_2, P_3, \ldots P_n$ in the above model remain constant, and on the other, income tends to vary among households, we may possibly derive the following type of relationship between quantity consumed and level of income:

$$C_1 = f_1(Y_1), C_2 = f_2(Y_2), C_3 = f_3(Y_3), \ldots C_n = f_n(Y_n)$$

Where *C* is quantity consumed, *Y* the level of income and *f* shows the functional relationship between the two i.e. quantity consumed (*C*) and the level of income (*Y*).

The function, as Stated above, assumes different values of quantity consumed depending upon the value of *Y* and it is possible to trace a curve in *n*-dimensional quantity space $[C_1, C_2, C_3, \ldots C_n]$. This curve is popularly known as Engel Curve.

The following important algebraic forms of Engel functions are available in the existing literature:

Sl.No.	Algebraic Form	Function Type
1	2	3
1	$q = a + bX$	Linear
2	$q = a + bX + cX^2$	Quadratic
3	$q = a - b/X$	Hyperbolic
4	$q = a + b \cdot \log X$	Semi-log
5	$\text{Log } q = a - b \cdot 1/X$	Log-inverse
6	$\text{Log } q = a + b \log X - c \cdot 1/X$	Log-log-inverse
7	$\text{Log } q = a + b \log X$	Log-linear
8	$\text{Log } q = a + b \log X - c (\log X)^2$	Log-quadratic

Where *q* is expenditure on a particular commodity and *X* is the total expenditure (both in per capita terms); *a* is the intercept term; and *b* and *c* are the regression parameters.

It is important to note that to estimate income/expenditure elasticities, a number of Engel functions have been tried by different research workers. However, out of the available formulations for the Engel functions, the relevance of specific types for studying specific commodities is governed by several statistical, economic and other theoretical considerations. In this regard, the current evidence highlights two important points. In the first instance, it is obvious that no unique Engel curve suffices for the complete range of consumer goods, and, in the second, different mathematical forms give rise to widely differing estimates of income/expenditure elasticities or marginal propensity to consume. Each of the available Engel functions has its own merits to commend itself over others. Likewise, it has its own share of limitations. The relative merits and demerits of these functional forms are extensively discussed in econometric literature. We do not intend to go into them. On the contrary, without wishing to lose merits of some formulations and to get into the statistical problems posed by others, we take a bold decision to estimate all the eight functional forms mentioned earlier.

Using our sample data, we have estimated Engel elasticities for different commodity groups. In general bivariate Engel functions have been tried. In the estimation of such Engel functions, per capita commodity expenditure q has been taken as the 'regressand' and per capita total expenditure X as the 'regressor'. Such per capita formulations, as is well known, imply neutrality as regards the economies of scale in consumption. In other words, by assuming that per capita commodity expenditure depends only on the per capita level of total expenditure (the well-known homogeneity hypothesis), an attempt has been made to take cognizance of the variations in the household size. For estimating the Engel functions, the following procedural adjustments have been made. Firstly, to take care of the wide intra-group variations in the total as well as commodity expenditure (both in per capita terms), the sample have been divided into as many as seventeen categories (Please see Appendix Table A-3.1) on the basis of per capita total expenditure. As a result of this exercise, we obtained as many as seventeen pairs of observations on q and X. Secondly, by using the number of household behind each pair of q and X as the relevant weights, weighted least square regressions have been run between q and X. Thirdly, and most importantly, it needs to be pointed out that with the objective of making the co-efficient of determination (R^2) strictly comparable between one estimated form and the other, we transformed the dependent variable q on the lines suggested by Box and Cox[9] while running the weighted regressions.

As said earlier, we have used 8 types of Engel functions. Amongst these, the final selection has, however, been made by striking a balance between statistical, economic and other considerations. In this regard, the following procedure has been adopted:

A higher value of co-efficient of determination (R^2), or adjusted coefficient of determination ($\bar{R}^2$), proper signs of regression coefficients as also their statistical significance have been the main criteria for narrowing our choice of functional forms. All-such functions for which regression parameter/parameters or $R^2/\bar{R}^2$ or both are not statistically significant at 95.0 per cent level of confidence have been dismissed straight because the regression equation in such cases is obviously useless. A three parametric Engel function having one statistically non-significant parameter owing to high correlation between the explanatory variables, has also been dropped by us. T test and F test have been employed to test the statistical significance of regression parameter/parameters and co-efficient of determination respectively. Functions qualifying T- and F-tests have been further tested for serial correlation by employing Durbin-Watson statistic[10]. Even with rigorous application of the above criteria, we were left with 2-3 functional forms for each commodity group. For making a final selection, other considerations such as their conforming to economic theory, computational convenience, etc. have been taken into account.

Finally, we have looked at the problem of poverty in terms of our income data. For working out the proportion of households below the poverty line in terms of income norms discussed earlier in this chapter, we have made use of the usual head-count ratio. Symbolically

$$P = \frac{m}{n}$$

Where

P measures the proportion of households below the poverty line in terms of per capita income formulations, *m* is the number of households below the poverty line and *n* is the total number of households.

For obvious reasons, the usual head-count ratio is beset with a number of limitations (for details, see chapter 6). In order to overcome such limitations, we have pressed into service the modified version of Sen's *P* measure[11] to work out the intensity of poverty in the two study areas. Although various modifications have been suggested to Sen's original index by Sen himself and others, thanks to the availability of disaggregated, household-level data with us, the following modified version (suggested by Sen himself) should serve us the best:

$$P_s = \frac{2}{(q+1)nZ} \sum_{i=1}^{q} (Z - Y_i)(q + 1 - i)$$

Where P_s is Sen's measure of the intensity of poverty, *n* the population size, Y_i the income of the *i*th individual arranged in ascending order of magnitude. *q* the number of people at or below the poverty line and *Z* the poverty level per capita income.

We have also looked at the problem of poverty in an alternative manner. By taking into account the percentage distribution of the poor households on the basis of their per capita net household income, we have compared the poverty levels as also the additional income required to cross over the poverty line between Punjab and Bihar.

NOTES

1. The terms like *Muklawa* in Punjab or *Gauna* in Bihar have the same meaning. They imply a type of post-marriage social agreement by which girls married at a very young age because of prevalence of child marriage are required to stay with their parents till they attain the age of puberty, understand the post-marriage sexual relations and become capable of managing their household affairs individually.
2. This is a very common practice and has been widely in use. For example, see G.K. Chadha (1979); *Production Gains of New Agricultural Technology,* Publication Bureau, Panjab University, Chandigarh, pp. 29-30; and R.K. Sharma (1983); *Impact of New Technology on Income Distribution Among Cultivating Households in Rural Haryana: A Regional Study,* Ph.D. Dissertation (Unpublished), Jawaharlal Nehru University, New Delhi, p. 160.
3. For example, see B.S. Minhas, (1970); "Rural Poverty, Land Redistribution and Development Strategy : Facts and Policy", *Indian Economic Review,* Vol. V (New Series), April, pp. 97-128. This approach of defining poverty line was suggested in 1962 by a distinguished working group appointed by the Planning Commission for the said purpose.
4. Various estimates for minimum nutritional requirement have been suggested by different authorities such as the Indian Council of Medical Research (ICMR), Second Pay Commission for Central Government Employees (1957-59) and FAO Rome etc. Broadly speaking, these estimates have varied between 2100 to 2400 calories per person per day.
5. Pranab K. Bardhan, (1973) "On the Incidence of Poverty in Rural India of the Sixties", *Economic and Political Weekly,* Vol. VIII, Nos. 4-6, Annual Number, February, pp. 245-254.
6. P.K. Bardhan (1973); *Ibid*; p. 247.
7. We have worked out these annual figures on the basis of Consumer Price Index for Agricultural Labourers for Punjab and Bihar. This index is readily available in, *Statistical Abstract of India for 1980),* New Series, No. 25, Government of India, p. 410.
8. We are aware of the fact that this measure when translated into welfare function terms, has been severely objected to by a large number of welfare economists. The argument put forward is that the sensitivity of the Lorenz

curve measure depends on the number of people in-between the income/expenditure levels rather than on the size of income/expenditure levels. Despite such limitations, this method has been most extensively used owing to the fact that it has many merits to commend itself over other measures. For instance, not only unlike most of them it is intuitively a simple measure or takes into account the full distribution, it is also not affected by the static value. And presumably, these properties commend the concentration ratio method for studying the income/consumption expenditure distribution. Consequently, we put our reliance on this simple but intuitively powerful and widely used method of Gini concentration ratio. For further details, see, J.N. Morgan. (1961); The Anatomy of Income Distribution, *Restat,* (as quoted by Thomas Stark).

9. G.E.P. Box and D.R. Cox (1964), "An Analysis of Transformation", *Journal of the Royal Statistical Society,* Series B, pp. 211-243.
10. It is worthwhile pointing out that in the present study, D.-W Statistic (short name for Durbin — Watson Statistic) provided by Theil and Nagar (1961) has been made use of for testing the presence of auto correlation. The value of n and k at 0.05 per cent level of significance have been computed. '*n*' refers to the number of observations and '*k*' the number of explanatory variables excluding the constant. For further details, see Devender B. Gupta (1973) *Consumption Pattern in India: A Study of Inter-Regional Variations,* Tata McGraw-Hills Publishing Co. Ltd., Bombay p. 20.
11. For further details of Sen's *P* measure, please see Chapter 6.

4

ON-FARM EMPLOYMENT/EARNINGS

The rising occupational diversification in rural India since the inception of planning era is a well recognised fact. While some of the old activities have tended to disappear gradually over the years, some others have expanded fast and some new ones have emerged as important sources of employment and earnings for the rural population including landless labour households. Further, some of the rural households are getting increasingly linked with the nearby sub-urban and urban towns for the purpose of their employment and earnings, depending upon the level of general development of the area and the availability of infra-structural facilities. In brief, the composition and the level of employment of rural labour households have undergone perceptible changes in most part of rural India; and accordingly, such households have reduced their extreme dependence on single source of earnings, namely agricultural employment.

As is to be expected, the occupational diversification has witnessed varying degree of change in different areas. On the one extreme are the Green Revolution areas which have undergone the most remarkable occupational changes for the rural labour households, and, on the other extreme are the areas which have witnessed rather limited change in the rural occupational structures, *inter alia*, primarily because agricultural growth and agricultural transformation there have been of a very low order. In areas of fast agricultural growth, the on-farm labour-absorption has increased because of many technological changes. This has increased the on-farm earning potential of rural labour households. Besides, allied farm activities such as dairying and poultry have also contributed towards a rise in their earnings.[1] Again, thanks to a growing network of village link roads, and the rising rural-urban economic nexus, many rural labour households are benefiting through urban employment, and so on. In sum, the structure of rural employment and earnings has undergone formidable changes in agriculturally growing areas under the combined impact of the internal dynamics of rural transformation and growing rural-urban linkages. The basic objective of the present chapter is to look into the combined impact of this interaction on the on-farm employment and earnings of different categories of non-cultivating rural labour households in the States of Punjab and Bihar. An attempt has been made to account for the wide variations observed between the Punjab and the Bihar on-farm employment and income scenarios.

The on-farm employment scenario can be visualized in many different ways. For example, nearness to an urban industrial town has its own influence on the on-farm off-farm balances; a more rapidly growing agriculture creates its own compulsions and possibilities regarding employment distribution between farm and non-farm activities, and so on. To lend concrete content to various possibilities, we suggest below some hypotheses which are tested empirically later in the chapter:

(i) The yearly on-farm mandays of employment and earnings per household keep on increasing as we move away from the town.

(ii) Earning per day of on-farm employment is inversely related to distance from the focal town both in areas of fast and slow agricultural growth; the level of earning per day of employment is, however, much higher in the former compared with the latter areas.

(iii) In general, as we move into the interior of the countryside, the avenues of on-farm employment are confined largely to agricultural wage employment; sources of on-farm self-employment (e.g. dairying, poultry, etc.) get reduced as the distance increases.

(iv) In each pair of nearly equally distanced villages of Punjab and Bihar, the incidence of employment/earnings on daily basis is higher in the former compared with the latter.

In the remaining part of this chapter, we seek empirical answers to the various hypotheses set out above. To facilitate a clear exposition of the agrarian realities of Punjab and Bihar, the following order of discussion has been observed. To begin with, the overall on-farm employment and its various components, namely on-farm wage employment, on-farm non-wage (self) employment, and, dairying and poultry, have been discussed between the two States. Further, this analysis has been extended both in respect of each of the sample villages of Punjab and Bihar, and, then between predominantly agricultural and predominantly non-agricultural labour households. This is followed by a discussion of wage-paid on-farm employment on daily basis, wherein the relative significance of each source of wage-paid on-farm employment on daily basis is brought out. In each discussion, earnings (total as well as per manday) and employment are set out side by side so that Punjab and Bihar differentials are brought out in clear perspective.

Level of On-Farm Employment/Earnings

Before taking up our hypotheses, we consider it useful to compare the overall position of Punjab labour households *vis-a-vis* their Bihar counterparts in respect of their total yearly on-farm employment/ earnings and its various components. Mean values of different components of total on-farm employment and earnings for all sample households of Punjab and Bihar are detailed in Table 4.1.

It is clear that about 97.0 per cent of our sample households in Bihar are engaged in on-farm employment of one type or the other, compared with a slightly low figure of 92.0 per cent in Punjab. It is interesting to note that while the total mandays of on-farm employment are slightly higher in Bihar (457.51 mandays) compared with Punjab (421.62 mandays), the position is diametrically opposite as regards per household and per manday of on-farm earnings. A non-cultivating rural labour household in Punjab is earning nearly 65.0 per cent more from on-farm employment than its counterpart in Bihar. Consequently, per day earning from on-farm employment is nearly 79.0 per cent higher in Punjab over Bihar. This clearly shows that a relatively greater disposition of work time and mandays of employment in on-farm activities by a Bihar household notwithstanding, the growing and dynamic agriculture of Punjab is comparatively more remunerative and is capable of increasing the level of earnings much faster than in Bihar.

TABLE 4.1: Pattern of On-Farm Employment and Earnings of Labour Households in Punjab and Bihar

(Mean Value, Per Annum)

Sl. No.	Employment/Earning Source	Variable	Punjab (PJBi)	Bihar (BIIRi)	Differential (di)
1	2	3	4	5	6
1.	Wage Employment	Emp	310.62 (73.67)	386.08 (84.39)	−19.55
		Ern	2782.51 (74.47)	2048.37 (90.43)	35.84
		Epd	8.96	5.31	68.74
		PPR	87.33	93.67	
2.	Non-Wage Employment	Emp	3.18 (0.75)	13.13 (2.87)	−75.78
		Ern	21.56 (0.58)	92.38 (4.08)	−76.66
		Epd	6.78	7.04	−3.69
		PPR	18.67	71.00	
3.	Dairying and Poultry	Emp	107.83 (25.58)	58.30 (12.74)	84.96
		Ern	932.36 (24.95)	124.36 (5.49)	649.73
		Epd	8.65	2.13	306.10
		PPR	82.00	67.67	
4.	Total On-Farm Employment	Emp	421.62 (100.00)	457.51 (100.00)	−7.84
		Ern	3736.43 (100.00)	2265.12 (100.00)	64.96
		Epd	8.86	4.95	78.99
		PPR	92.33	97.33	

Note: 1. Emp: Employment in Mandays (1 Manday = 8 hours).
2. Ern: Total Earnings (in Rs.).
3. Epd: Earning Per Manday of Employment.
4. PPR: Percentage of Positive Responses
5. $d_i = \frac{PJBi - BIIRi}{BIIR_i}$
6. i : Value of *ith* component of Total On-Farm Employment/Earnings.
7. Figures in the parentheses are percentages of the Total On-Farm Employment/ Earnings.

These Notations are used in the subsequent Chapters as well.

Let us look into the components of on-farm employment. To begin with, we discover that in Bihar, the involvement of sample households is about 94.0 per cent, compared with a slightly lower figure of about 87.0 per cent in Punjab as far as the most dominant constituent viz. wage-paid on-farm employment is concerned. In other words, on an average, a Punjab household is putting in about 20.0 per cent less effort in this type of on-farm employment, yet earning nearly 36.0 per cent more compared to its counterpart in Bihar. The most striking feature of the differential earnings between the Punjab and the Bihar households is that on the basis of earnings per manday of employment, the average Punjab household is nearly 70.0 per cent better off than the one in Bihar. As regards the other component of on-farm employment, viz. non-wage (self) employment, a Bihar household tends to give the impression of slight superiority in terms of mandays of work as well as per household and per day earnings. However, this is more apparent than real. It is important to point out that this source of on-farm employment in Bihar is contributed by self-cultivation of tiny pieces of land, cultivation of leased-in land, and gathering the remains of wheat and paddy after harvesting, while in Punjab, this type of employment is derived only as a marginal activity, confined to the fast disappearing practice of gathering the remains of wheat and paddy. Table 4.1 clearly shows that only about 18.0 per cent of sample households in Punjab are pursuing such sources of employment against as high as 71.0 per cent in Bihar. In any case, a relatively higher time spent on such activities in Bihar but a much lower on dairying and poultry compared with Punjab, brings out the structural weaknesses of the Bihar employment pattern. On an average, the Punjab non-cultivating rural labour households spends nearly 108 mandays in a year on dairying and poultry compared with only 58 in Bihar. The differences become still more sharp if we compare per household and per day net earnings between Punjab and Bihar. The figures for Punjab are Rs. 932.36 and Rs. 8.65 respectively, while these are only Rs. 124.36 and Rs. 2.13 respectively for Bihar. The higher employment and earning potential created in Punjab through a series of institutional measures has greatly facilitated private investment in dairy enterprises. The institutional lending being relatively more effective in Punjab compared with Bihar, the Punjab households have succeeded in augmenting their total earnings to a much greater extent. It is worthwhile pointing out that in our sample, about 82.0

per cent of households in Punjab are engaged in dairying and poultry against only 67.0[2] per cent in Bihar (Table 4.1). In fact, income and employment through dairying and poultry enterprises occupy a fairly big chunk of the total employment and earnings in Punjab, and, as many studies show, have the effect of mollifying the severity of overall income distribution in rural Punjab.[3]

The Village-wise Pattern

In the preceding analysis, we have compared the overall position of Punjab and Bihar labour households in terms of different components of their total yearly on-farm employment/earnings. One broad conclusion that emerges from our discussion is that in the matter of accrual of earnings from different components of on-farm employment, a labour household in Punjab is far better placed than its counterpart in Bihar. We may now test our three hypotheses by comparing the pattern of on-farm employment/earnings of labour households living near the focal town as also away from it in the two States. For this purpose, the village-wise pattern of different components of on-farm employment/earnings of Punjab-Bihar labour households is presented in Table 4.2. To lend statistical concreteness to our findings, for most of the components, the effect of distance is worked out through linear statistical relation such as:

$$Y_i = \alpha + \beta D_j$$

Where Y_i is the ith component of on-farm employment/income, observed cross-sectionally among the eight sample villages, D_j is the distance between the jth village and the designated focal town, α is the intercept and β measures the effect of distance. Table 4.2 throws up many interesting features.

Firstly, a word about the extent of involvement in on-farm employment (variable PPR under Sl. No. 4, Table 4.2). As we move away from the focal town, the rural labour households extend their dependence on on-farm employment nearly completely. Beyond a certain distance, the involvement of each rural labour household in on-farm employment is a must, the degree of involvement notwithstanding. This is true both in Punjab and Bihar. Secondly, the per household mandays of on-farm employment go on increasing, both in Punjab and Bihar, as we move into the interior of the countryside. The statistical functions give significant regression co-efficients. Thirdly and most importantly, Punjab and Bihar represent sharp contrasts in the matter of per household and per day earnings. For instance, while per household earnings from on-farm employment increase with distance in Punjab; in Bihar, on the other hand, the increase in per household earnings with increase in rural-urban distance is not statistically significant. As such, the hypothesis regarding the increasing importance of on-farm employment in villages from the focal town, gets empirical confirmation in Punjab; while its validity cannot be stressed in the case of Bihar. Again, while per day earning from on-farm employment is not much affected by the intervening effect of distance in Punjab, the labour households in the interior of rural Bihar earn significantly less on per day basis. This rejects a part of our hypothesis as regards the inverse relationship between per day earning of on-farm employment and distance from the focal town in the case of Punjab. The pattern of per day earning in Bihar can be explained by the fact that the phenomenon of daily commutation to nearby towns ceases to operate beyond a certain distance with its obvious effect on per day on farm earnings. In Punjab, on the other hand, the process of commutation does not get diluted even up to a fairly big distance from the focal town. In other words, in the case of Bihar, with a decrease in rural-urban proximity, the pull force of the urban areas becomes less operative and total on-farm employment for the labour households is more intimately tied up with agricultural activities as such.

We now look at the components of on-farm employment/ earnings. Both in Punjab and Bihar, the involvement of sample households in wage-employment component becomes higher as we move away from the focal town. However, between equally distanced pair of Punjab and Bihar villages, the involvement of rural labour households in this component is higher in Bihar villages compared with equally distanced villages in Punjab. This suggests a relatively higher dependence of Bihar households on this category of employment. Again, for this type of (wage-paid on-farm) employment, the mandays of work per household keep on increasing in both the States as we move into the interior; for each village in Bihar, the mandays are uniformly higher compared with a more or less equally distanced village in Punjab, and lastly, as we move away from the focal town, the difference in mandays of employment between the

TABLE 4.2: Village-wise Pattern of On-Farm Employment and Earnings of Labour Households in Punjab and Bihar

(*Mean Value, Per Annum*)

Sl. No.	Employment/ Earning Source	Vari- able	State	Village V1	V2	V3	V4	V5	V6	V7	V8	Regression Equation $Y_i = a + b D_j$	No. of Observa- tions (N)
1	2	3	4	5	6	7	8	9	10	11	12	13	14
1.	Wage Employment	Emp	PJB	177.14	209.72	247.67	324.14	310.91	368.94	455.83	448.96	Y_i = 223.43 + 14.74* D	262
				(58.42)	(71.08)	(70.14)	(72.14)	(67.06)	(77.48)	(79.70)	(78.42)	(4.77)	
			BHR	289.88	216.86	470.62	481.14	496.40	348.15	464.39	446.88	Y_i = 363.73 + 4.66* D	281
				(85.09)	(73.89)	(87.35)	(89.20)	(85.60)	(81.27)	(86.52)	(87.06)	(2.05)	
			di	-38.89	-3.29	-47.37	-32.63	-37.37	5.97	-1.84	0.47		
		Ern	PJB	1677.54	1907.33	2276.34	2862.67	2858.74	3345.84	3885.74	3836.43	Y_i =2154.62 +114.90* D	262
				(69.26)	(72.44)	(66.34)	(73.02)	(68.65)	(79.34)	(82.50)	(79.85)	(4.34)	
			BHR	1722.80	1266.97	2546.20	2435.80	2706.63	1895.45	2289.77	2245.46	Y_i =2122.25 + 6.22 D	281
				(87.40)	(76.58)	(93.37)	(93.92)	(90.72)	(88.04)	(95.37)	(95.15)	(0.58)	
			di	-2.63	50.54	-10.60	17.52	5.62	76.52	69.70	70.85		
		Epd	PJB	9.47	9.09	9.19	8.83	9.19	9.07	8.52	8.55	Y_i = 10.34 - 0.08* D	262
												(3.86)	
			BHR	5.94	5.87	5.41	5.06	5.45	5.44	4.93	5.03	Y_i = 6.05 - 0.05* D	281
												(6.08)	
			di	59.43	54.86	69.87	74.51	68.62	66.73	72.82	69.98		
		PPR	PJB	76.19	70.21	89.79	71.43	86.96	90.48	100.00	100.00		
			BHR	76.92	78.38	96.15	100.00	100.00	95.29	100.00	100.00		

Contd.

TABLE 4.2 *Contd.*

1	2	3	4	5	6	7	8	9	10	11	12	13	14
2.	Non-wage Employment	Emp	PJB	2.33	1.83	1.69	8.29	4.91	3.13	5.37	5.00	Y_i = 13.78 + 0.33 *D*	56
				(0.77)	(0.62)	(0.48)	(1.85)	(1.06)	(0.66)	(0.94)	(0.87)	(1.19)	
			BHR	13.62	14.70	8.81	14.14	10.53	16.36	10.68	10.75	Y_i = 20.89 - 0.24 *D*	213
				(3.99)	(5.01)	(1.64)	(2.62)	(1.81)	(3.82)	(1.99)	(2.09)	(1.46)	
			di	-82.89	-87.55	-80.82	-41.37	-53.37	-80.87	-49.72	-53.49		
		Ern	PJB	20.38	12.72	11.33	47.86	32.87	21.10	36.69	32.81	Y_i = 99.74 + 1.59 *D*	56
				(0.84)	(0.48)	(0.33)	(1.22)	(0.79)	(0.50)	(0.78)	(0.68)	(0.86)	
			BHR	115.94	128.37	56.50	109.46	62.27	120.52	62.40	50.65	Y_i = 185.19 - 5.45* *D*	213
				(5.88)	(7.76)	(2.07)	(4.22)	(2.09)	(5.60)	(2.60)	(2.15)	(3.01)	
			di	-82.42	-90.09	-79.95	-56.28	-47.21	-82.49	-41.20	-35.22		
		Epd	PJB	5.85	8.54	11.03	8.64	8.61	8.17	7.11	7.89	Y_i = 7.43 - 0.05 *D*	56
												(1.47)	
			BHR	8.51	8.73	6.41	7.74	5.91	7.37	5.84	4.71	Y_i = 8.30 - 0.18* *D*	213
												(3.19)	
			di	-31.26	-2.18	72.07	11.63	45.69	10.85	21.75	67.52		
		PPR	PJB	14.29	10.64	14.10	42.86	26.09	17.46	28.57	26.92		
			BHR	65.38	64.86	65.36	85.71	73.33	74.12	73.68	67.31		

Contd.

TABLE 4.2 *Contd.*

1	2	3	4	5	6	7	8	9	10	11	12	13	14
3.	Dairying and Poultry	Emp	PJB	123.76	83.49	103.72	116.86	147.83	104.10	110.74	118.58	Y_i = 135.44 - 0.54 *D*	246
				(40.81)	(28.30)	(29.38)	(26.01)	(31.88)	(21.86)	(19.36)	(20.71)	(1.07)	
			BHR	37.19	61.92	59.35	44.14	73.00	63.87	61.66	55.69	Y_i = 78.04 + 0.86 *D*	201
				(10.92)	(21.10)	(11.01)	(8.18)	(12.59)	(14.91)	(11.49)	(10.85)	(1.46)	
			di	232.78	34.84	74.76	164.75	102.51	62.99	79.60	112.93		
		Ern	PJB	724.14	712.91	1143.65	1009.71	1272.48	850.05	787.80	935.65	Y_i = 1313.42 - 19.82 *D*	246
				(29.90)	(27.08)	(33.33)	(25.76)	(30.56)	(20.16)	(16.72)	(19.47)	(1.44)	
			BHR	132.38	259.15	124.38	48.34	214.51	137.00	48.81	63.69	Y_i = 290.15 - 11.74* *D*	216
				(6.72)	(15.66)	(4.56)	(1.86)	(7.19)	(6.36)	(2.03)	(2.70)	(2.46)	
			di	447.02	175.10	819.48	1988.77	493.20	520.47	1514.01	1369.07		
		Epd	PJB	5.85	8.54	11.03	8.64	8.61	8.17	7.11	7.89	Y_i = 8.81 - 0.10 *D*	246
												(1.04)	
			BHR	3.56	4.19	2.10	1.10	2.94	2.14	0.79	1.14	Y_i = 2.64 - 0.11* *D*	201
												(2.32)	
			di	64.33	103.82	425.24	685.45	192.86	281.78	800.00	592.11		
		PPR	PJB	90.48	63.83	78.21	100.00	95.65	80.95	88.57	96.15		
			BHR	53.85	72.97	69.23	76.19	93.33	65.88	65.79	63.46		

Contd.

TABLE 4.2 *Contd.*

1	2	3	4	5	6	7	8	9	10	11	12	13	14
4.	Total On-Farm Employment	Emp	PJB	303.24	295.04	353.08	449.29	463.65	476.16	571.95	572.54	Y_i = 313.30 + 16.26* D	277
				(100.00)	(100.00)	(100.00)	(100.00)	(100.00)	(100.00)	(100.00)	(100.00)	(5.02)	
			BHR	340.69	293.49	538.77	539.43	579.93	428.39	536.74	513.33	Y_i = 389.09 + 7.99* D	292
				(100.00)	(100.00)	(100.00)	(100.00)	(100.00)	(100.00)	(100.00)	(100.00)	(3.30)	
			di	-10.99	0.53	-34.47	-16.71	-20.05	11.15	6.56	-11.53		
		Ern	PJB	2422.06	2632.97	3431.33	3920.24	4164.08	4216.99	4710.22	4804.89	Y_i = 3023.24 + 116.09* D	277
				(100.00)	(100.00)	(100.00)	(100.00)	(100.00)	(100.00)	(100.00)	(100.00)	(3.57)	
			BHR	1971.13	1654.49	2727.08	2593.60	2983.41	2152.98	2400.97	2359.80	Y_i = 2202.28 + 12.33 D	292
				(100.00)	(100.00)	(100.00)	(100.00)	(100.00)	(100.00)	(100.00)	(100.00)	(1.08)	
			di	22.88	59.14	25.82	51.15	39.57	95.87	96.18	103.61		
		Epd	PJB	7.99	8.92	9.72	8.73	8.98	8.86	8.24	8.39	Y_i = 8.74 - 0.02 D	277
												(0.53)	
			BHR	5.79	5.64	5.06	4.81	5.14	5.03	4.47	4.60	Y_i = 6.38 - 0.11* D	292
												(5.22)	
			di	38.00	58.16	92.09	81.50	74.71	76.14	84.34	82.39		
		PPR	PJB	90.48	78.72	91.03	100.00	100.00	93.65	100.00	100.00		
			BHR	96.15	91.89	96.15	100.00	100.00	96.47	100.00	100.00		

Note:
1. An explanation of various notations such as Emp, Ern, Epd, PPR, BHR and di is given in Table 4.1.
2. Y_i = the value of *i*th component of Total On-Farm Employment/Earnings.
3. α = intercept i.e. the value of Y when the effect of the distance is neutralised.
4. β = measures the slope.
5. D_i = distance between a particular village and the urban focal town.
6. Figures in ( ) are the percentages of Total On-Farm Employment/Earnings.
7. Figures in ( ) under column 13 are 't' values.
8. * denotes the significance of 't' values at 0.05 level.
9. Notations used in this table are used in the subsequent Chapters as well.

Punjab and Bihar villages becomes smaller. In other words, in terms of relative importance of wage-paid on-farm employment to the rural labour households, the villages in the interior whether in the advanced State of Punjab or in the slow growing areas of Bihar are structurally quite similar. This lends confirmation to our hypothesis implying a positive association between wage-paid on farm employment and rural-urban distance. In spite of the empirical confirmation of relationship, it needs to be pointed out that Punjab villages near the focal town are quite different from their counterparts in Bihar. But then the total household earning from this (wage-paid on-farm) source of employment increases in Punjab but is unaffected in Bihar. The Bihar pattern seems to emerge because, to an extent, the wage-payments especially to the attached farm servants are still determined by traditional ties rather than by economic forces. Again, per day earning declines as we shift away from the focal town, both in Punjab and Bihar. It is indeed an interesting pattern in as much as the mandays of employment are less but per day earning is higher, in villages near the focal towns. The plausible explanation is that in the villages near the towns, labour households have relatively greater prospects of employability including the possibility of higher wage rates both in agricultural as well as non-agricultural jobs. Undoubtedly, however, the cushion of high wage rate is available much more sharply to all villages in Punjab compared with those in Bihar.

A feature about this category of on-farm employment that deserves special mention is that while in Bihar, per household earnings register very wide fluctuations from village to village; in Punjab, on the other hand, they tend to rise uninterruptedly as we move from the first village to the last. While general dynamism of Punjab agriculture, operating in the last village not much less intensively as in the first is a patent explanation for the systematically rising pattern in this State, part of the explanation lies in differences in the mode of wage payment in the two States especially to the attached farm servants. While such farm labourers in Punjab receive wages generally in cash, they are commonly paid in terms of a rent-free tiny plot of cultivable land in Bihar. And given the fluctuating fortunes of agriculture as also the operation of a low level of production technology in Bihar, earnings from the latter are bound to be more fluctuating, less certain and smaller than the contractual cash wage payment available in the rural Punjab.

The superiority of wage-paid on-farm employment in Punjab over that in Bihar can be established more assertively through an alternative method of analysis. Intuitively, it may be rewarding to compare the aggregate picture, say at the village level or perhaps averaged over all sample villages, between Punjab and Bihar. For this purpose, we arrive at the village-level figures of employment and earnings by blowing up the mean household level figures; for each village, the average household-level figure (computed from the sample households) has been multiplied by the total number of relevant households in the village. This gives us figure for the village as a whole. This village-level figure divided by gross cropped area of the village gives us the figure in a shape comparable between Punjab and Bihar. In a similar way, we have derived overall estimates for all villages taken together each for Punjab and Bihar. It needs to be clarified here that the totals of employment and earnings in Punjab also include the figures for the migrant labour. The results of this exercise are given in Appendix Table A-4.1.

Before we proceed to analyse our results, a note of caution needs to borne in mind. It is possible that some households, over and above the labour households purposively included in our sample, might also be working as farm labourers, though for short intervals only. Since such households do not figure in our sample, our blown-up estimates of total on-farm wage employment are slightly underestimated. The degree of under-estimation should not, however, distort the relative picture of the two States in as much as the problem relates exclusively to the Punjab households where the absolute superiority is, in any case, of a very high order compared with the situation in Bihar.

Appendix Table A-4.1 shows that practically for each village in Bihar, labour use per acre of gross cropped area is higher compared with its counterpart in Punjab. However, the reverse is true in the matter of earnings per unit of gross cropped area. For instance, labour-use per acre of gross cropped area in Punjab is nearly 29.0 per cent lower than that in Bihar, but the level of earnings in the former is nearly 23.0 per cent higher than in the latter on per acre of gross cropped area basis. The phenomenon of lower mandays of employment and higher level of earnings per unit of gross cropped area may be attributed to the higher level of farm mechanisation especially for operations such as ploughing, harvesting and threshing, etc. However, it is the strength of Punjab agriculture that wage-paid on-farm employment on per acre of total cropped are as well as on 'time criterion' basis is comparatively much more productive in the progressive areas of Punjab than in backward Bihar.

In the matter of on-farm non-wage (self) employment also, the involvement of sample households in Punjab and Bihar is higher in the distantly located villages compared with the nearby villages from the focal town. Between the Punjab and Bihar villages at nearly comparable distances, the involvement is much higher in most of the Bihar villages over the Punjab villages. As pointed out earlier, a Bihar household apparently looks to have an edge over its Punjab counterpart in as much as the former puts in more labour and earns a higher level of per household earnings both in the nearby as well as distantly located villages. However, as far as per day earning from this employment category is concerned, we can observe that even though it is much lower in Punjab villages (Rs. 5.85) in the immediate proximity of the focal town, yet, on an average, it tends to decline as we move into the interior. In Bihar also, a more or less declining pattern of earning per day is discernible. Again, between Punjab and Bihar villages at comparable proximities from the focal town, while earnings per day are higher in the latter than in the former villages in the immediate proximity of the focal town, the reverse is true in the distantly located villages. This suggests that decrease in per day earning in Bihar villages is relatively more sharper than Punjab when we move away from the focal town in the rural areas.

As observed earlier in this chapter, a relatively greater time spent in such activities in Bihar but a much smaller in dairying and poultry compared with Punjab, reveals the structural weaknesses of on-farm employment pattern in Bihar. A village to village comparison shows that a higher percentage of rural labour households are involved in dairying and poultry practically in each village of Punjab compared with its counterpart in Bihar. The picture on dairying and poultry does not throw up a very neat and systematic pattern in terms of inter-village deviations. In fact, employment/earnings in dairying and poultry are not affected as much by distance from the focal town as by other *extraneous* factors such as institutional lending, availability of milk collection facilities, etc. However, a few broad features emerge fairly clearly from Table 4.2. Firstly, the share of dairying and poultry in total on-farm employment/earnings is relatively higher in villages near the town compared with distantly located villages. Secondly, between each pair of Punjab and Bihar villages, the proportion of employment/earnings accruing from dairying and poultry are much higher in the former compared with the latter. This shows that the pattern of on-farm employment/earnings is relatively more diversified for Punjab households compared with Bihar households in villages near as well as away from the focal town. Again, the level of per day earning from this source is uniformly higher in Punjab than in Bihar, the distance of a village from the focal town notwithstanding. Further, given the higher involvement of Punjab households compared with those in Bihar in dairying and poultry, almost in all pairs of Punjab-Bihar villages, it is obvious that 'dairying and poultry', is comparatively a much more lucrative economic proposition for Punjab households than those for Bihar. The relatively low proportion of employment/earnings from dairying and poultry in the interior of the countryside than in villages near the town strengthens our belief that agricultural wage employment is the most dominant component of rural on-farm employment/earnings in extremely remote villages.

On-Farm Employment/Earnings of PALH and PNLH Groups

We have looked into the pattern of on-farm employment/earnings from yet another standpoint. We have divided our sample rural labour households into two broad categories: predominantly agricultural labour households (hereafter PALH) and predominantly non-agricultural labour households (hereafter PNLH). To recapitulate, the rural labour households which derive more than 50.0 per cent of their total wage income from agricultural labour are designated as PALH.[4] The two-way classification on the above lines offers an opportunity to see the sources of employment and income of those rural households which have a high degree of dependence on agricultural wage employment against those which have non-agricultural sources to provide them the major wherewithal of their living. The changing agrarian reality in India is gradually causing a shift of the rural labour households from the PALH category to PNLH category under the impact of agricultural transformation on the one hand, and, the rising avenues of non-agricultural employments, rural as well as urban, on the other. It is natural to expect that in the transitional phase, as being witnessed currently in certain parts of India, the PNLH group would fair better in terms of more productive sources of employment. The present section seeks to examine the employment/income differences between the PALH and the PNLH groups.

Table 4.3 presents some aspects of on-farm employment for the two groups of households. In particular, some points need to be underlined. Firstly, there are significant differences in the pattern of on-farm employment/earning levels of PALH and PNLH groups of Punjab, compared with those of Bihar. In the case of PALH group, Bihar scenario reflects a relatively higher dependence on wage-paid on-farm employment compared with its Punjab counterpart, while the reverse is true about the group's involvement in dairying and poultry. In more concrete terms, while about 86.0 per cent of the total on-farm employment and nearly 93.0 per cent of on-farm earnings for the PALH group in Bihar are derived from agricultural wages alone, against approximately 80.0 per cent of employment and earnings for the same group in Punjab, the group's earning from dairying and poultry is a petty figure of 4.0 per cent in Bihar compared with nearly 20.0 per cent in Punjab. It is thus clear that the PALH group of Punjab has a more diversified and relatively more lucrative structure of on-farm employment, not to speak of their non-farm employment which we propose to take up in the following chapter. It is, therefore, no surprise that per day earning of the Punjab PALH group from dairying and poultry (i.e. Rs. 9.12) is mani-fold higher compared with its counterpart in Bihar (i.e. Rs. 1.73 only).

In the matter of per day earning from wage-employment (as agricultural labour), the PALH group in Punjab was better off than the one in Bihar, to the tune of about 70.0 per cent. As a matter of fact, the differentials in wage rates would be higher between the Punjab and Bihar PALH groups if we keep in mind the relatively higher mandays of employment per year (499.21) available to the Punjab households compared with those available to their Bihar counterparts (439.08). Summing over the decisive edge of Punjab households in dairying and poultry as well as agricultural wage-employment, we clearly discover that at the level of total on-farm employment, the differential in per day earning is markedly in favour of the PALH group of Punjab (Rs. 8.85 and Rs. 4.87 per day in Punjab and Bihar, respectively). Not only that the per day earning is nearly twice as much in Punjab as in Bihar, the mandays of yearly on-farm employment also are fairly higher in the former than in the latter. The overall picture shows many concrete advantages of the Punjab households as regards the employment time as well as per day earning from each component of the on-farm employment.

TABLE 4.3: Pattern of On-Farm Employment and Earnings of PALH and PNLH Groups in Punjab and Bihar

(Mean Value, Per Annum)

Sl. No.	Employment/ Earning Source	Vari-able	State	PALH	PNLH	All	di*
1	2	3	4	5	6	7	8
1.	Wage Employment	Emp	PJB	499.21 (80.01)	86.23 (47.67)	310.62	478.93
			BHR	439.08 (85.67)	107.83 (63.92)	386.08	307.20
			di	13.69	-20.03		
		Ern	PJB	4397.64 (79.61)	860.86 (53.48)	2782.51	410.84
			BHR	2311.10 (92.51)	669.02 (64.27)	2048.37	245.15
			di	90.28	28.67		
		Epd	PJB	8.81	9.98	8.96	-11.72
			BHR	5.26	6.20	5.31	-15.16
			di	67.49	60.97		
		PPR	PJB	100.00	72.26	87.33	
			BHR	100.00	60.42	93.67	
2.	Self-Employment	Emp	PJB	4.56 (0.73)	1.53 (0.85)	3.18	198.04
			BHR	12.74 (2.49)	15.15 (8.98)	13.13	-15.91
			di	-64.21	-89.90		
		Ern	PJB	30.74 (0.56)	10.63 (0.66)	21.56	189.18
			BHR	82.16 (3.29)	146.05 (14.03)	92.38	-43.75
			di	-62.59	-92.72		
		Epd	PJB	6.74	6.93	6.78	-2.74
			BHR	6.45	9.64	7.04	-33.09
			di	4.50	-28.11		
		PPR	PJB	24.54	11.68	18.67	
			BHR	91.67	62.50	87.00	

Contd.

TABLE 4.3 *Contd.*

1	2	3	4	5	6	7	8
3.	Dairying and Poultry	Emp	PJB	120.18 (19.26)	93.13 (51.48)	107.83	29.05
			BHR	60.70 (11.84)	45.71 (27.10)	58.30	32.79
			di	97.99	103.74		
		Ern	PJB	1095.52 (19.83)	738.23 (45.86)	932.36	48.40
			BHR	105.04 (4.20)	225.83 (21.70)	124.36	-53.49
			di	942.96	226.90		
		Epd	PJB	9.12	7.93	8.65	15.01
			BHR	1.73	4.94	2.13	-64.98
			di	427.17	60.53		
		PPR	PJB	91.41	72.26	82.00	
			BHR	70.24	54.17	67.67	
4.	Total On-Farm Employment	Emp	PJB	623.95 (100.00)	180.89 (100.00)	421.62	244.93
			BHR	512.53 (100.00)	168.69 (100.00)	457.51	203.83
			di	21.74	7.23		
		Ern	PJB	5523.91 (100.00)	1609.72 (100.00)	3736.43	243.16
			BHR	2498.30 (100.00)	1040.90 (100.00)	2265.12	140.01
			di	121.11	54.65		
		Epd	PJB	8.85	8.90	8.86	-0.56
			BHR	4.87	6.17	4.95	-21.07
			di	81.72	44.25		
		PPR	PJB	100.00	83.21	92.33	
			BHR	100.00	83.33	97.33	

Note: 1. For an explanation of various notations, Emp, Ern, Epd, PPR, di, please refer to Tables 4.1.

2. $di^* = \frac{PALH_i - PNLH_i}{PNLH_i}$

3. *i* = Value of *i*th component.

4. Figures in the parentheses are percentages of the Total On-farm Employment/ Earnings.

It is equally important to underline that like the PALH group, the PNLH group in Punjab fares much better in comparison with the same in Bihar. In particular, the differential in per day earning from dairying and poultry or from total on-farm employment reveals a significantly better position of the Punjab PNLH group. In brief, a fast growing agriculture of Punjab bestows more productive employment opportunities not only on those households which are largely dependent on agricultural wage employment but also on those which have a more diversified structure of employment. The latter group thus enjoys larger benefits of non-farm employment without being devoid of what they can chip-off from agriculture as well. For the PNLH group, the multiplicity of employment opportunities, in particular, income supplementation accruing to them through on-farm earnings are thus solid gains arising out of the Green Revolution that overtook the rural Punjab since the late sixties. Our analysis shows that such benefits to rural labour households of Bihar are yet to accrue on any significant scale.

Secondly, the per day earning from total on-farm employment is the same between PALH and PNLH groups in Punjab, while in Bihar, the latter group enjoys a much higher per day earning compared to the former. The equal per day earning in Punjab can perhaps be explained by the fact that the fast growing agriculture in the State throws up lots of demand for labour, real increase in agricultural wages and consequently a fairly high per day earning from on-farm employment. No special advantage seems to accrue to PNLH group, as far as per day earning is concerned. The relatively higher time involvement of PALH group in on-farm employment is *not* a disadvantage to those households which depend more on earnings from agricultural employment. In a broad sense, per day on-farm earnings do not accrue discriminately against those who depend more on it. The dynamics of agricultural transformation in Punjab thus bestows benefits of higher employment and earnings both on those which depend largely on agriculture as well as those which draw their major incomes from non-agricultural employment. This is the outcome of agricultural dynamics in Punjab. In Bihar, the decisive disadvantage of those who subsist largely on earnings from agricultural employment is clearly discernible in as much as per day earning from on-farm employment of the PNLH group is Rs. 6.17 compared with Rs. 4.87 for the PALH group.

On-Farm Employment/Earnings on Daily Basis

In the preceding section, an attempt was made to look into the pattern of overall on-farm employment/earnings. A few important variations in the pattern of on-farm employment/earnings were observed between the two States.

Among the three components of on-farm employment discussed above, the wage-paid component is indeed of extreme importance to the type of households we are dealing with. It may, therefore, be in the fitness of things to look a bit more deeply into this source of on-farm employment. One very important aspect could be to examine the proportion of wage-paid on-farm employment/earnings obtained on daily against regular basis, by villages in the close vicinity of the urban-focal town and those far out in the interior, by PALH group against PNLH group, and so on. The present section analyses some aspects of employment on daily basis, as a proportion of total wage-paid on-farm employment. An attempt is made to see if there exist significant variations in wage-paid agricultural employment/earning on daily basis as a proportion of total wage-paid on-farm employment/earnings: (a) between Punjab and Bihar, (b) between equally distanced pair of Punjab and Bihar villages, and, (c) between PALH and PNLH groups of the two study areas.

To begin with, we propose to look into the validity of our hypothesis that attempts to visualise higher incidence of employment/earnings on daily basis in total wage-paid on-farm employment/earnings in Punjab villages compared with those in Bihar. In this regard, Table 4.4 introduces us to the degree of on-farm employment on daily basis prevalent among the rural labour households. To recapitulate, we are discussing wage-paid on-farm (essentially agricultural labour) employment and our respondents are a mixture of agricultural labour households and other rural labour households. Among the latter households also, employment as agricultural labour is quite common, and given a more diversified structure of their employment, their employment as agricultural labour is relatively much more on daily basis. We have thus a mixture of household categories as also a mixture of economic exigencies prompting certain rural labour households to seek employment as agricultural labour more acceptably on daily rather than on regular basis.

Table 4.4 throws up a few points. The practice of working as attached farm servants — another expression for regular agricultural wage-paid employment, is of a very low order both in Punjab and Bihar. One does not discover a definite pattern as one moves into the interior; the low incidence is prevalent in all categories of villages. In fact, in certain villages, this type of employment is totally non-existent among the sample households. Whatever socio-politico reasoning may be framed for this aspect of on-farm employment, it is almost unquestionable that the rural labour households, especially agricultural labour households among them, have drifted away from attached jobs and attached obligations partly because the net year-round earnings from wage-paid agricultural labour work on daily basis as well as from non-agricultural jobs tend to be higher than the yearly earnings as an attached farm servant. The seasonality premiums, on certain agricultural operations do reflect themselves in terms of higher wage rates and consequently, the economic acumen of these households would fully justify their action of seeking unattached farm employment. This assertion gains credence if we look at the percentage of households seeking agricultural wage paid employment on purely daily basis. In Punjab villages, nearly 62.0 per cent of rural labour households are engaged in agricultural employment on purely daily basis against about 50.0 per cent in Bihar villages. Still more important is the fact that practically in each village in Punjab, the incidence of agricultural employment on purely daily basis is much higher compared with each corresponding village in Bihar. This substantiates our hypothesis that the incidence of employment/earnings on daily basis in the total wage-paid on-farm employment/earnings is higher in Punjab villages compared with Bihar villages. The growing strength of Punjab agriculture is perhaps a source for providing this prompting for daily-versus-regular division to the labour households. For obvious reasons, this cushion is available to Bihar households on a much smaller scale.

Another important and plausible explanation for the pattern of incidence of wage-paid agricultural employment on daily basis can also be traced on employer's side in the two States. The demand for attached farm labour on the part of Punjab farmer has significantly declined over the years due to several factors. First, on account of huge influx of migrant labour in Punjab during peak seasons of wheat harvesting, paddy transplantation and harvesting, farmers do not suffer from acute shortage of labour. Secondly, the introduction of higher degree of farm mechanisation in Punjab especially in the form

TABLE 4.4: Village-wise Percentage Distribution of Labour Households Between Wage-Paid On-Farm Employment on Regular and Daily Basis

Sl. No.	Percentage of Households recorded as:	State	Village								Average
			V1	V2	V3	V4	V5	V6	V7	V8	
1	2	3	4	5	6	7	8	9	10	11	12
1.	Purely Attached Farm Servants	PJB	—	9.09	7.14	—	15.00	8.77	2.86	7.69	7.25
		BHR	10.00	—	4.00	—	6.67	3.70	2.63	3.85	3.56
2.	On-Farm Labour Purely on Daily Basis	PJB	81.25	63.64	65.72	40.00	65.00	56.14	60.00	50.00	61.45
		BHR	40.00	68.97	28.00	19.05	33.33	71.61	39.47	44.23	49.82
3.	Mixed (On Attached as well as Daily Basis) Labour	PJB	18.75	27.27	27.14	60.00	20.00	35.09	37.14	42.31	31.30
		BHR	50.00	31.03	68.00	80.95	60.00	24.69	57.90	51.92	46.62
	Total On-Farm Wage-Paid Labour	PJB	100.00	100.00	100.00	100.00	100.00	100.00	100.00	100.00	100.00
		BHR	100.00	100.00	100.00	100.00	100.00	100.00	100.00	100.00	100.00

Note: 1. PJB = Punjab.
2. BHR = Bihar.

of tractors, harvesters and drills has not only reduced the timeliness of harvesting and threshing operations, but also has led to gradual disappearance of certain other field operations such as ploughing with bullocks, etc. Thirdly, because of work standardisation and rising incidence of contracts, the commercial calculus on the part of Punjab farmers has gained rising importance in Punjab over the years. In Bihar, on the other hand, such developments are conspicuous by their absence or their degree is still fairly low. As a result of this, the incidence of wage-paid agricultural employment on daily basis is higher in Punjab than in Bihar.

It is also quite important to note that the incidence of mixed employment (attached + daily basis) is also fairly high both in Punjab and Bihar. But the contrasts between the two States need to be underlined. In Punjab villages near the urban-focal town, the percentage of households availing of the mixed employment opportunities is much smaller than those in the far-away villages. In the nearby villages, women-folk have a relatively greater share in the agricultural labour employment, and as we recede from the focal town, on the one hand, the absolute dependence on agricultural employment increases and involvement of men-folk naturally increases, on the other. Hence the observed pattern in Punjab. In Bihar, there is a tendency for the households to avail of *all available avenues* of work, whether on purely daily basis or on contract basis or in the form of semi-attached servant, etc., the choice is rather limited. It is not a mere coincidence that the total mandays of employment for a Bihar household, in agricultural wage-employment are uniformly higher than in Punjab, although in terms of per day earning, it is far behind its Punjab counterpart (see Table 4.1 and 4.2). Yet another, and possibly more plausible, explanation lies with the rather loose definition of an attached-farm-servant in Bihar, in contrast with the rigid specifications given of such a worker in Punjab. In Bihar, many among the small and medium farmers, who do not engage themselves in cultivation because of certain social taboos, keep one or the other farm hand 'attached' to themselves, generally for one year and in many cases, *even for six months*. Moreover, there is no fixity of stay with the employer, as understood in the traditional sense; the fixity is only notional and the so-called 'attached-farm-servant' can seek work elsewhere while there is no work going on at the employer's farm.[5] Understandably, therefore, the Bihar picture on the incidence of mixed employment is to be understood in its own right; a simple comparison with Punjab would not be in order.

We have seen above that the percentage of households seeking agricultural wage-paid employment on the basis of "attached-to the farm-service" is extremely low, both in Punjab and Bihar. Analytically, therefore, it is important to look further into the picture of farm employment as agricultural labourers on daily basis. Table 4.5 through 4.8 deal with various aspects of on-farm employment on daily basis. It may be clarified at this point that from now onwards, all households reporting any degree of wage-paid agricultural employment on daily basis are put together. In other words, rural labour households are not differentiated on the basis of time duration of wage-paid agricultural employment on daily basis; obviously our sample households seeking employment on daily basis are an amalgam of labour households reporting agricultural employment on a purely daily basis and those with a varying mixture of households reporting on-farm employment on attached-cum-daily basis.

Table 4.5 presents the village-wise percentage of labour households reporting some agricultural employment on daily basis (PPR), and the proportion of agricultural employment (Emp)/earnings (Ern), actually accruing to them on daily basis. It seems generally true that as we move away into the interior, the proportion of households reporting agricultural employment on daily basis (PPR) keeps on rising, both in Punjab and Bihar. As a matter of fact, no definite relationship between employment time on daily basis (emp., Table 4.5) and wage-paid earnings on daily basis (Ern., Table 4.5) is discernible. Moreover, no clear differences are visible between Punjab and Bihar villages either in the matter of agricultural employment-time on daily basis or wage-paid earnings resulting from this type of employment. There are, however, different explanations for what is observed in Punjab against that observed in Bihar. First, Punjab has a well developed network of village link roads. Consequently, rural-urban nexus is much stronger in Punjab compared with that in Bihar. Therefore, the rural labour households can afford to keep their options open relatively more in Punjab than in Bihar. Secondly, because of the huge influx of migrant labour into Punjab, the farmers also prefer to employ farm labour on daily basis as it is relatively more economical for them to do so. In Bihar, on the other hand, agriculture offers limited demand, restricted largely to

TABLE 4.5: Percentage Share of Wage-Paid On-Farm Employment/Earnings on Daily Basis in the Total Wage-Paid On-Farm Employment and Earnings of Labour Households in Punjab and Bihar

Sl. No.	Head	State	Village								Average	PALH	PNLH
			V1	V2	V3	V4	V5	V6	V7	V8			
1	2	3	4	5	6	7	8	9	10	11	12	13	14
1.	Emp	PJB	59.17	40.43	44.23	49.54	56.98	46.39	59.61	51.16	49.57	44.50	84.49
		BHR	46.53	54.69	35.12	29.33	39.85	66.33	42.76	47.80	48.70	47.22	80.31
2.	Ern	PJB	62.89	43.75	49.80	57.79	64.26	51.73	64.68	55.11	54.58	49.11	87.83
		BHR	52.33	60.77	43.17	35.86	45.86	72.55	50.96	53.77	55.57	54.07	82.69
3.	PPR	PJB	76.19	63.83	83.33	71.43	73.91	82.54	97.14	92.31	81.00	88.34	72.26
		BHR	69.23	78.38	92.31	100.00	93.33	91.76	97.37	96.15	90.33	96.43	58.33

Note: 1. PJB = Punjab.
2. BHR = Bihar.
3. PALH = Predominantly Agricultural Labour Households.
4. PNLH = Predominantly Non-agricultural Labour Households.
5. PPR = Percentage of Positive Responses reporting Wage-paid agricultural employment on daily basis.

peak season operations. In total, the demand for farm labour in Bihar is fairly low and given the fact of increasing supply of labour, wage rate is bound to be low. Consequently, in Bihar, it is the farmer who prefers to employ farm labour on daily basis.

Table 4.6 gives some details of on-farm employment on daily basis in respect of six field crop operations. First, we look at the overall position, i.e. the average of all the six operations. Our sample data show that about 90.0 per cent of the households in Bihar are engaged in agricultural wage-paid on-farm employment on daily basis compared with a slightly lower figure of 81.0 per cent in Punjab. It may be noted that while the total mandays of employment are higher in Bihar (188.02 mandays), the position seems to be quite opposite with respect to per household and per day earnings. Averaged over all the six field crop operations, a typical rural labour household in Punjab is earning nearly 33.0 per cent more from wage-paid agricultural labour, on daily basis, than its Bihar counterpart. As a result of this, per day average earning is 63.0 per cent higher in Punjab over Bihar. The high and growing remunerativeness of agricultural employment in Punjab thus comes up again in terms of daily earning of rural households.

It we look into operation-wise employment and earnings on daily basis, it appears that while none of the sample households in Punjab reported any wage employment in ploughing, in Bihar on the other hand, nearly one-third of the sample households are engaged in it. It is on account of the fact that with the introduction of tractors, drills and other farm machinery, the operation of ploughing is nearly completely mechanised in Punjab. In Bihar, on the other hand, it is still done largely through bullock-driven ploughs. Further, on account of differences in the cropping pattern in the two States, while none of the sample households in Bihar reported any wage employment in cotton picking; in Punjab, nearly 18.0 per cent of the sample households were engaged in this operation.

In the case of sowing and weeding, the involvement of sample households was observed to be much higher in Bihar. It may be noted that while the mandays of employment as well as the corresponding level of per household earnings from sowing were lower in Punjab than in Bihar, the reverse seemed to be happening for weeding. However, per day earning from both these operations were much higher in Punjab than in Bihar. This again shows that although per household mandays of employment in sowing are lower in Punjab

TABLE 4.6: Pattern of On-Farm Employment and Earnings of Labour Households in Punjab and Bihar on Daily Basis

(Mean Value, Per Annum)

Sl.No.	Operation	Head	Punjab	Bihar	d_i
1	2	3	4	5	6
1.	Ploughing (*Jutai*)	Emp	—	17.03 (9.06)	—
		Ern	—	95.43 (8.38)	—
		Epd	—	5.60	—
		PPR	—	32.33	—
2.	Sowing and Transplantation (*Ropni* and *Biya Kabarna*)	Emp	19.50 (12.67)	56.59 (30.05)	-65.49
		Ern	179.49 (11.82)	328.57 (28.87)	-45.37
		Epd	9.20	5.82	58.08
		PPR	52.00	86.33	
3.	Weeding (*Sohni*)	Emp	57.79 (37.53)	25.60 (13.62)	125.74
		Ern	463.32 (30.50)	115.54 (10.15)	301.00
		Epd	8.02	4.51	77.83
		PPR	59.33	86.67	
4.	Harvesting, Threshing and Winnowing (*Katni*, *Dauni* and *Usaoni*)	Emp	60.64 (39.38)	86.11 (45.80)	-29.58
		Ern	744.92 (49.04)	583.37 (51.25)	27.69
		Epd	12.28	6.77	81.39
		PPR	76.67	88.67	
5.	Other Agricultural Operations such as Watering, Manuring etc. (*Patwan*, *Patauni*, *Khad*, *Cheetna*, etc.)	Emp	11.38 (7.39)	2.78 (1.47)	309.35
		Ern	101.24 (6.67)	15.36 (1.35)	559.11
		Epd	8.90	5.52	61.23
		PPR	26.33	17.67	
6.	Cotton Picking	Emp	4.67 (3.03)		
		Ern	29.98 (1.97)		
		Epd	6.42		
		PPR	18.33		
	Overall Wage-Paid On-Farm Employment on Daily Basis	Emp	153.98 (100.00)	188.02 (100.00)	-18.10
		Ern	1518.67 (100.00)	1138.26 (100.00)	33.42
		Epd	9.86	6.05	62.98
		PPR	81.00	90.33	

Note: Notations used in this table are explained in Table 4.1.

partly due to the introduction of large scale seed-drill machinery and partly because this operation in Punjab villages, especially the transplantation of paddy, is generally transferred to and carried out by the migrant labour, yet the growing agriculture of Punjab has kept per day earning from this operation sufficiently higher than that in Bihar. With respect to lower mandays of employment and earning per household in weeding operation in Bihar, it may be observed that in the first instance, this operation is largely restricted to paddy cultivation, and in the second, it is carried out on half day basis. In Punjab, this operation is carried out in the case of several crops such as vegetables, paddy, wheat and so on. Hence, due to bigger demand for labour in respect of weeding operation in Punjab, per day earning from this operation was nearly 78.0 per cent higher in Punjab over Bihar.

In harvesting and threshing operation also, relatively larger involvement and higher mandays of employment in Bihar, do not place a Bihar household in a better position *vis-a-vis* his Punjab counterpart. It is fairly evident that a Punjab household while putting in nearly 30.0 per cent less labour time, is earning nearly 28.0 per cent more than its Bihar counterpart. Earning on per day basis for this operation makes the contrast dramatically sharp; per day earning is more than 81.0 per cent higher in Punjab than that in Bihar. This is despite the fact that there is huge influx of migrant labour and a much higher degree of mechanisation in Punjab for this operation too.

Village-wise Pattern of Daily Wage-paid Employment

Some features for the village-wise pattern of agricultural wage-paid employment/earnings on daily basis are set out in Table 4.7. Firstly, as far as the extent of participation in overall wage-paid on-farm employment (PPR under Sl. No. 7, Table 4.7) on daily basis is concerned, we observe that in both the States, the rural labour households tend to increasingly participate as we move away from the focal town. Secondly, as is evident from the statistically significant regression co-efficients, mandays of agricultural employment on daily basis tend to increase in both the States as the rural-urban proximity declines. Thirdly, while per household earning in Punjab tends to rise significantly with increase in rural-urban distance, the same is not true in the case of Bihar. However, as far as per day earning is concerned, it is clear that it registers a significant decline in both the States as we move into the remote villages away from the focal town.

TABLE 4.7: Village-wise Pattern of On-Farm Employment and Earnings of Labour Households in Punjab and Bihar on Daily Basis

(*Mean Value, Per Annum*)

Sl. No.	Operation	Vari-able	State	Village V1	V2	V3	V4	V5	V6	V7	V8	Regression Equation $Y_i = \alpha + \beta D_j$	No. of Observa-tions (N)
1	2	3	4	5	6	7	8	9	10	11	12	13	14
1.	Ploughing (*Jutai*)	Emp	PJB	—	—	—	—	—	—	—	—		
			BHR	8.65	7.62	13.92	13.48	26.33	20.14	13.97	25.35	Y_i = 42.93 + 0.87* D	97
				(6.42)	(6.42)	(8.43)	(9.55)	(13.31)	(8.72)	(7.04)	(11.87)	(1.96)	
		Ern	PJB	—	—	—	—	—	—	—	—		
			BHR	53.75	46.89	85.90	77.10	144.17	111.55	81.23	132.97	Y_i = 269.93 + 2.26 D	97
				(5.96)	(6.09)	(7.81)	(8.82)	(11.62)	(8.11)	(6.96)	(11.02)	(0.96)	
		Epd	PJB	—	—	—	—	—	—	—	—		
			BHR	6.21	6.15	6.17	5.72	5.47	5.54	5.81	5.25	Y_i = 6.24 - 0.05* D	97
												(7.63)	
		PPR	PJB	—	—	—	—	—	—	—	—		
			BHR	23.08	16.22	30.77	23.81	40.00	38.82	28.95	42.31		
2.	Sowing and Transplantation (*Ropni* and *Biya Kabarna*)	Emp	PJB	25.67	16.85	11.38	15.00	23.43	21.03	29.94	23.62	Y_i = 40.01 - 0.26 D	156
				(24.49)	(19.87)	(10.39)	(9.34)	(13.23)	(12.29)	(11.02)	(10.28)	(0.74)	
			BHR	39.81	35.24	48.92	42.24	58.80	71.48	62.08	60.27	Y_i = 52.10 + 1.29* D	259
				(29.51)	(29.72)	(29.60)	(29.93)	(29.73)	(30.95)	(31.26)	(28.22)	(3.33)	
			di.	-35.52	-52.19	-76.74	-64.49	-60.15	-70.58	-51.77	-60.81		

Contd.

TABLE 4.7 *Contd.*

1	2	3	4	5	6	7	8	9	10	11	12	13	14
		Ern	PJB	218.85	142.45	105.30	144.61	231.28	203.87	279.38	207.26	Y_i = 353.23 - 0.83 *D*	156
				(20.75)	(17.07)	(9.29)	(8.74)	(12.59)	(11.78)	(11.11)	(9.80)	(0.25)	
			BHR	265.75	233.14	317.35	251.49	339.83	398.59	346.71	333.64	Y_i = 346.73 + 3.27 *D*	259
				(29.48)	(30.28)	(28.87)	(28.79)	(27.38)	(28.99)	(29.71)	(27.63)	(1.44)	
			di	-17.65	-38.90	-66.82	-42.50	-31.94	-48.85	-19.42	-37.88		
		Epd	PJB	8.53	8.45	9.25	9.64	9.87	9.69	9.33	8.78	Y_i = 8.71 + 0.05* *D*	156
												(3.31)	
			BHR	6.68	6.61	6.49	5.95	5.78	5.58	5.59	5.54	Y_i = 6.59 - 0.07* *D*	259
												(12.18)	
			di	27.69	27.84	42.53	62.02	70.76	73.66	66.91	58.48		
		PPR	PJB	57.14	46.81	32.05	42.86	43.48	60.32	77.14	73.08		
			BHR	69.23	72.97	88.46	95.24	93.33	89.41	92.11	88.46		
3.	Weeding (*Sohni*)	Emp	PJB	31.43	30.79	39.99	61.43	55.26	60.89	116.37	96.19	Y_i = 48.02 + 5.30* *D*	178
				(29.99)	(36.31)	(36.51)	(38.26)	(31.19)	(35.58)	(42.82)	(41.88)	(5.22)	
			BHR	23.08	20.81	27.96	18.24	24.67	29.75	27.42	24.21	Y_i = 30.14 - 0.06 *D*	260
				(17.11)	(17.55)	(16.92)	(12.93)	(12.47)	(12.88)	(13.81)	(11.33)	(0.34)	
			di	36.18	47.96	43.03	236.79	124.01	104.67	324.40	297.32		

Contd.

TABLE 4.7 *Contd.*

1	2	3	4	5	6	7	8	9	10	11	12	13	14
		Ern	PJB	260.67	253.89	335.56	510.04	457.63	506.60	878.64	717.37	Y_i = 440.26 + 36.57* D	179
				(24.71)	(30.43)	(29.60)	(30.83)	(24.91)	(29.27)	(34.93)	(33.93)	(4.30)	
			BHR	118.00	109.78	139.54	84.73	113.22	132.07	109.07	97.23	Y_i = 160.02 - 2.58* D	260
				(13.09)	(14.26)	(12.70)	(9.70)	(9.12)	(9.60)	(9.35)	(8.05)	(3.26)	
			di	120.91	131.27	140.48	501.96	304.20	283.58	705.57	637.81		
		Epd	PJB	8.29	8.25	8.39	8.30	8.28	8.32	7.55	7.46	Y_i = 8.28 - 0.06* D	178
												(4.12)	
			BHR	5.11	5.28	4.99	4.65	4.59	4.44	3.98	4.02	Y_i = 5.30 - 0.08* D	260
												(14.54)	
			di	62.23	56.25	68.14	78.49	80.39	87.39	89.70	85.57		
		PPR	PJB	47.62	53.19	51.28	71.43	43.48	65.08	82.86	69.23		
			BHR	65.38	75.68	92.31	95.24	93.33	89.41	89.47	90.38		

Contd.

TABLE 4.7 *Contd.*

1	2	3	4	5	6	7	8	9	10	11	12	13	14
4.	Harvesting, Threshing and Winnowing (Katni, Dauni and Usaoni)	Emp	PJB	42.38	31.34	47.28	74.14	76.52	70.29	92.94	83.92	Y_i = 49.09 + 3.32* D	230
				(40.43)	(36.96)	(43.16)	(46.17)	(43.19)	(41.06)	(34.20)	(36.54)	(4.65)	
			BHR	61.62	53.11	72.54	65.00	85.47	105.34	92.66	101.13	Y_i = 78.62 + 1.76* D	266
				(45.68)	(44.78)	(43.89)	(46.07)	(43.21)	45.62)	(46.66)	(47.35)	(2.85)	
			di	-31.22	-40.99	-34.82	14.06	-10.47	-33.27	0.30	-17.02		
		Ern	PJB	532.27	394.00	597.68	916.64	964.87	865.29	1099.46	983.00	Y_i = 646.59 + 38.98* D	230
				(50.45)	(47.22)	(52.72)	(55.41)	(52.52)	(50.00)	(43.70)	(46.50)	(4.05)	
			BHR	452.77	368.95	544.18	447.93	629.92	710.11	616.44	630.74	Y_i = 593.36 + 6.14 D	266
				(50.22)	(47.92)	(49.51)	(51.28)	(50.75)	(51.64)	(52.83)	(52.24)	(1.52)	
			di	17.56	6.79	9.83	104.64	53.17	21.85	78.36	55.85		
		Epd	PJB	12.56	12.57	12.64	12.36	12.61	12.31	11.83	11.71	Y_i = 12.77 - 0.05* D	230
												(2.30)	
			BHR	7.35	6.95	7.50	6.89	7.37	6.74	6.65	6.24	Y_i = 7.50 - 0.05* D	266
												(4.49)	
			di	70.88	80.86	68.53	79.39	71.10	82.64	77.89	87.66		
		PPR	PJB	71.43	59.57	78.21	71.43	65.22	79.37	97.14	84.62		
			BHR	61.54	72.97	92.31	100.00	93.33	90.59	97.37	96.15		

Contd.

TABLE 4.7 *Contd.*

1	2	3	4	5	6	7	8	9	10	11	12	13	14
5.	Other Agricultural Operations such as Watering, Manuring, etc. (*Patwan, Patauni, Khad, Cheetna,* etc.)	Emp	PJB	3.24 (3.09)	2.49 (2.94)	7.99 (7.29)	6.00 (3.74)	15.52 (8.76)	13.11 (7.66)	24.17 (8.90)	20.58 (8.96)	Y_i = 41.46 + 0.16 D (0.39)	79
			BHR	1.73 (1.28)	1.81 (1.53)	1.92 (1.16)	2.14 (1.52)	2.53 (1.28)	4.22 (1.83)	2.45 (1.23)	2.63 (1.23)	Y_i = 15.78 - 0.00 D (0.00)	53
			di	87.28	37.57	316.15	180.37	513.44	210.66	886.53	682.51		
		Ern	PJB	29.41 (2.77)	22.23 (2.66)	76.20 (6.72)	57.14 (3.45)	141.40 (7.70)	117.62 (6.79)	206.12 (8.19)	172.86 (8.18)	Y_i = 406.58 - 1.96 D (0.57)	79
			BHR	11.23 (1.25)	11.22 (1.45)	12.17 (1.11)	12.31 (1.41)	14.00 (1.13)	22.79 (1.66)	13.45 (1.15)	12.81 (1.06)	Y_i = 101.44 - 1.35 D (1.48)	53
			di	161.89	98.13	526.13	364.18	910.00	416.10	1432.49	1249.41		
		Epd	PJB	9.02	8.93	9.54	9.52	9.11	8.97	8.53	8.40	Y_i = 9.78 - 0.08* D (7.00)	79
			BHR	6.49	6.19	6.33	5.74	5.52	5.40	5.49	4.86	Y_i = 6.41 - 0.08* D (5.90)	53
			di	38.98	44.26	50.71	65.85	65.04	66.11	55.37	72.84		
		PPR	PJB	4.76	6.38	20.51	14.29	30.43	31.75	51.43	50.00		
			BHR	11.54	10.81	15.38	14.29	20.00	23.53	18.42	17.31		

Contd.

TABLE 4.7 *Contd.*

1	2	3	4	5	6	7	8	9	10	11	12	13	14
6.	Cotton Picking	Emp	PJB	2.10	3.32	2.90	4.00	6.43	5.84	8.31	5.38	Y_i = 25.18 + 0.03 *D*	55
				(2.00)	(3.92)	(2.65)	(2.49)	(3.63)	(3.41)	(3.06)	(2.34)	(0.13)	
			BHR	—	—	—	—	—	—	—	—		
		Ern	PJB	13.97	21.89	18.94	25.97	41.82	37.32	52.19	33.62	Y_i = 168.30 - 0.46 *D*	55
				(1.32)	(2.62)	(1.67)	(1.57)	(2.28)	(2.16)	(2.07)	(1.59)	(0.30)	
			BHR	—	—	—	—	—	—	—	—		
		Epd	PJB	6.67	6.59	6.54	6.49	6.50	6.39	6.28	6.25	Y_i = 6.63 - 0.02 *D*	55
												(1.42)	
			BHR	—	—	—	—	—	—	—	—		
		PPR	PJB	9.52	12.77	11.54	14.29	26.09	22.22	31.43	23.08		
			BHR	—	—	—	—	—	—	—	—		

Contd.

TABLE 4.7 *Contd.*

1	2	3	4	5	6	7	8	9	10	11	12	13	14
7.	Overall Wage-Paid On-Farm Employment on Daily Basis	Emp	PJB	104.81	84.79	109.54	160.57	177.17	171.16	271.74	229.69	$Y_i = 97.15 + 10.35^* D$	243
				(100.00)	(100.00)	(100.00)	(100.00)	(100.00)	(100.00)	(100.00)	(100.00)	(5.13)	
			BHR	134.88	118.59	165.27	141.10	197.80	230.94	198.58	213.60	$Y_i = 167.94 + 3.86^* D$	271
				(100.00)	(100.00)	(100.00)	(100.00)	(100.00)	(100.00)	(100.00)	(100.00)	(2.93)	
			di	-22.29	-28.50	-33.72	13.80	-10.43	-25.89	36.84	7.53		
		Ern	PJB	1054.97	834.45	1133.66	1654.41	1837.00	1730.69	2513.43	2114.11	$Y_i = 1072.56 + 89.35^* D$	243
				(100.00)	(100.00)	(100.00)	(100.00)	(100.00)	(100.00)	(100.00)	(100.00)	(4.50)	
			BHR	901.50	769.98	1099.15	873.56	1241.14	1375.11	1166.90	1207.40	$Y_i = 1139.70 + 11.57 D$	271
				(100.00)	(100.00)	(100.00)	(100.00)	(100.00)	(100.00)	(100.00)	(100.00)	(1.46)	
			di	17.02	8.37	3.14	89.39	48.01	25.86	115.39	75.10		
		Epd	PJB	10.07	9.84	10.35	10.30	10.37	10.11	9.25	9.20	$Y_i = 10.79 - 0.07^* D$	243
												(2.68)	
			BHR	6.68	6.49	6.65	6.19	6.27	5.95	5.88	5.65	$Y_i = 6.67 - 0.06^* D$	271
												(9.75)	
			di	50.75	51.62	55.64	66.40	65.39	69.92	57.31	62.83		
		PPR	PJB	76.19	63.83	83.33	71.43	73.91	82.54	97.14	92.31		
			BHR	69.23	78.38	92.31	10.00	93.33	91.76	97.37	96.15		

Note: 1. For an explanation of various notations used in this Table, please see Table 4.1 and 4.2.
2. In Column No. 2, names of the respective operations in Bihar are given in the brackets
3. * denotes the significance of 't' values at 0.05 level.

We may now look at different operations of wage-paid agricultural employment/earnings on daily basis. We begin with the sowing operation. It may be observed from Table 4.7 that rate of involvement in sowing operation (Variable PPR) is higher in both the States in the extremely remote villages than in the villages in the close proximity of the focal town. Secondly, while mandays of employment in this operation are not significantly affected by the intervening distance of rural-urban proximity in Punjab; in Bihar on the other hand, these register an increasing pattern. Thirdly, while per household earnings remain invariant with respect to distance in both the States, per day earning represents a diametrically opposite pattern between Punjab and Bihar. The Punjab-Bihar contrasts as observed in this operation owe their explanation to many factors.

It is important to note that while this operation in Punjab is largely confined to vegetables and paddy transplantation; in Bihar, on the other hand, it is mainly carried out for paddy, wheat, etc. While female labour in Punjab and Bihar villages near the focal town largely participates in the transplantation of vegetables and paddy respectively; the male labour in the latter increasingly participates both in the transplantation of paddy and sowing of wheat. In Punjab however while wheat is sown largely by means of farm machinery called seed-drill, the resident labour of distantly located villages from the focal town has also to compete with the migrant labour as far as the transplantation of paddy is concerned. This is due to the fact that the latter is preferred more because of its higher competence in this operation. Consequently, mandays of employment in this operation become invariant with respect to distance from the focal town in Punjab, while in Bihar an increasing employment time is in evidence. Further because of the practice of differential rate of earnings to male and female labour (generally higher wages to the former and lower to the latter), per day earning in Punjab tends to rise as against a declining pattern in the case of Bihar.

Further, at every conceivable distance from the focal town, earning per day in Punjab villages is much higher than in Bihar villages. Still further, the differential in per day earning between each pair of Punjab and Bihar villages tends to widen with every increase in the distance. In other words, as we move into the interior of the countryside, the per day earning from the operation of sowing and transplantation gets diluted in Bihar. In Punjab on the other hand, it shows a slight tendency to increase for reasons detailed earlier.

As for as weeding operation is concerned, while involvement in this operation is much higher in the extremely remote villages compared with the nearby villages (Variable PPR under Sl. No. 3), there are important differences between Punjab and Bihar in this respect. Firstly, rate of participation in weeding operation is higher in Bihar villages compared with Punjab villages both located in close proximity of the focal town and in those away from it. Secondly, while mandays of employment in this operation in Punjab tend to rise as we move away from the focal town, in Bihar, it remains unaffected by distance. Further, while per household earnings tend to rise with increase in rural-urban distance in Punjab, in Bihar, on the other hand, the reverse is noticeable. However, per day earning in this operation tends to decline in both the States. It is mainly because of lower per day earning in this operation in the extremely remote villages that such a pattern emerges. Mandays of employment in weeding operation in Punjab tend to vary positively with respect to distance because weeding of wheat offers enough employment to the resident labour of remote villages.

It is interesting to observe that between each pair of Punjab and Bihar villages, mandays of employment as well as earnings (both on household and per day basis) are much higher in Punjab than in Bihar, both in villages near the town and away from it. This is due to the fact that in Bihar, this operation is confined to paddy only. Employment in this operation in Bihar is on half day basis, sustained largely by female labour. Hence the pattern as observed in Bihar. In Punjab, employment in this operation is confined to vegetables, wheat, paddy etc. It is mainly carried out by men on full day basis who, in turn, are paid relatively higher wages. Also, the participation of migrant labour in this operation is very low in Punjab.

The operation of harvesting and threshing is the most important operation among wage-paid agricultural employment on daily basis. It needs to be pointed out that while harvesting is carried out largely in terms of contractual arrangements, threshing is done on daily basis in both the States. While mandays of employment in this operation tend to rise in both the States with increase in rural-urban distance; per day earnings registers a declining pattern. Again, while earnings at the household level tend to vary positively with distance because of larger mandays of employment in the extremely remote villages of Punjab; in Bihar, on the other hand, they remain invariant with respect to distance.

It is striking to observe that between each pair of Punjab and Bihar villages, the mandays of employment are higher in Bihar than in Punjab practically at all rural-urban distances. However, in the case of per household and per day earnings from this operation, an opposite pattern is visible between the two States. The lower mandays of employment in Punjab owe their explanation to the fact that on the one hand this operation is largely carried out with the help of threshing machinery on a large scale, it is still done with the help of a pair of bullocks in Bihar. Consequently, smaller number of mandays of employment are available to the resident labour of Punjab in this operation. Still further, the huge influx of migrant labour in this operation in Punjab, also offers another patent explanation for reducing the absolute number of mandays of employment in this operation. It is a unique feature of Punjab agriculture that despite such adversaries (in terms of mandays of employment for the resident labour) it compensates much more in the form of earning levels.

Employment/Earnings of PALH and PNLH Groups on Daily Basis

We may as well look at the differences of agricultural employment/earnings on daily basis, between PALH and PNLH groups of the two study areas. Table 4.8 presents some details in this regard. A few important features emerge as follows.

First, at the level of all crop operations put together, the involvement of PALH group in Bihar is much higher compared with its Punjab counterpart. This larger involvement does not place the PALH group of Bihar in a better position compared with that of Punjab, either in terms of per household mandays of employment or earnings, both total as well as per day. It is indeed striking that the PALH group in Punjab, putting in just about 7.0 per cent extra labour time, is earning nearly 73.0 per cent more at the household level and about 61.0 per cent higher at per day level than its Bihar counterpart. Second, while 30.0 per cent of total wage-paid agricultural employment on daily basis and nearly 29.0 per cent of total earnings for the PALH group in Bihar are obtained from sowing operation alone against about 12.0 per cent and 11.0 per cent for the same group in Punjab, the group's earning from weeding is a meagre figure of 10.0 per cent in Bihar, compared with nearly 33.0 per cent in Punjab. Still further, the differential of per day earning for either of these two operations reveals that both are relatively more lucrative for PALH group of Punjab compared with its Bihar counterpart.

TABLE 4.8: **Pattern of Wage-Paid On-Farm Employment and Earnings on Daily Basis of PALH and PNLH Groups in Punjab and Bihar**

(Mean Value, Per Annum)

Sl. No.	Operation	Variable	State	PALH	PNLH	All	di*
1	2	3	4	5	6	7	8
1.	Ploughing	Emp	PJB	—	—	—	—
			BHR	19.56	3.73	17.03	424.40
				(9.43)	(4.31)	(9.06)	
		Ern	PJB	—	—	—	—
			BHR	109.45	21.88	95.43	400.23
				(8.76)	(3.95)	(8.38)	
		Epd	PJB	—	—	—	—
			BHR	5.60	5.87	5.60	-4.60
		PPR	PJB	—	—	—	—
			BHR	36.90	8.33	32.33	—
2.	Sowing	Emp	PJB	26.12	11.63	19.50	124.59
				(11.76)	(15.96)		
			BHR	62.24	26.35	56.50	136.20
				(30.02)	(30.43)		
			di	-58.03	-55.86		
		Ern	PJB	244.69	101.91	179.49	140.10
				(11.33)	(13.48)		
			BHR	359.35	166.96	328.57	115.23
				(28.76)	(30.18)		
			di	-31.91	-38.96		
		Epd	PJB	9.37	8.76	9.20	6.96
			BHR	5.77	6.34	5.82	-8.99
			di	62.39	38.17		
		PPR	PJB	65.03	36.50	52.00	
			BHR	92.06	56.25	86.33	

Contd.

TABLE 4.8 *Contd.*

1	2	3	4	5	6	7	8
3.	Weeding	Emp	PJB	88.33	21.46	57.79	311.60
				(39.76)	(29.45)		
			BHR	27.61	15.04	25.60	83.58
				(13.32)	(17.37)		
			di	219.92	42.69		
		Ern	PJB	705.81	174.81	463.32	303.76
				(32.68)	(23.12)		
			BHR	122.89	76.93	115.54	59.74
				(9.83)	(13.91)		
			di	474.34	127.23		
		Epd	PJB	7.99	8.15	8.02	-1.96
			BHR	4.45	5.11	4.51	-12.92
			di	79.55	59.49		
		PPR	PJB	73.62	42.34	59.33	
			BHR	92.46	56.25	86.67	
4.	Harvesting	Emp	PJB	82.18	35.02	60.64	134.67
				(36.99)	(48.06)		
			BHR	94.72	40.92	86.11	131.48
				(45.69)	(47.25)		
			di	-13.24	-14.42		
		Ern	PJB	997.97	443.85	744.92	124.84
				(46.20)	(58.70)		
			BHR	640.41	283.88	583.37	125.59
				(51.24)	(51.32)		
			di	55.83	56.35		
		Epd	PJB	12.14	12.67	12.28	-4.18
			BHR	6.76	6.94	6.77	-2.59
			di	79.59	82.56		
		PPR	PJB	84.05	67.88	76.67	
			BHR	95.24	54.17	88.67	
5.	Other Agricultural Operations	Emp	PJB	19.45	1.78	11.38	992.70
				(8.75)	(2.45)		
			BHR	3.20	0.56	2.78	471.43
				(1.54)	(0.65)		
			di	507.81	217.86		
		Ern	PJB	172.73	16.17	101.24	968.21
				(7.99)	(2.14)		
			BHR	17.60	3.56	15.36	394.38
				(1.41)	(0.64)		
			di	881.42	354.21		

Contd.

TABLE 4.8 *Contd.*

1	2	3	4	5	6	7	8
		Epd	PJB	8.88	9.09	8.90	-2.31
			BHR	5.50	6.33	5.52	-13.11
			di	61.45	43.60		
		PPR	PJB	44.17	5.11	26.33	
			BHR	20.24	4.17	17.67	
6.	Cotton Picking	Emp	PJB	6.10 (2.74)	2.97 (4.08)	4.67	105.39
			BHR	—	—	—	—
		Ern	PJB	38.94 (1.80)	19.33 (2.56)	29.98	101.45
			BHR	—	—	—	—
		Epd	PJB	6.38	6.51	6.42	-2.00
			BHR	—	—	—	—
		PPR	PJB	23.31	12.41	18.33	
			BHR	—	—	—	
7.	Overall Wage-Paid On-Farm Employment on Daily Basis	Emp	PJB	222.17 (100.00)	72.86 (100.00)	153.98	204.93
			BHR	207.33 (100.00)	86.60 (100.00)	188.02	139.41
			di	7.16	-15.87		
		Ern	PJB	2159.62 (100.00)	756.09 (100.00)	1518.67	185.63
			BHR	1249.70 (100.00)	553.20 (100.00)	1138.26	125.90
			di	722.81	36.58		
		Epd	PJB	9.72	10.38	9.86	-6.36
			BHR	6.03	6.38	6.05	-5.49
			di	61.79	62.70		
		PPR	PJB	88.34	72.26	81.00	
			BHR	96.43	58.33	90.33	

Note: 1. Notations used in this table are explained in Table 4.1.

2. $di^* = \dfrac{PALH_i - PNLH_i}{PNLH_i}$

3. i = Value of ith component.

4. Figures in the parentheses are percentages of the Overall Wage-Paid On-Farm Employment/Earnings on Daily Basis.

Again for harvesting and threshing, the PALH group in Punjab puts in nearly 13.0 per cent less labour time but earns nearly 56.0 per cent more than its Bihar counterpart at the household level and nearly 80.0 per cent at the per day level. Like many other operations, for that matter other aspects of agricultural employment, larger labour-time spent by the rural labour in Bihar does not bring it commensurate earnings, either on household or on per day basis. The strength of growing agriculture in Punjab, more pointedly in terms of labour capability in earning more on per day basis, comes up sharply again and again.

Like PALH group, the PNLH group in Punjab also fares much better in comparison with the same in Bihar. In particular, we can see that while putting in nearly 16.0 per cent less effort than its Bihar counterpart, it is earning nearly 37.0 per cent more at the household level and 63.0 per cent more at the per day level than the latter. Similarly in the case of sowing, per day earning of PNLH group in Punjab is recorded to be nearly 38.0 per cent more than its Bihar counterpart, even though it showed slightly lower employment time. Again in weeding operation, the PNLH group of Punjab is better placed than it Bihar counterpart in all respects. In harvesting and threshing operation, the participation of Punjab PNLH group is about 68.0 per cent compared with a low figure of about 54.0 per cent for the similar group in Bihar. But while putting in about 14.0 per cent less effort than its Bihar counterpart, a household belonging to PNLH group in Punjab is found to be earning nearly 56.0 per cent more at the household level and about 83.0 per cent more on per day basis than its Bihar counterpart. This suggests that employment and earnings of PNLH group of Punjab obtained on daily basis are much higher, in all crop operations, and hence in an overall sense, this group has a considerable edge over its counterpart in Bihar.

The preceding discussion highlights that regardless of relatively greater disposition of work time and mandays of employment by a Bihar household in some aspects of on-farm employment, the growing and dynamic agriculture of Punjab is comparatively more remunerative and capable of increasing the level of earnings much faster than in Bihar. Further, a relatively higher time spent in non-wage (self) employment activities in Bihar but a much lower in dairying and poultry activities compared with Punjab, brings out the structural weaknesses of Bihar agriculture. Still further, on account of a more effective and a much less biased functioning of rural institutions in general, and those floated for the weaker sections in particular, dairying has emerged as an important source of employment/earning with rural labour households in Punjab; in Bihar, however, much headway has not as yet appeared in this regard. Consequently, employment/earning through dairying and poultry enterprises occupies a fairly large chunk of total on-farm employment/earnings in Punjab, which in turn, tends to mollify the severity of overall income distribution in rural Punjab. Evidently, the on-farm employment/earning structure is comparatively more diversified in the progressive State of Punjab than in the backward Bihar.

The sharp contrast of earnings per day of employment as observed in Punjab and Bihar clearly reveals what a growing and dynamic agriculture is capable of doing. Finally, differences at the level of total earnings from on-farm employment between Punjab and Bihar clearly signify that sheer labour effort does not matter much in the modern system of agricultural production; rural institutions and technology have their own role to play in augmenting employment/earning opportunities for the rural labour households. In fine, the differential pattern of on-farm employment/earnings (both on overall as well as per day basis) as observed between Punjab and Bihar owes its explanation to a host of factors such as differences in the level of farm technology, strength of rural-urban nexus due to varying levels of infra-structural facilities and institutional set-up, and so on.

NOTES

1. This fact has been brought out in quite a number of studies. In particular, see G.K. Chadha (1986), *The State and Rural Economic Transformation: The Case of Punjab 1950–85*, Sage Publications, New Delhi; and Harbans Singh (1986), *Employment, Income and Consumption of Rural Labour Households in a Green Revolution Region: A Case Study of Punjab and Haryana*, Ph.D. Thesis, Jawaharlal Nehru University, New Delhi.
2. It may be clarified here that in Bihar, Percentage of positive responses for earnings from dairying and poultry was higher than those for employment from this source. It is owing to the fact that in 15 sample households (all belonging to PALH group in the discussion to follow), either the working members while carrying out the work for their employers on attached basis were also tending their own cattle or some local relative while looking after the cattle of the entire village was doing this job.

3. See, for example, G.S. Bhalla and G.K. Chadha (1983), *Green Revolution and the Small Peasant: A Study of Income Distribution among Punjab Cultivators*, Concept Publishing Company, New Delhi, Chapter 4, Table 4.5, p. 90.
4. The classification of these households has been rigorously defined in Chapter 2 of the present study.
5. This type of employer-labourer relationship has been described as 'beck-and-call' system. For further discussion, please see Daniel and Alice Thorner. "Types of Employer-Labourer relationship in Indian Agriculture," in *Indian Journal of Agricultural Economics 1940—64, Selected Readings*, Indian Society of Agricultural Economics, Bombay pp. 287-302.

5

NON-FARM EMPLOYMENT/EARNINGS

In the foregoing chapter, an attempt was made to study the pattern of on-farm employment/earnings of Punjab and Bihar labour households. Significant differences were observed between Punjab and Bihar households in the matter of on-farm employment/ earnings. The edge of Punjab households was clearly in evidence in every aspect of on-farm employment/earnings; in particular, the considerably higher per day earning of the Punjab households in all varieties of on-farm employment clearly testified to the dynamics of agricultural transformation in this State, and the lack of it in Bihar.

The rural labour households in most of the developing economies have their share in non-farm activities too. As a matter of fact non-farm employment, although still at fairly moderate level, has been gaining steadily in importance during the recent past. Naturally, therefore, attempts have been made in recent years to study the pattern, extent and employment potential of such activities. The rising interest in this area of research is explained by a number of factors.

Firstly, in as much as a big majority of rural households including rural labour households are reported to be living below the poverty line, any ameliorative measure, if indeed its poverty reduction effect is to be felt on an enduring basis, must look beyond agricultural employment, naturally the non-farm avenues of employment are to be drawn upon as much as possible. This, however does not negate the short term possibility of augmenting on-farm labour absorption through a well devised strategy comprising technological, institutional and organisational measures. Rather, there has been concrete evidence about its having taken place already in a number of Asian countries which have been experiencing technological break-throughs of varying intensities over the years. What we wish to emphsise is that on-farm employment by itself, does not have the potential of offering a lasting solution to the problem of rural unemployment/underemployment and poverty. This view derives additional force from the fact, confirmed by many studies, that on-farm employment is always less productive and less remunerative than non-farm employment. Secondly and equally importantly, most peasant economies in Asia are typically characterised by continuous population pressures, an ever declining man-land ratio and lopsided unbalanced economic development. Moreover, land distribution pattern is also becoming increasingly skewed in most such economies. Under such circumstances, it is not surprising therefore that rapid expansion of non-farm employment opportunities is being looked upon as an important policy alternative for bringing improvements in the income levels as also in the levels of living of the rural labour households.

It needs to be mentioned here that although the importance of non-farm activities has been increasingly felt in development strategies of most Asian countries, yet detailed field studies of the characteristics of, and, reasons for non-farm employment have been few and only very recent. Besides, it has been pointed out that not only there is an underestimation of participation in non-farm employment, there are also a number of other important questions to be answered in relation to involvement in these activities amongst household members. For instance, if the number engaged in non-farm work tends to vary with the size of the household and if the number so involved and duration of work vary inversely with farm size? Is the incidence of non-farm employment highest amongst household heads or wives and children? What is the incidence by age and sex? And finally, what are the perceived motivations for non-farm employment? A number of studies have addressed themselves to some of these questions presumably because answers to such questions help to have a better appreciation of non-farm activities as important source of total employment/earnings. While it is neither possible nor it is intended to have a detailed review of each and every research work undertaken so far on the issue under consideration, it is nonetheless useful to examine some of the important aspects of non-farm employment as brought out by some recent studies.[1] It needs to be pointed out that most studies of non-farm employment to-date have relied to a great extent on information drawn from population census, agricultural census and labour surveys as conducted from time to time, between 1950–81.

It may serve us well to look at some of the broad conclusions emerging from studies on non-farm employment. These are: (a) on account of the increase in the quantum of off-farm employment, there has occurred a considerable movement out of the full-time farming into part-time farming, (b) income earned through non-farm activities constitutes a very important component of farm household income, (c) there exists an inverse relationship between farm size and off-farm employment, (d) growth of non-farm activities is expected to go a long way in boosting, and as such lead to less inequitable income distribution which is considered essential for the setting up of an egalitarian socio-economic set up, and (e) wage-paid non-farm activities — the dominant component of non-farm employment, reflect the crucial significance of the level of wages in determining the income levels and living conditions of those as may be heavily dependent on such activities. Further, as regards the factors underlying the growth of non-farm activities, these studies underline a host of socio-economic, institutional and other factors which are usually designated as 'push-pull' factors.[2] A cross-country examination, however, reveals that the factual evidence on the broad conclusions mentioned above has been rather mixed due to several factors. Consequently, the differing nature, incidence and productivity/gainfulness of non-farm activities across different countries is observed to be occurring largely due to inter-country differences in the path and levels of industrialisation, concentration of industrial activities, levels of urbanisation, rural infra-structural facilities, stage of technological and economic development, etc. Such inter-country differences, however, notwithstanding, what is required is to devise a mechanism which may bring substantial continuous improvement in the earning levels accruing from non-farm activities. It is likely to prove to be an effective strategy not only in raising the level of earnings and subsequent improvement in the consumption patterns of those who may be heavily dependent on such activities, but also in significantly lowering the much needed population pressure in the farm sector of over populated predominantly agricultural poor economies.

Similarly, a number of other well-known scholars[3] have undertaken to examine various issues regarding non-farm employment. A broad impression that one forms on the basis of such studies regarding the empirical experience of a number of Asian countries is that the level and the nature of non-farm activities depend, *inter alia*, upon the State of development of the farm sector itself. In this regard, it has been argued that a fast growing agriculture is capable of generating: (a) high and rising levels of on-farm employment and income, (b) new and expanding avenues of non-farm employment and income, especially for the weaker sections of rural society, (c) rising demand for purchased inputs to meet the growing requirements of technological changes, and for non-farm consumption goods arising out of higher income levels and structural changes in rural consumption patterns, and (d) considerable agro-industrialisation, which by its very nature, is very widely dispersed in space and strengthens the rural-urban economic relationship. In brief, the rising agricultural production and productivity makes a far reaching impact not only on on-farm and non-farm employment and income levels but also in strengthening further the inter-sectoral linkages. It is another matter that its impact has varied from country to country and for that matter between different regions of the same country depending upon the local conditions. Consequently inter-country differences reveal themselves rather sharply both as regards the extent of non-farm employment available to their rural households and as regards the division of employment time between on- and off-farm activities. Although inter-country differences and the factors accounting for them have their own lessons to offer, yet it is the availability of non-farm employment on an enduring basis, which is to day the primary concern of policy-makers in most developing economies of Asia for ameliorating the economic lot of the poor.

The preceding discussion makes it fairly obvious that since non-farm sector is absorbing a growing proportion of human labour in many Asian countries to-day, it has, therefore, come to acquire an importance of its own in discussions of the rural economy. Although many empirical attempts have been made to collate the quantitative information on the size and structure of the rural non-farm sector, yet very few systematic attempts have been made to characterise or analyse its role in the developmental process. Besides, most such empirical attempts have largely veered around the farming households endeavouring to prove or disprove the inverse relationship between farm size and the quantum of non-farm employment. Moreover, while considerable research has already taken place elsewhere in many South-East Asian countries, in India on the other hand, no systematic attempt has so far been made to study the pattern of non-farm employment/earnings especially for the non-cultivating rural labour households. In this regard, it is relevant to point out that under the spurt of technological breakthrough in Indian agriculture and the growing rural-urban contact, the non-farm sector, as a source of wage-paid employment/earnings, has come to assume an importance of its own in the total yearly employment/earnings of the rural labour households. More precisely, a growing number of rural labour households or their male working members are increasingly seeking employment in non-farm activities both in the countryside itself as also in the nearby urban and sub-urban areas. In spite of the fact that importance of non-farm activities has been recognised as a source of wage-paid employment/earnings for the rural labour households, yet in the absence of some serious research effort, this important phenomenon has largely gone unnoticed. It is so at least for the present. Consequently, there exists an important research gap. As such, an attempt is made to examine the pattern of non-farm employment/earnings of the rural labour households of Punjab and Bihar. In this context, we propose to examine empirically, the following set of hypotheses:

(1) The yearly mandays of non-farm employment/earnings per household as also the level of earnings per day are inversely related to distance from the focal town both in Punjab and Bihar.
(2) In each pair of Punjab and Bihar villages located at comparable proximities from the focal town, mandays of non-farm employment per household and corresponding level of per household and per day earnings are relatively higher in the fast growing areas of Punjab than in Bihar.
(3) The incidence of wage-paid urban employment/earnings keeps on declining both in Punjab and Bihar, as we move into the interior of the countryside from the focal town. In other words, the avenues of non-farm employment/earnings get increasingly confined to wage-paid rural employment in both the States as the distance between a village and the urban focal town increases.
(4) Between the PALH and PNLH groups, per household mandays of employment/earnings in non-farm activities are higher for Punjab groups compared with similar groups in Bihar.

To observe analytical conformity with the discussion in the previous chapter, we begin with the overall as well as different components of total yearly non-farm employment/earnings followed by a similar analysis between each pair of nearly equally distanced villages of Punjab and Bihar as also between PALH and PNLH groups of the two States. With the objective of bringing Punjab-Bihar differentials into sharp focus, earnings (on total as well as per day basis) have also been presented side by side. To lend further substance to our inferences, percentages of different components have been worked out and regression analysis has also been done, wherever necessary.

Level of Non-Farm Employment/Earnings in Punjab and Bihar

Table 5.1 contains the mean values of different components of total non-farm employment/earnings.

It is clear from the above Table that a substantially larger benefit of non-farm employment accrues to rural labour households of Punjab, compared with those of Bihar. In the Punjab Sample, as many as 74.0 per cent of the households report non-farm employment of one type or the other against only 47.0 per cent in Bihar (Variable PPR under Sl. No. 4, Table 5.1). It is equally significant that the quantum of non-farm employment and the consequent earnings (both on per household and per day basis) are relatively much higher in Punjab than in Bihar. For example, an average non-cultivating rural labour household in Punjab, in comparison with his counterpart in Bihar, enjoys about 88.0 per cent of extra employment time and nearly 276.0 per cent more of earnings, from non-farm avenues of employment. Consequently, for every day of non-farm employment, a Punjab household earns nearly double the amount. Thus the decisive edge of the Punjab households manifests itself, in every possible way, at the level of total non-farm employment (Sl. No. 4, Table 5.1). Strikingly, their edge over Bihar households is discernible uniformly for each of the three components of non-farm employment. Whether it relates to the percentage of households availing themselves of each type of non-farm employment or to the mandays of employment actually availed of or to the total earning accruing from each employment category or to the earning derived for each day of work put in under each variety of non-farm activities, the Punjab households are much better off. Still more striking is the fact that urban wage employment plays a more decisive role in Punjab compared with the other two categories of non-farm employment. Let us look a little more closely at this component of employment.

TABLE 5.1: Pattern of Non-Farm Employment and Earnings of Labour Households in Punjab and Bihar

(Mean Value, Per Annum)

Sl. No.	Employment/Earning Source	Variable	Punjab (PJB)	Bihar (BHR)	Differential (di)
1	2	3	4	5	6
1.	Rural Wage Employment	Emp	33.79 (18.48)	26.33 (27.13)	28.33
		Ern	418.37 (17.11)	145.18 (22.35)	188.17
		Epd	12.38	5.51	124.68
		PPR	30.67	20.67	
2.	Urban Wage Employment	Emp	136.69 (74.77)	64.71 (66.68)	111.23
		Ern	1924.25 (78.72)	472.14 (72.69)	307.56
		Epd	14.08	7.30	92.88
		PPR	47.00	22.33	
3.	Others Including Self Employment	Emp	12.33 (6.75)	6.00 (6.19)	105.50
		Ern	101.84 (4.17)	32.21 (4.96)	216.18
		Epd	8.26	5.37	53.82
		PPR	10.67	8.00	
4.	Total Non-Farm Employment	Emp	182.81 (100.00)	97.05 (100.00)	88.37
		Ern	2444.46 (100.00)	649.53 (100.00)	276.34
		Epd	13.37	6.69	99.85
		PPR	74.33	47.33	

Note: 1. For an explanation of various notations Emp, Ern, Epd, PPR and di used in this Table, please see Table 4.1.
2. Figures in the parentheses are percentages of the Total Non-farm Employment/Earnings.

It is not an unimportant fact that urban wage employment is available to about 47.0 per cent of the sample households in Punjab compared with only 22.0 per cent in Bihar (Variable PPR under Sl. No. 2, Table 5.1). Urban wage employment thus eludes a preponderant majority of rural labour households in Bihar. More revealing is the fact that mandays of urban employment available to a typical household in Punjab are more than double of those available to a Bihar household, and each manday of such employment brings double the earning in Punjab than in Bihar. In terms of the contribution that the urban wage employment makes to total earnings from non-farm employment, the Punjab and the Bihar scenarios are not much different from each other, yet in terms of the actual earning accruing to a household from this source, the Punjab households get more than fourfold (Rs. 1924.25) than what the Bihar households get (Rs. 472.14).

The higher employment/earning potential in urban wage employment has been created in Punjab much faster partly through rapid growth of urban-industrial centres and partly through widespread network of village link roads, which to a large extent, have appeared as an off-shoot of the Green Revolution. Thus following the internal dynamics of rural transformation in Punjab, rural-urban contact has tremendously grown in Punjab which, in turn, has opened up many avenues of highly remunerative wage-paid urban employment in the State. However, in these developments, Bihar is languishing far too behind.

A similar relative picture of Punjab's superiority is discernible for rural wage employment, and to a slightly lesser extent, for other non-farm employments. For example, in rural wage non-farm employment, a Punjab household, on an average, gets about 28.0 per cent more of employment, derives about 188.0 per cent higher earnings, and for every day of work, its earning is Rs. 12.38 compared with only Rs. 5.51 in Bihar. Moreover, a much larger percentage of households in Punjab (nearly 31.0%) earn wages through rural non-farm employment compared with Bihar (nearly 21.0%). To a large extent, rural wage employment under non-farm activities is an offspring of the level of agricultural development itself. A fast growing agriculture has the potential of creating many non-farm avenues of employment in the rural areas themselves. Examples are construction and trade activities, transport and banking, repairs and services, etc.

The unquestionable blessings of the Green Revolution in Punjab manifest themselves in higher quantum of rural employment under numerous non-farm activities. To this must be added the higher quantum of wage employment available to Punjab households outside the villages and one cannot escape the conclusion that the structure as well as the level of non-farm employment opportunities available to rural labour households in Punjab are far more superior than in Bihar. The fact of higher remunerativeness in Punjab for rural as well as urban wage-paid employment needs to be stressed in particular.

In sum, the overall comparison between Punjab and Bihar labour households (Table 4.1 read with Table 5.1) reinforces our conclusion that while the differentials in terms of employment-time are not so marked between the Punjab and the Bihar households, those in terms of earning are strikingly in favour of the Punjab workers. In other words, while the Bihar workers seem to be ostensibly engaged in work of one type or the other, they are way behind their brethren in the Punjab when it comes to net gains of such employment. Practically, every category of non-farm employment, like that observed for farm-employment in Chapter 4, yields the Bihar workers a significantly lower return. No wonder, therefore, the phenomenon of low-productive employment is quite widespread in Bihar. Perhaps, labour exploitation, as reflected by under-paid employment, may also be responsible for the above situation.

The Village-wise Pattern

After having examined the pattern of non-farm employment/ earnings between Punjab and Bihar at the State level, we may now look into its village-wise pattern in the two study areas. Specifically, we propose to examine the first three of the four hypotheses outlined earlier in this chapter. These hypotheses are tested by comparing the mean values and per cent shares of employment/earnings for overall as also for individual components of non-farm employment. Besides, analysis has also been carried out in terms of regression analysis.

To begin with, Table 5.2 describes the village-wise pattern of non-farm employment. The objective here again is to capture the impact of distance on overall as well as on different components of non-farm employment/earnings. The important points that emerge from Table 5.2 are as under.

TABLE 5.2: Village-wise Pattern of Non-Farm Employment and Earnings of Labour Households in Punjab and Bihar

(*Mean Value, Per Annum*)

Sl. No.	Employment/ Earning Source	Variable	State	Village V1	V2	V3	V4	V5	V6	V7	V8	Regression Equation $Y_i = \alpha + \beta D_j$	No. of Observations (N)
1	2	3	4	5	6	7	8	9	10	11	12	13	14
1.	Rural Wage Employment	Emp	PJB	48.38	79.43	13.14	69.14	42.04	30.43	11.91	22.19	$Y_i = 214.05 - 11.16^* D$	92
				(15.97)	(31.41)	(5.65)	(24.83)	(20.08)	(21.71)	(24.52)	(50.12)	(5.16)	
			BHR	5.19	2.30	3.81	4.81	89.07	63.08	4.26	11.92	$Y_i = 115.30 + 1.11 D$	62
				(2.45)	(0.79)	(2.87)	(40.08)	(82.22)	(83.08)	(49.08)	(80.00)	(0.22)	
			di	832.18	3353.48	244.88	1337.42	−52.80	−51.76	179.58	86.16		
		Ern	PJB	540.48	901.85	178.53	1299.50	773.47	314.37	94.19	302.29	$Y_i = 2623.46 - 135.34^* D$	92
				(12.10)	(25.96)	(5.88)	(34.42)	(26.17)	(17.21)	(19.37)	(61.29)	(4.18)	
			BHR	32.58	12.15	19.96	23.43	398.39	373.53	18.71	54.06	$Y_i = 676.23 + 2.40 D$	62
				(2.02)	(0.58)	(2.25)	(36.24)	(80.58)	(83.03)	(46.50)	(83.19)	(0.10)	
			di	1558.53	7322.63	794.44	5446.31	94.15	−15.84	403.42	459.17		
		Epd	PJB	11.17	11.35	13.59	18.80	18.40	10.33	7.91	13.62	$Y_i = 12.38 - 0.21^* D$	92
												(2.67)	
			BHR	6.28	5.28	5.24	4.87	4.47	5.92	4.39	4.54	$Y_i = 6.29 - 0.08^* D$	62
												(2.10)	
			di	77.87	114.96	159.35	286.04	311.63	74.49	80.18	200.00		
		PPR	PJB	23.81	29.79	20.51	57.14	30.43	39.68	40.00	26.92		
			BHR	11.54	8.11	7.69	14.29	20.00	41.18	13.16	15.38		

Contd.

TABLE 5.2 *Contd.*

1	2	3	4	5	6	7	8	9	10	11	12	13	14
2.	Urban Wage Employment	Emp	PJB	244.14	173.32	198.71	182.71	153.09	100.13	24.94	9.81	$Y_i = 320.85 - 4.80^* D$	141
				(80.56)	(68.54)	(85.42)	(65.63)	(73.13)	(71.43)	(51.32)	(22.16)	(2.04)	
			BHR	206.65	285.57	114.58	—	—	5.82	—	—	$Y_i = 321.57 - 10.06 D$	67
				(97.55)	(98.60)	(86.25)	(—)	(—)	(7.67)	(—)	(—)	(0.75)	
			di	18.14	− 39.31	73.42	—	—	1620.45	—	—		
		Em	PJB	3839.74	2571.61	2693.12	2268.14	2006.61	1440.54	296.57	98.08	$Y_i = 4761.40 - 106.67^* D$	141
				(85.97)	(74.01)	(88.68)	(60.09)	(67.88)	(78.84)	(61.00)	(19.88)	(2.96)	
			BHR	1580.19	2088.08	752.97	—	—	43.76	—	—	$Y_i = 2408.53 - 93.07 D$	67
				(97.98)	(99.08)	(84.99)	(—)	(—)	(9.73)	(—)	(—)	(0.91)	
			di	142.99	23.16	257.67	—	—	3191.91	—	—		
		Epd	PJB	15.73	14.84	13.55	12.41	13.11	14.39	11.89	10.00	$Y_i = 15.46 - 0.20^* D$	141
												(2.55)	
			BHR	7.65	7.31	6.57	—	—	7.52	—	—	$Y_i = 7.40 - 0.08 D$	67
												(0.74)	
			di	105.62	103.01	106.24	—	—	91.36	—	—		
		PPR	PJB	71.43	59.57	66.67	85.71	52.17	38.10	5.71	7.69		
			BHR	76.92	81.08	57.69	—	—	2.35	—	—		

Contd.

TABLE 5.2 *Contd.*

1	2	3	4	5	6	7	8	9	10	11	12	13	14
3.	Others including Self-Employment	Emp	PJB	10.52	0.13	20.79	26.57	14.22	9.62	11.74	12.27	$Y_i = 146.24 - 3.31\,D$	32
				(3.47)	(0.05)	(8.93)	(9.54)	(6.79)	(6.86)	(24.16)	(27.72)	(1.14)	
			BHR	—	1.76	14.46	7.13	19.27	7.02	4.42	2.98	$Y_i = 114.49 - 3.63\,D$	23
				(—)	(0.61)	(10.88)	(59.92)	(17.78)	(9.25)	(50.92)	(20.00)	(1.66)	
			di	—	-92.61	43.78	269.54	-26.21	37.04	165.61	311.74		
		Ern	PJB	86.19	1.06	165.29	207.14	175.87	72.22	95.42	92.88	$Y_i = 1223.76 - 28.98\,D$	32
				(1.93)	(0.03)	(5.44)	(5.49)	(5.95)	(3.95)	(19.63)	(18.83)	(1.02)	
			BHR	—	7.14	113.08	41.22	96.00	32.56	21.53	10.92	$Y_i = 768.69 - 33.66^{*}\,D$	23
				(—)	(0.34)	(12.76)	(63.75)	(19.42)	(7.24)	(53.50)	(16.81)	(2.02)	
			di	—	-85.15	46.17	402.52	83.20	121.81	343.20	750.55		
		Epd	PJB	8.19	8.15	7.95	7.80	12.37	7.51	8.13	7.57	$Y_i = 7.69 + 0.06\,D$	32
												(0.91)	
			BHR	—	4.06	7.82	5.73	4.98	4.64	4.87	3.66	$Y_i = 5.93 - 0.11^{*}\,D$	23
												(2.15)	
			di	—	100.74	1.66	36.13	148.39	61.85	66.94	106.83		
		PPR	PJB	4.76	2.13	16.67	14.29	8.70	7.94	17.14	11.54		
			BHR	—	5.41	11.54	9.52	13.33	8.24	10.53	7.69		

Contd.

TABLE 5.2 *Contd.*

1	2	3	4	5	6	7	8	9	10	11	12	13	14
4.	Total Non-Farm Employment	Emp	PJB	303.05	252.87	232.64	278.43	209.35	140.17	48.60	44.27	Y_i = 361.02 — 15.04* D	223
				(100.00)	(100.00)	(100.00)	(100.00)	(100.00)	(100.00)	(100.00)	(100.00)	(7.70)	
			BHR	211.85	289.62	132.85	12.00	108.33	75.93	8.68	14.90	Y_i = 306.39 — 13.53* D	141
				(100.00)	(100.00)	(100.00)	(100.00)	(100.00)	(100.00)	(100.00)	(100.00)	(5.03)	
			di	43.05	—12.69	75.11	2220.25	93.25	84.60	459.91	197.11		
		Ern	PJB	4466.40	3474.52	3036.94	3774.79	2955.95	1827.13	486.19	493.25	Y_i = 5036.38 — 228.34* D	223
				(100.00)	(100.00)	(100.00)	(100.00)	(100.00)	(100.00)	(100.00)	(100.00)	(7.98)	
			BHR	1612.77	2107.37	886.01	64.65	494.39	449.85	40.24	64.98	Y_i = 2261.49 —119.13* D	141
				(100.00)	(100.00)	(100.00)	(100.00)	(100.00)	(100.00)	(100.00)	(100.00)	(6.49)	
			di	176.94	64.87	242.77	5738.96	497.90	306.16	1108.23	659.08		
		Epd	PJB	14.74	13.74	13.05	13.56	14.12	13.04	10.00	11.14	Y_i = 14.84 — 0.32* D	223
												(6.19)	
			BHR	7.61	7.28	6.67	5.39	4.56	5.92	4.64	4.36	Y_i = 7.44 — 0.18* D	141
												(8.24)	
			di	93.69	88.74	95.65	151.58	209.65	120.27	115.52	155.50		
		PPR	PJB	85.71	85.11	83.33	85.71	82.61	73.02	54.29	38.46		
			BHR	84.62	89.19	73.08	19.05	33.33	48.24	18.42	21.15		

Note: For an explanation of various notations Emp, Ern, Epd, PPR, PJB, BHR and di as used in this table, please refer to Tables 4.1 and 4.2.

* Denotes the significance of 't' values at 0.05 level.

Firstly, as far as the rate of participation in total yearly non-farm employment (Variable PPR under Sl. No. 4, Table 5.2) is concerned, both in Punjab and Bihar, the percentage of rural labour households to whom non-farm employment is available keeps on declining as we move deep into the interior. There is, however, a big qualitative difference between the two States. While in Punjab, a very high percentage of households get non-farm employment even in the far out villages, in Bihar this employment is available only to a handful of households when we reach villages located not very far away from the focal town; the situation worsens as we move further deep into the countryside. Thus in Bihar, the remotely located villages have very meagre access to non-farm employment while such opportunities are available to a very high percentage of households in Punjab. The rural-urban distance creates limited friction in Punjab.

Secondly, as is evident from statistically significant regression co-efficients, the per household mandays of non-farm employment go on decreasing as we move away from the town both in Punjab and Bihar. It cannot, however escape our notice that while in Punjab, the mandays of employment decline uniformly as we move away from the town, say from one village to the next, the Bihar pattern reveals severe ups and downs. To this must be added the fact that, in general, in every village of Punjab, the mandays of total non-farm employment are higher than its counterpart in Bihar. These facts clearly suggest that non farm employment is available on a much wider scale for rural labour households of Punjab compared with those of Bihar. Also, while the Punjab situation suggests a firm pattern, the Bihar situation reflects a lot of adhocism and undependable nature of non-farm activities. More concrete explanations in this regard are framed later when we look into the component-wise picture in Punjab and Bihar villages.

Thirdly, per household and per day earnings from non-farm employment are also inversely related to the distance from the focal town, both in Punjab and Bihar. However, the differentials in per day earnings between the two study areas need to be underlined. While the decline in per day earning till we reach villages located 12-13 km away from the urban focal town in Punjab is extremely small, in Bihar, the decline sets in practically beyond the very first village and continuously goes on thereafter. It is, therefore, natural to expect that the gap in per day earning between the Punjab and the Bihar villages keeps on rising as we move away from the focal town; in other words, the remoter villages of Bihar are relatively more worse off than their counterparts in Punjab, compared with those near the town. For instance, per day earning from total non-farm employment in the remotest village of Punjab is nearly 46.0 per cent higher than that in the one nearest to the urban focal town in Bihar and, if a comparison is made between the first village of Punjab and the last village of Bihar, the differential is as high as nearly 238.0 per cent. Similarly, there are equally yawning gaps in the matter of per day earnings from different components of non-farm employment, which in turn, reflect the superiority of Punjab labour households over those of their counterparts in Bihar, in villages near the town as well as away from it. Thus, the hypotheses envisaging an inverse relationship between employment/earnings per household as well as per day from non-farm employment and rural-urban distances as also the superiority of Punjab households over those of Bihar households at all conceivable distances from the urban focal town, are sustained by our sample data.

We might as well look into the position regarding different components of overall non-farm employment/earnings. In this connection, Table 5.2 has the following important features to offer:

Firstly, apart from the fact that variations do exist from village to village, the involvement of sample households in wage-paid rural employment is higher in remote villages from the local town in the two study areas. However, between each pair of Punjab and Bihar villages, the percentage of positive responses is higher in the case of the former compared with the latter. Secondly, it is important to note that per household mandays of rural wage employment/earnings tend to decline in Punjab with increase in rural-urban distance. In Bihar, on the other hand, employment/earnings from this component of non-farm employment remain unaffected with respect to distance from the focal town. Thirdly, in both the States, per day earning tends to decline significantly (as is evident from statistically significant regression co-efficients for per day earning) as the rural-urban distance increases. While the declining relationship may be accepted in a statistical sense, we must also admit that the pattern is not smooth or clean, either in Punjab or in Bihar, when we move from first village to the last. There are ups and downs, in some cases of considerable magnitude, in total or per day earning from rural wage employment, as we cover the urban rural continuum in space. The implication is that the non-farm wage employment in rural areas is not yet developed in a sustained fashion; there is the element of seasonal spurt or occasional upsurge in one activity or the other, in one village now and in another villager later, and so on, that seem to cause up and down swings on village-to-village basis. The adhocism in the availability of non-farm wage-employment in rural India is clearly emerging in our analysis. It is, however, a different matter that every village in Punjab reveals a markedly better picture than its comparable counterpart in Bihar. As we see a little later, it is in the nature of urban employment, especially in industrial or construction activities, that the degree of regularity is more assured. Fourthly, a few minor exceptions notwithstanding, for each village in Punjab, the mandays of wage-paid rural employment and the consequent level of earnings (both on per household and per day basis) are higher against those in equally distanced villages in Bihar. Lastly, such differences in employment/earnings between the Punjab and Bihar villages tend to narrow down as we move into the interior. The differences observed between Punjab and Bihar with respect to wage-paid rural employment/earnings at the per household level in relation to distance from the focal town can be explained by two factors. Firstly, it can be maintained that in low growth areas (Bihar in our case), the growth process itself keeps the level of wage-paid rural employment/earnings in the non-farm sector low. Moreover, within the low growth regions, whatever non-farm activity permeates into the villages near the town has shifted its locale largely to the nearby urban and sub-urban areas. In remote villages on the other hand, such activities seemingly, have not made any dent either in terms of mandays of employment or earnings at the household level. Compared with it, in Punjab mandays of wage-paid rural employment/earnings are higher in villages near the focal town compared with the distantly located villages. This is on account of a peculiar characteristic of first two sample villages of Punjab in having four iron and steel mills located in their vicinity. These iron and steel mills which are notionally rural but operationally urban have generated a large number of mandays of wage-paid rural non-farm employment to the sample households in these villages. It can, therefore, be argued that in the case of Punjab, while the locale of many non-farm activities has shifted to the nearby urban and sub-urban areas, considerable non-farm activity has been generated within such villages as are located near the urban industrial centres.

The inter-State differences in the accrual of urban employment also come up sharply. For Punjab, our data lends full support to the hypothesis on the declining incidence of urban-wage employment for villages away from the focal town, while in Bihar, this avenue of employment cases to be available beyond a certain distance. A few striking features need to be underlined.

Firstly, the ratio of participation (Variable PPR under Sl. No. 2, Table 5.2) in both the States, becomes lower as we move away from the focal town. Secondly, while availability of this component of employment/earnings extends even up to the last sample village of Punjab; it becomes nearly non-existent after the third village in Bihar. Consequently, even though the involvement of Bihar labour households is higher than those of Punjab households in the first two villages nearer to the focal town, the Punjab pattern lends substance to the fact that rural-urban nexus is stronger in Punjab than in Bihar. Next, for this type of employment, while the mandays of employment and earnings (both per household and per day) tend to decline as we move away from the focal town, it is not so in Bihar. In the latter, mandays of employment/earnings on per household or on per day basis remain invariant with respect to distance from the focal town. In the Punjab case, we can maintain that as the pull of the urban areas becomes weaker with increase in distance from the focal town, the involvement as well as incidence of employment in wage-paid urban activities tend to decline. This decline in the proportion of wage-paid non-farm urban employment/earnings is also visible in Punjab as we move away from the focal town into the interior of the countryside. Both employment/earnings accruing from wage-paid non-farm urban employment are nearly 3-4 times larger for a village in close proximity of the focal town compared with remotely located village.

As regards employment/earnings in 'other activities including self-employment' only a marginal involvement is observed both in Punjab and Bihar. Nevertheless, the relatively superior performance of the Punjab households stands out clearly, more or less along the lines observed earlier for rural or urban non-farm wage employment.

To conclude our discussion on village-wise availability of on-farm employment, a few broad observations may be in order. In every aspect of non-farm employment/earning, whether of rural wage-employment or urban wage-employment type, the Punjab households, whether living nearer an urban focal town or quite away from it, show a much better economic performance, compared with their Bihar counterparts. In particular, the non-farm employment opportunities both in the rural as well as the urban areas are availed of by a much higher percentage of rural labour households in the Punjab compared with Bihar. Not only that, the mandays of actual employment availed of and total earnings, therefore, are also much higher in Punjab, in every conceivable urban-rural distance syndrome. Most strikingly, per day earning is also uniformly higher everywhere in Punjab when we compare Punjab with Bihar. The strong economic base of the rural Punjab, giving rise to higher rural (wage-paid) non-farm employment, coupled with expanding industrial and other economic activities in the urban Punjab, giving rise to higher urban (wage-paid) employment to people in the nearby villages, is the crucial element of Punjab's model of economic development. In contrast, the Bihar situation reflects weakness at the village level as well as in terms of rural-urban linkages.

The relatively happier situation in Punjab cannot, however, hide a very crucial aspect which, in fact, applies more acutely to Bihar as well. This has to do with the nature of non-farm employment avenues available to rural labour households. As yet, in Punjab, and much more so in Bihar, modern industrial activities are generally absent in the rural areas. Those which are available are mostly in the household sector which, by their very nature, are available on a noticeable scale in one village or the other, while other villages are bereft of many such enterprises. Other sources of non-farm employment in rural areas viz. construction, repair of agricultural implements, loading and unloading of grains in the rural grain markets, etc. do not possess a regular employment potential. Sometimes, one such activity may receive a spurt in one or two villages while other villages are going without it during that period. The total effect of such sporadic non-farm activities is that mandays of rural employment from them at best reveal a fluctuating pattern as one moves from an urban centre towards the villages in the interior. The availability of rural non-farm employment is thus full of adhocism. This adhocism is in evidence in Punjab, and of course, very much in Bihar. In contrast, the urban employment does not pose this situation in Punjab; in Bihar, villages beyond a certain distance are totally devoid of this employment opportunity.

Non-Farm Employment/Earnings of PALH/PNLH Groups

To test out hypothesis on the superior position of PALH and PNLH groups of Punjab over those of Bihar, we look into the pattern of their non-farm employment/earnings. The picture on PALH and PNLH groups of our sample households throws up a few significant conclusions, as in Table 5.3.

TABLE 5.3: Pattern of Non-Farm Employment and Earnings of PALH and PNLH Groups in Punjab and Bihar

(Mean Value, Per Annum)

Sl. No.	Employment/ Earning Source	Vari- able	State	PALH	PNLH	All	di*
1	2	3	4	5	6	7	8
1.	Rural Wage Employment	Emp	PJB	23.89	45.56	33.79	90.71
				(37.45)	(14.04)		
			BHR	18.20	69.02	26.33	279.23
				(43.33)	(17.88)		
			di	31.26	-33.99		
		Ern	PJB	233.73	638.05	418.37	172.99
				(35.05)	(13.99)		
			BHR	99.95	382.66	145.18	282.85
				(41.18)	(13.74)		
			di	133.85	66.74		
		Epd	PJB	9.78	14.00	12.38	43.15
			BHR	5.49	5.54	5.51	0.91
			di	78.14	152.71		
		PPR	PJB	39.88	19.71	30.67	
			BHR	20.63	20.83	20.67	
2.	Urban Wage Employment	Emp	PJB	29.49	264.24	136.69	796.03
				(46.22)	(81.46)		
			BHR	16.83	316.06	64.71	1777.96
				(40.07)	(81.88)		
			di	75.22	−16.40		
		Ern	PJB	349.87	3797.42	1924.25	985.38
				(52.47)	(83.29)		
			BHR	105.21	2398.52	472.14	2179.75
				(43.35)	(86.11)		
			di	232.54	58.32		
		Epd	PJB	11.86	14.37	14.08	21.16
			BHR	6.25	7.59	7.30	21.44
			di	89.76	89.33		
		PPR	PJB	12.88	87.59	47.00	
			BHR	10.71	83.33	22.33	

Contd.

TABLE 5.3 *Contd.*

1	2	3	4	5	6	7	8
3.	Others Including Self-Employment	Emp	PJB	10.42 (16.33)	14.59 (4.50)	12.33	40.02
			BHR	6.97 (16.60)	0.94 (0.24)	6.00	−86.51
			di	49.50	1452.13		
		Ern	PJB	83.24 (12.48)	123.98 (2.72)	101.84	48.94
			BHR	37.54 (15.47)	4.22 (0.15)	32.21	−88.76
			di	121.74	2837.91		
		Epd	PJB	7.99	8.50	8.26	6.38
			BHR	5.39	4.49	5.37	−16.70
			di	48.24	89.31		
		PPR	PJB	11.66	9.49	10.67	
			BHR	9.13	2.08	8.00	
4.	Total Non-Farm Employment	Emp	PJB	63.80 (100.00)	324.39 (100.00)	182.81	408.45
			BHR	42.00 (100.00)	386.02 (100.00)	97.05	819.10
			di	51.90	-15.97		
		Ern	PJB	666.84 (100.00)	4559.45 (100.00)	2444.46	583.74
			BHR	242.70 (100.00)	2785.39 (100.00)	649.53	1047.67
			di	174.76	63.69		
		Epd	PJB	10.45	14.06	13.37	34.55
			BHR	5.78	7.22	6.69	24.91
			di	80.80	94.74		
		PPR	PJB	52.76	100.00	74.33	
			BHR	37.30	100.00	47.33	

Note: 1. For an explanation of various notations used in this table, please refer to Tables 4.1 and 4.3.

2. Figures in the parentheses are percentages of the Total Non-farm Employment/ Earnings.

Firstly, the PALH group in Punjab fares uniformly much better than its counterpart in Bihar, for individual components as well as the total of non-farm employment/earnings. For example, on an average, a rural labour household in Punjab enjoys 31.0 per cent higher of wage-paid rural (non-farm) employment, more than 75.0 per cent higher of urban wage-paid employment, about 50.0 per cent of self-employment and 52.0 per cent of total non-farm employment. The differential gets magnified when we shift our focus from employment to earnings. On an average, a rural household in Punjab gets about 134.0 per cent, 233.0 per cent, 122.0 per cent and 175.0 per cent higher earnings from rural wage employment, urban wage employment, self-employment, and total non-farm employment respectively. Similarly, in terms of per day earning, the edge of PALH households of Punjab over those of Bihar is to the tune of 78.0 per cent, 90.0 per cent 48.0 per cent and 81.0 per cent, for the four categories of non-farm employment mentioned above.

Secondly, as regards the PNLH groups, the Punjab-Bihar comparison poses certain contrasts. For example, while for most components of employment, mandays worked by an average household in Punjab were slightly lower compared with those worked in Bihar, the relative picture is significantly opposite as regards the earnings, especially on per day basis. For example, while a typical PNLH household in Bihar compared with its counterpart in Punjab, show about 51.0 per cent more mandays of wage-paid rural employment, its total and per day earnings from the same are nearly 67.0 per cent and 153.0 per cent lower than those accruing to a Punjab household. Similarly, for wage-paid urban employment, an average Bihar PNLH household puts in nearly 20.0 per cent more of labour-time compared with its counterpart in Punjab, it trails behind the latter to the extent of about 58.0 per cent and 89.0 per cent, respectively, as regards total and per day earnings. Again, in terms of total non-farm employment, while a Bihar household expends about 19.0 per cent more of labour-time, its total earnings are lower by as much as 64.0 per cent, and per day earnings by as much as 95.0 per cent. The lower mandays of employment and higher level of per household and per day earnings accruing to a PNLH household in Punjab than the one in Bihar, therefore, clearly signify that non-farm employment (including its individual components) is comparatively more remunerative in the progressive State of Punjab than in the backward Bihar. However, as regards our hypothesis regarding the superiority of PALH and PNLH groups of Punjab over their counterparts in Bihar in the matter of employment/earnings from non-farm employment, our analysis rejects it only to the extent that PNLH group of Bihar seems to be availing itself of more employment time in different types of non-farm activities. The superiority of the Punjab groups is clearly visible in the matter of gainfulness of overall non-farm employment as also in its individual components. Our results clearly convey the superiority of PALH and PNLH groups of Punjab compared with their counterparts in Bihar. We observe that practically in all respects and from standpoint, the Bihar households are trailing far behind their counterparts in Punjab in the matter of per household as well as per day earning. Both per household and per day earnings are manifold higher in the progressive area of Punjab compared with those in the backward Bihar.

The foregoing discussion makes it fairly evident that per household mandays of employment as also the level of per household/per day earning in overall non-farm employment are higher in Punjab than in Bihar. Further, a non-cultivating rural labour household in Punjab maintains its edge over its counterpart in Bihar in the matter of employment/earnings from different components of non-farm employment/earnings. This suggests that as the interaction between internal dynamics of rural transformation and rural-urban linkages has been much stronger in Punjab than in Bihar, the labour household of the former avail of a much more diversified and lucrative structure of non-farm employment and earnings than the latter. This is due to the fact that this interaction has generated many productive and highly remunerative avenues of wage-paid rural and urban employment as also non-wage self-employment activities. Finally, since the impact of this interaction has been greater in Punjab than in Bihar, a labour household in the former is relatively much better off than one in the latter, both in terms of the quantum of employment and level of earnings. As regards the village-wise pattern of non-farm employment/earnings, we can maintain that because of a strong and growing rural-urban linkages, while the opportunity of wage-paid urban employment/earnings is available to rural labour households even in the remote villages of Punjab; in Bihar, on the other hand, this phenomenon ceases to operate just after a small distance from the urban focal town. Lastly, relatively higher mandays of non-farm employment available to a PNLH household in Bihar do no place it in any advantageous position compared with its counterpart in Punjab. The sharp contrast observed in per household and per day earning levels, on the other hand, reveals the strength of Punjab economy so that a PNLH household in the State while working for a relatively smaller labour time, both for wage-paid rural and urban employment (and hence the total non-farm employment) earns relatively much more, than its counterpart in Bihar, both on per household and per day basis.

NOTES

1. Some of the most outstanding research contributions on the theme of non-farm employment/earnings are available in R.T. Shand ed. (1986): *Off-farm Employment in the Development of Rural Asia*, Vol. 1 and II. National Centre for Development Studies, Australian National University. In particular, see Rizwanul Islam: "Non-farm employment in Rural Asia: Issues and Evidence", pp. 153-173; Ryohie Kada, "Off-farm Employment and the Rural-Urban Interface in Japanese Economic Development", pp. 75-93. Samuel P.S.Ho., "Off-farm Employment and Farm Households in Taiwan", pp. 95-133; and Fun Koo Park, "Off-farm Employment in Korea: Current Status and Future Prospects", pp. 135-152. Also see, Enyinna Chuta and Carl Liedholm (1979), *Rural Non-Farm Employment: A Review of the State of Art*, MSU Development Paper No. 4, Department of Agricultural Economics, Michigan State University, East Lansing, Michigan.
2. Some such factors may be the availability of non-farm employment opportunities due to the beginning of construction work or setting up of the factories in the nearby areas, desire/need of additional income for personal use, inadequacy of agricultural income for making a living, need for extra income for the construction of a house or for making investment in the farm, to avail the benefits of institutional lending for the promotion of non-farm activities, small size of the holding with limited prospects for its further expansion, use of surplus labour time on account of the introduction of technological innovations, etc. For further details, please see Swapna Mukhopadhyay and Ping Lim Chee ed, (1985), *The Rural Non-Farm Sector in Asia*, Asian and Pacific Development Centre, Kuala Lumpur, Malaysia.
3. Faisal Kasryno, "Impact of Off-farm Employment on Agricultural Labour Absorption and Wages in Indonesia", pp. 273-307; G.K. Chadha, "The Off-farm Economic Structure of Agriculturally Growing Regions: A Study of Indian Punjab", pp. 147-175; and P. Hanumantha Rayappa, "Some Dimensions of Off-farm Employment in Rural Karnataka, India", pp. 177-192, all in R.T. Shand ed, (1986), *op. cit.*

6

TOTAL YEARLY EMPLOYMENT/ EARNINGS AND POVERTY

The preceding two chapters deal respectively with on- and non-farm employment and earnings of the resident labour households of Punjab and Bihar. The aim of the present chapter is two-fold. Firstly, it attempts to put together the contents of the previous two chapters to arrive at the total yearly employment/earnings. The relative importance of each of the two components of employment, namely on-farm and non-farm employment, in the total yearly employment/ earnings is discussed in the first place. Secondly, an attempt is made to estimate the incidence and level of poverty among the non-cultivating rural labour households in the two States. It needs to be pointed out that we are dealing with such a set of rural households as are commonly designated as 'poor'. Consequently, if differences are observed in the incidence and level of poverty taking place among the labour households of Punjab and Bihar, these should help us to test the validity of 'trickle-down' or 'percolation' thesis; around which a lively debate has ensued in the recent years.

In this regard, the following hypotheses are tested empirically.

Hypothesis I

(a) The non-cultivating rural labour households living near an urban industrial town enjoy larger number of total mandays of employment and a higher level of earnings in a year compared to similar households away from the town.

(b) The total mandays of employment and the level of earnings are higher for the Punjab households compared with those from Bihar, at all conceivable distances from the urban focal town.

Hypothesis II

(a) Both in the Punjab and Bihar, per capita net household income of labour households in villages near the towns is much higher than that of households away from the town.
(b) The per capita net household income of such households in Punjab is much higher than that of the corresponding households in Bihar at all distances from the focal town.

Hypothesis III

(a) In both the States, the proportion of rural labour households below the poverty line keeps on declining as we move from the interior of the countryside towards the urban industrial town.
(b) The proportion of such households, is lower in the Punjab villages compared with nearly equally distanced Bihar villages.

The above-mentioned hypotheses necessarily imply that the gains of rapid economic growth in general, and those emanating from the interaction between the agricultural transformation and growing rural-urban linkages in particular, have trickled-down more vigorously in the progressive areas of Punjab than those in Bihar. But is it really so? We seek confirmation to these hypotheses through our sample data.

The chapter is divided into two sections. Section A brings out a comparative picture of the Punjab and Bihar labour households in terms of their total yearly employment/earnings as well as its on-and non-farm components. To capture the impact of urban-rural distance, this analysis has been extended in terms of regression analysis. For facilitating more useful comparisons between Punjab and Bihar, discussion has also been carried out in terms of per earner and per capita estimates. Section B, attempts to study the impact of the above mentioned interaction on the incidence and intensity of rural poverty prevailing among the labour households of Punjab and Bihar.

SECTION A

Total Yearly Employment/Earnings

To being with, let us look at total employment and earning position of Punjab labour households, vis-a-vis their counterparts in Bihar.

Table 6.1 provides the essentials in this regard. The conclusions drawn previously in Chapters 4 and 5 regarding the better employment and earning performance of Punjab households over their counterparts in Bihar are further confirmed at the level of total employment. It is evident that the Punjab households enjoy only a marginal advantage over the Bihar households as regards the mandays of total yearly employment; the difference is less than 10.0 per cent. However, the real advantage of the Punjab households comes out sharply in terms of per household and per day earnings. For the total yearly employment, an average rural labour household in Punjab enjoys more than double the earning compared with its counterpart in Bihar. Also, for every day of employment, the Punjab household earns nearly double the amount accruing to the Bihar household. This suggests that the growing and dynamic economy of Punjab is capable of providing much more remunerative employment to its rural labour households, although the sheer number of days for which employment is available to such households does not differ much between Punjab and Bihar. In other words, the relative employment situation in Bihar may not look to be bad from the point of view of 'time criterion', yet it signals a situation of acute backwardness from the view-point of 'income criterion'. The same amount of human labour in Bihar brings only about one-half of monetary return compared with Punjab. The Bihar scenario thus reveals a relative deprivation for the labour class, presumably for the employer as well.

The division of total employment into on-farm and non-farm components throws up very striking contrasts between the two study areas. Table 6.1 shows that on-farm employment overwhelmingly dominates in both the States. However, the absolute number of on-farm employment in Punjab (about 422.0 mandays) are relatively smaller compared with the corresponding figure in Bihar (about 458.0 mandays). Also the per cent share of this component in the total yearly employment (about 83.0%) in the latter is much higher compared with that of the former (about 70.0%). On the contrary, the situation regarding the non-farm employment is tilting heavily in favour of Punjab. For example, the absolute number of mandays of non-farm employment as well as the per cent share of this component in the total employment in Punjab (about 183.0 mandays and 30.0%, respectively) are much higher than those in Bihar (about 97.0 mandays and about 18.0% respectively).

TABLE 6.1: Pattern of Total Yearly Employment and Earnings of Labour Households in Punjab and Bihar

(Mean Value)

Sl. No.	Employment/Earning Source	Variable	Punjab (PJB)	Bihar (BHR)	Differential (di)
1	2	3	4	5	6
1.	On-Farm Employment	Emp	421.62 (69.76)	457.51 (82.50)	−7.84
		Ern	3736.43 (60.45)	2265.12 (77.72)	64.96
		Epd	8.86	4.95	78.99
		PPR	92.33	97.33	
2.	Non-Farm Employment	Emp	182.81 (30.24)	97.05 (17.50)	88.37
		Ern	2444.46 (39.55)	649.53 (22.28)	276.34
		Epd	13.37	6.69	99.85
		PPR	74.33	47.33	
3.	Total Employment	Emp	604.43 (100.00)	554.56 (100.00)	8.99
		Ern	6180.89 (100.00)	2914.65 (100.00)	112.06
		Epd	10.23	5.26	94.49
		PPR	100.00	100.00	

Note: For an explanation of various notations Emp, Ern, Epd, PPR and di, please see Table 4.1.

It is also clear that while the lion's share in total yearly earnings is reported to be coming in the two States from on-farm employment, but the share of earnings from this head falls short of their corresponding share in employment from this component.

The per cent share of non-farm earnings in the total yearly earnings is much higher in Punjab (about 40.0%) than in Bihar (about 22.0%). In terms of absolute levels, a Punjab household records an extra of about 276.0 per cent over its Bihar counterpart.

Finally and most notably, while per day earnings from on- and non-farm components in Punjab are uniformly and substantially higher than in Bihar, yet the edge of Punjab households is much more marked in non-farm component (about 100.0%) against on-farm component (about 79.0%).

The preceding discussion of Punjab and Bihar differentials

highlights some important points. In the first instance, relatively bigger proportion of total yearly employment/earnings is available in non-farm employment in Punjab compared with Bihar. On the other hand, the proportion of on-farm employment/earnings in Bihar is much bigger than that of Punjab. Secondly, a slightly lower number of mandays of on-farm employment in Punjab, *vis-a-vis* that in Bihar, is more than compensated by relatively higher mandays of non-farm employment. Consequently, man days of total yearly employment are higher in Punjab than in Bihar. Thirdly and most importantly, the stable and consistently expanding agriculture in Punjab has enabled its labour households to maintain an edge in all correlates of employment over their corresponding counterparts in Bihar by offering the former more remunerative employment opportunities. This suggests and further lends credence to our view that the total yearly employment/earnings are structurally more diversified in the agriculturally progressive Punjab, compared with Bihar. And lastly, the sharp contrasts observed at the level of per household and per day earnings between Punjab and Bihar offer ample evidence that labour effort alone does not matter much in the modern system of agricultural production; rural institutions and technology-in-use also play a very crucial role in augmenting the level of production and thereby increasing employment opportunities and rising earning levels for the rural labour households.

The Villagewise Pattern

As in the preceding two chapters, we look into the pattern of Punjab-Bihar differentials at the village level. In particular, we would like to see the effect of distance from the urban focal town on total yearly employment as well as its two constituents viz on- and non-farm employment/earnings, in the study areas of Punjab and Bihar. In this context, let us test empirically the possibility of the existence of inverse relationship between mandays of employment/earnings and rural urban distance as also the superiority of Punjab villages over Bihar villages at all comparable distances.

The details of the villagewise pattern are set out in Table 6.2. This table reveals a few important points. First, as far as per household mandays of overall employment are concerned, Punjab and Bihar villages represent an important contrast. Interestingly, while in Punjab per household mandays (Emp.) of total yearly employment are statistically invariant with respect to the distance from the focal town, in Bihar, on the other hand, they tend to decline significantly. This differential in per household mandays of total yearly employment can be explained by a host of factors operating simultaneously in the two States. First in Punjab, while on the one hand, migrant labour in villages near the town have largely substituted the male local labour in the matter of wage-paid on-farm employment, the latter has also to compete with the former in the matter of wage-paid non-farm urban employment, especially in activities such as construction, industrial work, weighing as well as loading/unloading of grain in the grain markets, etc. Consequently, the possibility of availing more mandays of employment inside the agriculture as also in the urban wage paid non-farm employment gets restricted. However, such a phenomenon of migrant labour is conspicuous by its absence in Bihar. Second in Punjab, the shortage of power and cement (both these items affect the level and pattern of urban development) in the urban towns, are reported to contribute their share in restraining the total economic activity and thereby employment to the people from nearby villages. Thirdly and more importantly, another explanation emerges from a very careful scrutiny of regression results for total employment-time in conjunction with those for on-as well as non-farm employment-time. While regression co-efficient for on-farm and non-farm employment are both statistically significant, yet they record movement in the opposite directions of each other i.e. while regression co-efficient for on-farm employment records an increasing pattern, a decline is noticeable with regard to that for non-farm employment. In other words, the increase in on-farm employment is subsumed by a corresponding decrease in non-farm employment with the net result that as rural-urban distance increases, mandays of total yearly employment per households do not vary significantly. Compared with this, in Bihar, the mandays of total yearly employment are inversely related to distance from the focal town. This Punjab-Bihar contrast, regarding the availability of total yearly employment with respect to distance from the focal town, rejects our hypothesis in the case of Punjab; in Bihar, on the other hand, it is duly confirmed by our sample data. It is probably owing to the fact that employment opportunities in the interior of Bihar are confined largely to the agricultural sector. And given the low level of development in Bihar agriculture on the one hand, and the poor rural-urban linkages on the other, the mandays of employment register a declining trend as distance from the focal town increases.

TABLE 6.2: Villagewise Pattern of Total Yearly Employment and Earnings of Labour Households in Punjab and Bihar

(Mean Value)

Sl. No.	Employment/ Earning Source	Vari- able	State	Village V1	V2	V3	V4	V5	V6	V7	V8	Regression Equation $Y_i = \alpha + \beta D_j$	No. of Obser- vations- (N)
1	2	3	4	5	6	7	8	9	10	11	12	13	14
1.	On-Farm Employ- ment	Emp	PJB	303.24	295.04	353.08	449.29	463.65	476.16	571.94	572.54	Y_i = 313.30 + 16.26*D	277
				(50.02)	(53.37)	(60.31)	(61.74)	(68.89)	(77.26)	(92.17)	(92.63)	[5.02]	
			BHR	340.69	293.49	538.77	539.43	579.93	428.39	536.74	513.33	Y_i = 389.09 + 7.99*D	292
				(61.66)	(50.33)	(80.22)	(97.82)	(84.26)	(84.94)	(98.41)	(97.18)	[3.30]	
			di	−10.99	0.53	−34.47	−16.71	−20.05	11.15	6.56	−11.53		
		Ern	PJB	2422.06	2632.97	3431.33	3920.24	4164.08	4216.99	4710.22	4804.89	Y_i = 3023.24 + 116.09*D	277
				(35.16)	(43.11)	(53.05)	(50.95)	(58.48)	(69.77)	(90.64)	(90.69)	[3.57]	
			BHR	1971.13	1654.49	2727.08	2593.60	2983.41	2152.98	2400.97	2359.80	Y_i = 2202.28 + 12.33D	292
				(55.00)	(43.98)	(75.48)	(97.57)	(85.78)	(82.72)	(98.35)	(97.32)	[1.08]	
			di	22.88	59.14	25.82	51.15	39.57	95.87	96.18	103.61		
		Epd	PJB	7.99	8.92	9.72	8.73	8.98	8.86	8.24	8.39	Y_i = 8.74 - 0.02D	277
												[0.53]	
			BHR	5.79	5.64	5.06	4.81	5.14	5.03	4.47	4.60	Y_i = 6.38 - 0.11* D	292
												[5.22]	
			di	38.00	58.16	92.09	81.50	74.71	76.14	84.34	82.39		
		PPR	PJB	90.48	78.72	91.03	100.00	100.00	93.65	100.00	100.00		
			BHR	96.15	91.89	96.15	100.00	100.00	96.47	100.00	100.00		

Contd.

TABLE 6.2 *Contd.*

1	2	3	4	5	6	7	8	9	10	11	12	13	14	
2.	Non-Farm Employment	Emp	PJB	303.05	252.87	232.64	278.43	209.35	140.17	48.60	44.27	Y_i	= 361.02 - 15.04* *D*	223
				(49.48)	(46.13)	(39.69)	(38.26)	(31.11)	(22.74)	(7.83)	(7.37)		[7.70]	
			BHR	211.85	289.62	132.85	12.00	108.33	75.93	8.68	14.90	Y_i	= 306.39 - 13.53* *D*	141
				(38.34)	(49.67)	(19.78)	(2.18)	(15.74)	(15.06)	(1.59)	(2.82)		[5.03]	
			di	43.05	−12.69	75.11	2220.25	93.25	84.60	459.91	197.11			
		Ern	PJB	4466.40	3474.52	3036.94	3774.79	2955.95	1827.13	486.19	493.25	Y_i	= 5036.38 - 228.34* *D*	223
				(64.84)	(56.89)	(46.95)	(49.05)	(41.52)	(30.23)	(9.36)	(9.31)		[7.98]	
			BHR	1612.77	2107.37	886.01	64.65	494.39	449.85	40.24	64.98	Y_i	= 2261.49 - 119.13* *D*	141
				(45.00)	(56.02)	(24.52)	(2.43)	(14.22)	(17.28)	(1.65)	(2.68)		[6.49]	
			di	176.94	64.87	242.77	5738.96	497.90	306.16	1108.23	659.08			
		Epd	PJB	14.74	13.74	13.05	13.56	14.12	13.04	10.00	11.14	Y_i	= 14.84 - 0.32* *D*	223
													[6.19]	
			BHR	7.61	7.28	6.67	5.39	4.56	5.92	4.64	4.36	Y_i	= 7.44 - 0.18* *D*	141
													[8.24]	
			di	93.69	88.74	95.65	151.58	209.65	120.27	115.52	155.50			
		PPR	PJB	85.71	85.11	83.33	85.71	82.61	73.02	54.29	38.46			
			BHR	84.62	89.19	73.08	19.05	33.33	48.24	18.42	21.15			

Contd.

TABLE 6.2 *Contd.*

1	2	3	4	5	6	7	8	9	10	11	12	13	14	
3.	Total Employment	Emp	PJB	606.29	547.91	585.72	727.71	673.00	616.33	620.54	616.81	Y_i = 571.18 +	3.90D	300
				(100.00)	(100.00)	(100.00)	(100.00)	(100.00)	(100.00)	(100.00)	(100.00)		[1.30]	
			BHR	552.54	583.11	671.62	551.43	688.27	504.32	545.42	528.23	Y_i = 601.48 -	4.68* *D*	300
				(100.00)	(100.00)	(100.00)	(100.00)	(100.00)	(100.0)	(100.00)	(100.00)		[1.98]	
			di	9.73	−6.04	−12.79	31.97	−2.22	22.21	13.77	16.77			
		Ern	PJB	6888.47	6107.49	6468.27	7695.03	7120.03	6044.12	5196.42	5298.14	Y_i = 6872.18 -	81.04* *D*	300
				(100.00)	(100.00)	(100.00)	(100.00)	(100.00)	(100.00)	(100.00)	(100.00)		[2.57]	
			BHR	3583.90	3761.86	3613.08	2658.24	3477.79	2602.83	2441.21	2424.78	Y_i = 3776.86 -	86.08* *D*	300
				(100.00)	(100.00)	(100.00)	(100.00)	(100.00)	(100.00)	(100.00)	(100.00)		[6.90]	
			di	92.21	62.35	79.02	189.48	104.73	132.21	112.86	118.50			
		Epd	PJB	11.36	11.15	11.04	10.57	10.58	9.81	8.37	8.59	Y_i = 12.56 -	0.23* *D*	300
													[6.90]	
			BHR	6.49	6.45	5.38	4.82	5.05	5.16	4.48	4.59	Y_i = 6.45 -	0.11* *D*	300
													[9.62]	
			di	75.04	72.87	105.20	119.29	109.50	90.12	86.83	87.15			
		PPR	PJB	100.00	100.00	100.00	100.00	100.00	100.00	100.00	100.00			
			BHR	100.00	100.00	100.00	100.00	100.00	100.00	100.00	100.00			

Note: Various notations used in this table are explained in Tables 4.1 and 4.2
* denotes significance of 't' values at 0.05 level.

On the basis of the preceding analysis, we can maintain that in the case of Punjab, the proximity of a village from the focal town notwithstanding, per household mandays of total yearly employment do not differ much from one village to another. Secondly, per household and per day earnings from total yearly employment tend to decline with increase in rural-urban distance. In other words, as we go into the interior, the total yearly earning of an average labour household goes on declining, and with it does the per day earning. Since this is happening in both the States, we are led to believe that rural labour households in the interior end up with lower annual incomes mainly because of lower earnings per day of work. It is, however, a different matter that in every comparable location, the progressive situation of Punjab shows a significantly higher daily earning compared with Bihar.

We may also have a look at village-pairs between Punjab and Bihar. Such an analysis helps us to test our hypothesis on the superiority of Punjab households over that of Bihar households in the matter of total yearly employment/earnings irrespective of the distance from the urban focal town. It is evident that variations in employment time and earnings exist practically all along the continuum of rural-urban distance. However, the differentials in total mandays of employment are relatively less sharp compared with differentials in per households and per day earnings. Further, the distantly located villages in Punjab record comparatively higher increases both in per household and per day earnings over similar Bihar villages than the villages located in immediate proximity from the focal towns in the two States. This lends further substance to our contention that the impact of the dynamics of rural economic transformation and rural-urban linkages is comparatively much stronger in Punjab than in Bihar. Consequently, the decline in the level of per household and per day earnings is more pronounced in Bihar against Punjab. This lends confirmation to our hypothesis suggesting superiority of Punjab households over that of their counterparts in Bihar in the matter of total yearly employment/earnings at all distances from the focal town.

Let us now examine the pattern of total yearly employment/earnings of PALH and PNLH groups cross-sectionally by making use of the information in Table 6.3.

TABLE 6.3: Pattern of Total Yearly Employment and Earnings of PALH and PNLH Groups in Punjab and Bihar

(Mean Value)

Sl. No.	Employment/ Earning Source	Variable	State	PALH	PNLH	All	di*
1	2	3	4	5	6	7	8
1.	On-Farm Employment	Emp	PJB	623.95	180.89	421.62	244.93
				(90.72)	(35.80)	(69.75)	
			BHR	512.53	168.69	457.51	203.83
				(92.43)	(30.41)	(82.50)	
			di	21.74	7.23		
		Ern	PJB	5523.91	1609.72	3736.43	243.16
				(89.23)	(26.09)	(60.45)	
			BHR	2498.30	1040.90	2265.12	140.01
				(91.15)	(27.20)	(77.71)	
			di	121.11	54.65		
		Epd	PJB	8.85	8.90	8.86	−0.56
			BHR	4.87	6.17	4.95	−21.07
			di	81.72	44.25		
		PPR	PJB	100.00	83.21	92.33	
			BHR	100.00	83.33	97.33	
2.	Non-Farm Employment	Emp	PJB	63.80	324.39	182.81	−80.33
				(9.28)	(64.20)	(30.25)	
			BHR	42.00	386.02	97.05	−89.12
				(7.57)	(69.59)	(17.50)	
			di	51.90	−15.97		
		Ern	PJB	666.84	4559.45	2444.46	−85.37
				(10.77)	(73.91)	(39.55)	
			BHR	242.70	2785.39	649.53	−91.29
				(8.85)	(72.80)	(22.29)	
			di	174.76	63.69		
		Epd	PJB	10.45	14.06	13.37	−25.68
			BHR	5.78	7.22	6.69	−19.94
			di	80.80	94.74		
		PPR	PJB	52.76	100.00	74.33	
			BHR	37.30	100.00	47.33	

Contd.

TABLE 6.3 *Contd.*

1	2	3	4	5	6	7	8
3.	Total Employ-ment	Emp	PJB	687.75	505.28	604.43	36.11
				(100.00)	(100.00)	(100.00)	
			BHR	554.53	554.71	554.56	−0.03
				(100.00)	(100.00)	(100.00)	
			di	24.02	−8.91		
		Ern	PJB	6190.74	6169.16	6180.89	0.35
				(100.00)	(100.00)	(100.00)	
			BHR	2741.00	3826.29	2914.65	−28.36
				(100.00)	(100.00)	(100.00)	
			di	125.86	61.23		
		Epd	PJB	9.00	12.21	10.23	−26.29
			BHR	4.94	6.90	5.26	−28.41
			di	82.19	76.96		
		PPR	PJB	100.00	100.00	100.00	
			BHR	100.00	100.00	100.00	

Note: For explanation of various notations used in this table, See Table 4.1 and 4.3.

As is expected, PALH and PNLH groups are better off from each other in the matter of on-farm and non-farm employment/earnings respectively. It is, therefore, important to look into the pattern of their total yearly employment/earnings between the identical groups of the two States as also between the two groups within each State. It is interesting to observe the following important points emerging from Table 6.3.

First, the PALH group in Punjab puts in nearly 24.0 per cent extra labour but earns about 126.0 per cent more from total yearly employment at the household level than its counterpart in Bihar. Consequently, per day earning of the former is 82.0 per cent higher than that of the latter. Second, the superiority of the Punjab's PALH group over that of Bihar operates in more or less the same manner for each of the on-farm and non-farm components of total employment. The Punjab's PALH group is thus much better off in every aspect of its total employment status. Third, the differences in the employment and earning pattern of PNLH groups of the two States are rather striking. It is indeed important to note that a household belonging to PNLH group in Punjab, on an average, puts-in nearly 9.0 per cent less labour than its Bihar counterpart, but earns nearly 61.0 per cent more in a year at the household level and roughly 77.0 per cent at the per day level. Further, what is even more interesting is that the per household mandays of non-farm employment for PNLH group in Punjab are smaller than in Bihar by nearly 16.0 per cent[1]. But these relatively higher number of mandays of non-farm employment do not make a Bihar household better off compared with its Punjab counterpart. On the other hand, the differentials of per household and per day earning make it obvious that PNLH group of Punjab has a relatively more remunerative structure of total yearly employment than its Bihar counterpart.

It might as well as interesting to see the differences between PALH and PNLH groups within each of the two States. It is very interesting to see that the PALH group in Punjab enjoys nearly 36.0 per cent more of employment-time compared with the PNLH of the same State. Thanks of this extra employment-time, the PALH group in Punjab manages to ward off any corrosion in their total yearly earning compared with the PNLH group, it is indeed the most striking feature of the Punjab's model of economic development that households depending largely on agricultural employment (PALH group) are not beaten back by households whose major earnings accrue from non-farm employment. Farm employment is fairly competitive with non-farm employment in Punjab and those households which are primarily dependent on the former do not have to suffer an undue disadvantage. To put the record straight, the remunerativeness of farm employment in Punjab is discernible in terms of our 1980-81 household level data in spite of the huge pace of mechanization witnessed during the Green Revolution years as also the intervening effects of migrant labour consistently since the early 1970's. The blessings of a growing agricultural economy are thus unmistakably at play in Punjab. In sharp contrast. in Bihar, the PALH group fares rather poorly in comparison with the PNLH group. The tardy growth and fluctuating fortune of Bihar agriculture makes the PALH group much weaker than the PNLH group.

Lastly, the dependence of PALH group on non-farm employment and likewise the dependence of PNLH group on on-farm employment invites a special comment. In both the States, more than 90.0 per cent of total employment time of the PALH group is forthcoming through on-farm employment; non-farm employment for this group does not account for more than 10.0 per cent of total employment time. On the contrary, in Punjab and Bihar respectively, more than 35.0 per cent and 30.0 per cent of total employment time of the PNLH group is forthcoming through on-farm employment. It is clear that in both the States, the dependence on agriculture and related activities is fairly big even by those households which are getting a major part of their yearly income from sources outside agriculture. In other words, non-farm employment opportunities may have grown during the sixties and the seventies but dependence on agriculture is still of a fairly high order, in agriculturally growing as well as backward areas. Consequently, the growth profile of agriculture including its capability to provide higher employment and wages still holds larger explanation to the employment and income status of rural labour households in India. And these are precisely the features which differentiate the Punjab situation sharply from that of Bihar.

Per Earner Employment and Per Capita Income

So far, our analysis of employment and earnings has remained confined at the household level. It is possible that an analysis of this type may bypass many important characteristics of the household such as average number of earners per household, household size, etc; which are otherwise significant aspects of household economy. We must take cognizance of these features also for developing a proper understanding of the earnings, level of living and family welfare, on a comparable basis, between two areas characterized by difference in such family attributes. We, therefore, work out per earner employment and then per capita yearly income for the Punjab and the Bihar households. Table 6.4 throws up a few significant features.

It may be observed from this table that, on an average, every earner in a typical rural labour household of Punjab invests nearly 14.0 per cent more human effort in a year but is able to derive as much as 122.0 per cent extra earning compared with his counterpart in Bihar. Similarly, for an average non-cultivating rural labour household in Punjab, the level of per capita income is nearly 2.20 times higher that of the one from Bihar. Taking into consideration the fact that Punjab and Bihar experiences of agricultural growth represent two sharply contrasting situations, it follows that the gains of rapid economic growth tend to trickle down to all strata of the society when growth is high and sustained, as in Punjab. Thus, in contradiction to a popular belief that agricultural growth leads to immiserization of the working class, our data clearly establishes a positive association between the level of economic development and the level of per earner or per capita earning of even the lowliest among the rural households.

TABLE 6.4: Net Household and Per Capita Income of Labour Households in Punjab and Bihar

(Mean Value, Per Annum)

Sl. No.	Indicator	Punjab (PJBi)	Bihar (BHRi)	Differential (di)
1	2	3	4	5
1.	Total Yearly Mandays of Employment	604.43	554.56	8.99
2.	Per Earner Mandays of Employment	268.64	234.98	14.32
3.	Net Earnings from Total Yearly Wage Employment (in Rs.)	6180.89	2914.65	112.06
4.	Net Earnings Per Earner (in Rs.)	2747.06	1235.02	122.43
5.	Transfer Payments(in Rs.)	114.64	46.02	149.11
6.	Net Household Income	6295.53	2960.67	112.64
7.	Per Capita Income	1140.49	518.51	119.96

Note: $di = \frac{PJBi - BHRi}{BHRi}$

To lend further evidence to the above conclusion we go down to the villagewise pattern on the lines of Table 6.4. The results of this exercise are presented in Table 6.5. In this regard, we propose to test the validity of our hypothesis envisaging higher economic gains, percolating from rural economic transformation and rural-urban linkages as evidenced by per capita income in our case, for households living near the town compared with their distantly located counterparts and also the edge of Punjab households over their counterparts in Bihar at comparable distances from the focal town.

TABLE 6.5: Villagewise Pattern of Net Household and Per Capita Income of Labour Households in Punjab and Bihar

(Mean Value, Per Annum)

Sl. No.	Indicator	State	Village V1	V2	V3	V4	V5	V6	V7	V8	Regression Equation $Y_i = \alpha + \beta D_j$
1	2	3	4	5	6	7	8	9	10	11	12
1.	Total Mandays of Employment	PJB	606.29	547.91	585.72	727.71	673.00	616.33	620.54	616.81	
		BHR	552.54	583.11	671.62	551.43	688.27	504.32	545.42	528.23	
2.	Per Earner Man-days of Employment	PJB	271.88	291.44	272.43	275.65	259.85	265.66	247.23	264.73	Y_i = 293.38 - 1.490D [−1.80]
		BHR	255.81	266.26	261.33	301.33	235.71	202.54	219.04	235.82	Y_i = 278.45 - 3.05*D [4.11]
3.	Net Earnings from Total Wage Employment (Rs.)	PJB	6888.47	6107.49	6468.27	7695.03	7120.03	6044.12	5196.42	5298.14	
		BHR	3583.90	3761.86	3613.08	2658.24	3477.79	2602.83	2441.21	2424.78	
		di	92.21	62.35	79.02	189.48	104.73	132.21	112.86	118.50	

Contd.

TABLE 6.5 *Contd.*

1	2	3	4	5	6	7	8	9	10	11	12
4.	Net Earnings per Earner (Rs.)	PJB	3089.00	3248.66	3008.50	2914.78	2749.05	2605.22	2070.29	2273.88	Y_i = 3609.06 - 79.01* D [7.02]
		BHR	1659.21	1717.74	1405.87	1452.59	1191.02	1045.31	980.41	1082.49	Y_i = 1775.04 - 45.74* D [10.91]
		di	86.17	89.12	114.00	100.66	130.81	149.23	111.17	110.06	
5.	Transfer Payments (Rs.)	PJB	76.00	211.83	38.46	17.14	149.78	181.81	83.69	72.77	
		BHR	24.92	33.62	71.54	72.19	44.27	44.05	11.84	70.77	
		di	204.98	530.07	−46.24	−76.26	238.33	312.74	606.84	2.83	
6.	Net Household Income (Rs.)	PJB	6964.47	6319.32	6506.73	7712.17	7269.81	6225.93	5280.11	5370.91	Y_i = 6986.58 - 81.01* D [2.50]
		BHR	3608.82	3795.48	3684.62	2730.43	3522.06	2646.88	2453.05	2495.55	Y_i = 3816.62 - 85.45* D [6.72]
		di	92.98	66.50	76.59	182.45	106.41	135.22	115.25	115.22	
7.	Per Capita Income	PJB	1198.70	1253.83	1204.95	1173.85	1099.82	1140.28	932.88	1019.15	Y_i = 1355.22 - 17.72* D [3.07]
		BHR	621.14	685.10	655.63	540.68	574.56	451.69	421.49	441.69	Y_i = 721.26 - 16.92* D [7.75]
		di	92.98	83.01	83.79	117.11	91.42	152.45	121.33	130.74	

Note: For various notations used in this Table, please refer to Tables 4.1 and 4.2

* shows the significance of 't' values at 0.05 leve .

Table 6.5 clearly shows that per earner yearly earning registers a declining trend both in Punjab and Bihar in terms of distance from the urban areas. However, there are significant differences between the two as far as the level of per earner mandays of yearly employment are concerned. While per earner employment pattern in Bihar seems to be inversely related to the distance from the focal town; in Punjab, on the other hand, distance does not affect the mandays of total yearly employment on per earner basis. It is mainly due to the fact that in Punjab, the level of urbanisation being relatively higher, strong rural-urban linkages operate mainly because of well-developed infrastructural facilities like road conditions and transport services etc. In Punjab, the impact on the rural areas can be seen up to a much larger distance, compared with Bihar where such facilities are relatively much less developed. Again, net household income as well as per capita income in both the States tend to decline in relation to rural-urban distance. It is particularly important to point out that per capita income in the remotest village in the Punjab is more than 60.0 per cent higher than that in the one nearest to the urban-focal town in Bihar, and if we compare the per capita income of the first village of Punjab with that of the farthest village of Bihar, the gap is nearly three times over. Even pairwise comparison shows that at every possible distance, the Punjab households enjoy double or higher level of per capita income. In brief, the economic benefits of the Green Revolution in Punjab supported by the rising employment opportunities from non-agricultural activities have accrued to rural labour households in villages as far as 15-16 km away from a typical urban focal town; in comparison, villages as near as 2-3 km from a typical urban focal town in Bihar pale into insignificance. The implication is clear. Let there be agricultural growth all around, labour household benefit in the interior of the countryside. And let there be non-farm including industrial employment opportunities, its benefit does certainly percolate to rural labour households living even at places as far away as 15-16 km in the interior of the countryside provided commutability is assured to their working members through a well-developed road and transport system. This lends confirmation to our hypothesis regarding the higher per capita income level of labour households living in villages near the focal town against those living in distantly located villages as also the superiority of Punjab households over their counterparts in Bihar in each pair of Punjab-Bihar villages in this respect.

Finally, let us look at the above picture for the two groups of households viz. PALH and PNLH. Table 6.6 sets out the Punjab-Bihar comparison. The relative edge of Punjab households again comes out so very clearly. For example, an average earner of the PALH group in Punjab enjoys about 20.0 per cent more of employment-time but earns nearly 118.0 per cent more than its Bihar counterpart. Net household income of the Punjab group is higher by approximately 125.0 per cent than that of Bihar group. Consequently, per capita income is nearly 122.0 per cent higher in the case of Punjab group over its counterpart in Bihar.

TABLE 6.6: Net Household and Per Capita Income of PALH and PNLH Groups in Punjab and Bihar

(Mean Value, Per Annum)

Sl.No.	Head	State	PALH	PNLH	ALL	di*
1	2	3	4	5	6	7
1.	Total Yearly	PJB	687.75	505.28	604.43	36.11
	Mandays of Employment	BHR	554.53	554.71	554.56	–0.03
		di	(24.02)	(–8.91)		
2.	Per Earner Mandays of	PJB	276.20	257.80	268.64	7.14
	Employment	BHR	231.05	256.81	234.98	–10.03
		di	(19.54)	(0.39)		
3.	Net Earnings from	PJB	6190.74	6169.16	6180.89	0.35
	Total Yearly Employ-	BHR	2741.00	3826.29	2914.65	–28.36
	ment (Rs.)	di	(125.86)	(61.23)		
4.	Net Earnings Per	PJB	2486.24	3147.53	2747.06	–21.01
	Earner (Rs.)	BHR	1142.08	1771.43	1235.02	–35.53
		di	(117.69)	(77.68)		
5.	Transfer Payments	PJB	78.80	157.29	114.64	–49.90
		BHR	45.81	47.17	46.02	–2.88
		di	(72.01)	(233.45)		
6.	Net Yearly Household	PJB	6269.54	6326.45	6295.53	–0.90
	Income	BHR	2786.81	3873.46	2960.67	–28.05
		di	(124.97)	(63.33)		
7.	Per Capita Yearly	PJB	1096.07	1198.19	1140.49	–8.52
	Income	BHR	493.24	641.30	518.51	–23.09
		di	(122.22)	(86.84)		

Note: For an explanation of various notations, PJB, BHR, PALH, PNLH, di & di*, please refer to Tables 4.1 and 4.3.

Compared with it, an average earner belonging to the PNLH category in Punjab enjoys nearly the same quantity of employment-time but in terms of earnings, he is better off to the tune of about 78.0 per cent compared with his Bihar counterpart. Again, net household income of PNLH group in Punjab is nearly 63.0 per cent higher than that of the corresponding group in Bihar. In per capita terms, the Punjab's edge is as high as 87.0 per cent.

To summarize, it is clear that the rural labour households of Punjab are much better off that those of Bihar, practically in every aspect of employment and earnings. Even those among them which depend on agricultural wage employment for a major portion of their earnings (PALH group) are much better off than those households of Bihar which are engaged largely in non-agricultural activities. Finally, non-agricultural economic base of a weak agricultural economy cannot be strong enough to compensate for the weak earning potential from agricultural employment with the result that neither the PALH nor the PNLH group of Bihar can compete with its counterpart in Punjab.

Table 6.7 proposes a comparison between the Punjab and the Bihar households in yet another way. We find that, on an average, per capita net household income level of an average labour household in Punjab (Rs. 1140.49) is roughly 120.0 per cent higher than that of its counterpart in Bihar. Second, the level of per capita net household income of Punjab labour households is consistently higher than that of the Bihar households, at every step of the income distribution ladder. The bottom 20.0 per cent of the rural labour households of Punjab earn, on per capita basis, nearly 2.4 times the per capita income of Bihar households. In other words, the 'poorest' 20.0 per cent of rural labour households in the Punjab are roughly 2.4 times better off than their counterparts in Bihar. The next 20.0 or even 40.0 per cent on the ladder also show nearly equally yawning gaps between the two States. The above relative picture throws clear signals for the incidence of poverty in the two States. Naturally, we should expect poverty in an extremely severe form in Bihar, while in Punjab, it should be of a much milder nature. The analysis later in this chapter duly confirms all this.

Distribution of Net Household Income

In the preceding analysis, it has been observed that net household income as also the per capita income levels of labour households in Punjab are significantly higher than those of such households in Bihar. We now propose to compare the distribution of net household income of Punjab and Bihar households in terms of Lorenz curve technique. The estimates of the distribution of net household income of Punjab and Bihar labour households have been presented in Table 6.8. At the end of the table, we have also given the concentration ratio coefficients in terms of Gini's index. This table, brings out the following important points.

TABLE 6.7: Average Per Capita Yearly Income of the Rural Labour Households in Punjab and Bihar.

(Mean Value in Rs.)

Sl. No.	Households	Per Capita Yearly Income		
		Punjab (PJBi)	Bihar (BHRi)	Differential (di)
1	2	3	4	5
1.	Bottom 20.00 per cent	804.04	338.74	137.36
2.	Next 20.00 per cent	900.46	487.87	84.57
3.	Next 20.00 per cent	1072.39	492.30	117.83
4.	Next 20.00 per cent	1243.25	498.06	149.62
5.	Top 20.00 per cent	1450.06	692.87	109.28
	All Labour Households	1140.49	518.51	119.96

Firstly, distribution of net household income is uneven among he labour households of Punjab as well as of Bihar. It is evident from the fact that while the poorest nearly 7 to 8 per cent of persons in Punjab and Bihar share roughly 5.0 per cent of net household income; the richest nearly 14.0 per cent of persons of both the study areas account for approximately 4 times more than their bottom 7-8 per cent counterparts. For instance, the richest 14.0 per cent persons of Punjab and Bihar share nearly 20.0 per cent of net household income. Secondly, and possibly more important is the fact that the distribution of net household income among the labour household of Punjab is not much different from that among such households in Bihar. It is, rather, more or less the same between the two States. It is, therefore, quite natural to expect that Lorenz curves for net household income distribution for Punjab and Bihar labour households are located nearly equally from the diagonal line representing the perfect egalitarian set-up. It may, however, be noted that the super-imposition of Lorenz curves derived from distribution of net household income in respect of Punjab and Bihar labour households is not possible. This is owing to the fact that differences in the cumulative percentages of net household income distributions are exceedingly small between the two States. Consequently, net household income concentration ratios for Punjab and Bihar households do not register much variation. It is a sheer coincidence that the concentration ration 'g' works out to be .122 both for Punjab and Bihar labour households.

TABLE 6.8: Distribution of Net Household Income of Labour Households in Punjab and Bihar

Sl. No.	Decile Group	Punjab		Bihar	
		Percentage of Persons	Percentage of Income	Percentage of Persons	Percentage of Income
1	2	3	4	5	6
1.	First	6.82	4.86	8.23	4.93
2.	Second	8.27	5.79	8.58	6.05
3.	Third	8.69	6.50	8.06	7.04
4.	Fourth	8.99	7.47	7.71	7.79
5.	Fifth	8.81	8.45	8.93	8.57
6.	Sixth	10.20	9.44	9.92	9.34
7.	Seventh	9.35	10.75	11.33	10.33
8.	Eighth	11.83	12.35	11.62	11.71
9.	Ninth	13.16	14.76	11.56	14.46
10.	Tenth	13.88	19.63	14.06	19.78
	All	100.00	100.00	100.00	100.00
		Concentration Ratio (g) = .122		Concentration Ratio (g) = .122	

From the preceding discussion, it can be concluded that even though, there are not significant variations between Punjab and Bihar as regards the distribution of net household income; such variations do exist among the labour households in both the study areas. It suggests that even within the broad category of labour households, some labour households have become better off than their other brethren both in the agriculturally advanced and backward States.

SECTION B

The Interaction and Rural Poverty

In the preceding section, an attempt has been made to study the pattern of variations discernible in the total yearly employment/ earnings, per capita income and the distribution of net household income of labour households in Punjab and Bihar. In the present section, it is proposed to study the impact of the dynamics of rural transformation and growing rural-urban linkages on the incidence of poverty among the rural labour households in the study areas of Punjab and Bihar. In other words, we want to test the authenticity of the hypothesis implying positive relationship between the proportion of rural labour households below the poverty line and rural-urban distance and the higher incidence in Bihar than in Punjab in each pair of Punjab-Bihar villages. Before we proceed to analyse our sample data to confirm or reject this hypothesis, the point we want to clarify is that in the present study, poverty estimates have been obtained on the basis of per capita net household income.

Empirical Focus on the Poverty Theme

The frequency with which a concern for poverty is being expressed today in national as well as international circles has now reached a point where almost any type of programme is justified in the name of its abolition. This is mainly because of the growing realisation in the developed as well as the developing economies including our own that the benefits of rapid economic growth, wherever achieved, have not percolated to the poor. Consequently, recent years have witnessed a plethora of research writings on the theme of poverty. Apart from studying poverty in its historical perspective[2], some scholars have, recently, also endeavoured to explore its nexus with unemployment. Following a lively debate in India, two divergent views have emerged on the issue of unemployment-poverty nexus. The first view while assuming poverty and unemployment to be mutually interdependent i.e one causing the other, brings out a positive relationship between the two.[3] The second view runs contrary to the first, and as such, comes out with either negative or no association[4] between poverty and unemployment. The underlying reasoning behind this latter viewpoint is that the poor can ill afford to remain unemployed. Consequently, they are forced to seek work at whatever level of earnings it is available. Given this type of situation, one would expect the excess labour supply to find expression in 'distress wage' rather than in open unemployment. Though seemingly plausible arguments have been advanced and several convincing explanations have been offered from both the sides in support of the views mentioned above, yet the evidence gathered so far has failed to confirm and establish very clearly and unabatedly either the positive or the negative association between unemployment and poverty. Consequently, it is extremely difficult to support or reject either of the two views. It can, therefore, be inferred that the debate on unemployment-poverty nexus has, at best remained inconclusive and surely far from clear.

Besides the above mentioned important strides in its domain, the research on the theme of poverty has broadly traversed along two lines. First, on the theoretical plane, various indices and measures to estimate poverty have been hotly debated by quite a number of distinguished scholars in the framework of some commonly accepted axiomatic conditions.[5] Secondly, and more importantly, several empirical attempts[6] have been made in the recent past by various research workers to measure the extent and intensity of poverty. Consequently, empirical research on poverty is rich not only in terms of contents but also in terms of methodological contributions. For example, while a few researchers have employed the NCAER sample survey data,[7] but most of the studies have been based on NSS data. Some individual research workers have also studied the problem of poverty on the basis of primary data gathered through their own effort. Further, while some studies deal with the rural poor,[8] some others relate to the rural as well as urban poor.[9] There is another set of studies which has approached the problem of poverty either from State level[10] or from all India point of view. Some scholars have also attempted to measure poverty over time to study the temporal change[11] occurring in its magnitude. Some studies have used the 'estimate' formulated by an expert committee[12] set up by the Planning Commission in 1962 for the said purpose. Some other researchers[13] have also based their estimates on the levels recommended by the Pay Commission in 1957. Recently, many studies[14] have also used Bardhan's estimates for measuring poverty which, in turn; are obtained as equivalents of Rs. 20.0 p.m. at all India prices as recommended by the expert committee mentioned above. There are also some other studies which have estimated poverty on the basis of minimum calorie intake.[15] Then on the basis of said estimates, these studies have estimated the cost of the minimum diet.

All those persons whose income/expenditure levels falls short of that 'minimum' have been defined as the poor. But as the extent of poverty is a dynamic phenomenon, the measurement of its magnitude over time requires the expenditure/income figures in constant terms. Thus account has to be taken of changes in the level of prices which, in turn, necessitates the choice of an appropriate deflator. In this regard it is important to note that whereas some studies prefer to use National Income Deflator,[16] there are many others which have preferred to use the Consumer Price Index for Agricultural Labour, complied by Central Ministry of Labour[17] for various regions of the country. This Consumer Price Index is said to be more representative of the prices paid by the poorer people.

The underlying feature of almost all such studies on poverty is that they have sketched their independent estimates of the proportion of population suffering from economic deficiency. Also that not only different studies tend to disagree to the prevailing extent of poverty so much so that different measures and indices when applied to the same data yield different estimates of poverty. Also there has been a conflicting evidence with regard to the trend in the proportion of population below the poverty line. Over and above, doubts have been expressed in official as well as non-official circles regarding the reliability of data[18] on which poverty estimates are based in India.

Absolute Poverty in Punjab and Bihar

Before estimating poverty on the basis of our sample data, an important fact needs to be recognised that the concept of poverty can be envisaged in absolute as well as in relative sense. A person could be treated as poor if either the consumption expenditure or the income level of his household is below the socially accepted minimum poverty line (absolute poverty) or belongs to the lowest say 20.0 per cent of the households according to income or expenditure distribution (relative poverty). However, the central problem in the measurement of poverty is to determine the poverty line or the critical cut-off point of income of expenditure below which one may be treated as poor and which at the same time may reflect some socially accepted 'minimal' standard of living.

Two main approaches are noticeable concerning the problem of defining a poverty line at a point of time. While the first approach attempts to define the poverty line or the cut-off point in terms of the income level of some minimum expenditure level required to purchase a bundle of goods, the other views it in terms of nutritional norms such as the intake of calories and proteins to keep a person fit in the working condition. The pros and cons of these two approaches have been detailed by many research workers and we do not intend to repeat them here.

As one of our preoccupations in the present study is the estimation of prevailing poverty levels in the two States, it is not out of place to mention the procedural details followed in the present study. To begin with, we have made use of the simple headcount method to estimate the incidence of poverty in Punjab and Bihar. Following Bardhan,[19] a per capita monthly expenditure (income in the present case) of Rs. 15.00 at 1960-61 all-India prices has been taken as the cut-off point. Further, taking note of inter-State and rural-urban price differentials, the equivalents of Rs. 15.00 for rural Punjab and Bihar have been worked out at Rs. 15.90 and Rs. 15.80 respectively at 1960-61 prices. The annual equivalents for these figures are Rs. 190.80 for Punjab and Rs. 189.60 for Bihar at 1960-61 prices. The corresponding figures for 1980-81 work out to be Rs. 833.80 in Punjab and Rs. 811.49 in Bihar, on an annual basis. All such households whose per capita annual income falls short of Rs. 833.80 in Punjab and Rs. 811.49 in Bihar have been identified as poor households. The villagewise and the overall incidence of poverty among non-cultivating rural labour households of the two States are presented in Table 6.9. The following important facts need to be mentioned in this behalf.

Firstly, it is indeed revealing to note that the incidence of poverty in Bihar (nearly 88.0 per cent of the rural labour households), is much higher than in Punjab (about 22.0 per cent of such households). Secondly, both in Punjab and Bihar, the incidence of poverty is relatively greater in far-off village than in villages nearer the urban focal town. Lastly, between each pair of nearly equally distanced villages of Punjab and Bihar, the incidence of poverty is terribly higher in the Bihar villages than in the Punjab villages. This confirms and lends empirical substance of our hypothesis on poverty implying positive association between the incidence of poverty and rural-urban distance and relatively lower incidence of poverty in Punjab villages than that in those of Bihar, at all conceivable distances from the focal town.

The preceding analysis makes it fairly obvious that the Punjab labour households have had a share in the gains resulting from economic development in general and agricultural transformation in particular. Consequently, Punjab model of economic growth has been successful in making a real dent on the problem of poverty in the State. However, such a phenomenon seems to be non-existent in agriculturally backward areas, exemplified in our study by Bihar.

TABLE 6.9: Non-Cultivating Rural Labour Households Below the Poverty Line in Punjab and Bihar on Per Capita Net Household Income Basis

(Rs. 833.80 in Punjab and Rs. 811.49 in Bihar at 1980-81 Prices)

Sl. No.	Village	PUNJAB			BIHAR		
		A	B	C	A	B	C
1.	V1	21	4	19.05	26	18	69.23
2.	V2	47	8	17.02	37	26	70.27
3.	V3	78	15	19.23	26	20	76.92
4.	V4	7	1	14.29	21	19	90.48
5.	V5	23	4	17.39	15	13	86.67
6.	V6	63	13	20.63	85	82	96.47
7.	V7	35	14	40.00	38	38	100.00
8.	V8	26	6	23.08	52	48	92.31
9.	All	300	65	21.67	300	264	88.00

Note: A. Total number of sample households.
B. Number of sample house-holds below the poverty line.
C. B as percentage of A.

It might be stressed that the head count measure of the incidence of poverty registers a decline in poverty if a number of persons belonging to an income class at the margin and below the poverty line move above it. Though the implications of this measure of the incidence of poverty are easy to grasp in the sense that it leaves a rough idea readily about the magnitude of poverty in concrete number which, in turn, facilitates the working out of the commitments involved in operational strategy of poverty eradication, yet it suffers from a number of limitations. Such limitations make it essentially a crude index of poverty for many obvious reasons. In the first instance, the incidence of poverty estimated through this technique is highly sensitive to the choice of a particular cut-off point, and secondly it does not attach any weight whatsoever to the distribution of population below the poverty line. For example, despite a rapid increase in the income or expenditure level of a person below the poverty line, he will continue to be treated as poor so long as his income or expenditure level does not exceed the magic figure defined as the cut-off point. Thus, this method measures the incidence of poverty irrespective of the degree of shortfall from the postulated cut-off point. Still further, this measure is not sensitive to the redistribution of income among the poor. For instance, in the event of a pure transfer of income from persons with higher incomes to those with lower incomes within the population below the poverty line, the usual head-count ratio does not record a change so long as the amount so transferred does not help the beneficiaries to cross over the poverty line. Similarly, if a transfer of income from above poverty line persons to those below it takes place without affecting the number of persons below the poverty line, the usual head-count ratio does not register a decline in poverty. This does not make a sense in terms of social welfare norms. Obviously, there is a greater welfare gain if extremely abject poverty becomes less abject than if some poverty cases at the margin are transformed to borderline above poverty line cases. Sen's '*P*' measure endeavours to overcome the problems inherent in the head-count ratio by making use of weighting system. Consequently, it has been extensively employed by a number of research workers.

Sen's Poverty Measure 'P'[20]

Closely akin to Gini's measure, Sen's '*P*' measure of poverty has been extensively employed by studies on poverty. It is essentially an ordinal measure which takes into account the head-count ratio, the poverty-gap ratio and the Gini-coefficient of the income or expenditure distribution of the poor. Further, while using rank order weights in a manner which is sensitive to the gap between the below poverty line income/expenditure level of the poor and the cut-off point itself, it assigns higher weight per unit to the income/expenditure below the poverty line. As such, it seems to reflect a more realistic picture of the incidence and intensity of poverty.

It needs to be recognised here that Sen's '*P*' measure is concerned not only with the incidence of poverty but also with its intensity. It is employed in working out the amounts by which the income or expenditure of the poor falls short of the specified cut-off point of poverty in terms of income or expenditure. The bigger is the shortfall from the cut-off point, the greater shall be the weight per unit of that shortfall in the poverty measure suggested by Sen. Thus Sen's '*P*' measure differs from the Gini-coefficient in two important respects, viz., (a) in being concerned only with the population below the poverty line, and (b) in calculating the income or expenditure differences from the cut-off point and not from the average income of the distribution itself.

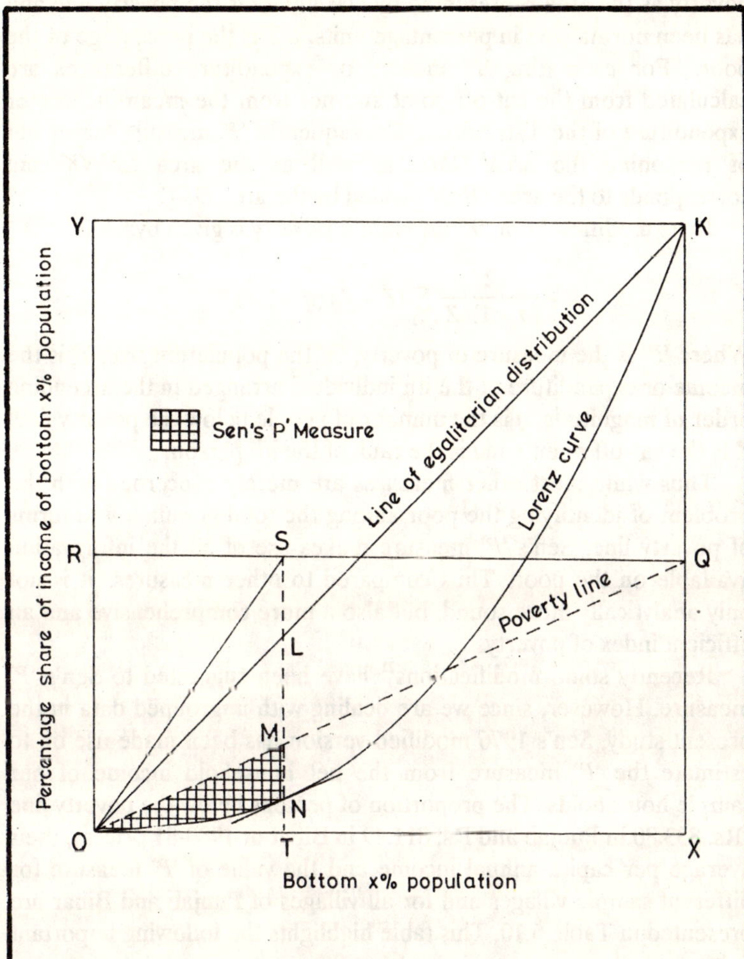

FIG. 6.1: Sen's "Poverty Measure 'P'"

The graphic presentation (Fig. 6.1) of '*P*' measure has been borrowed from Sen himself. In the said figure '*P*' measures the poverty as the area represented by *OMN*. *OQ* is the poverty line and has been normalized in percentage units. *OT* is the percentage of the poor. For estimating '*P*' income or expenditure differences are calculated from the cut-off point and not from the mean income or expenditure of the distribution. Consequently, '*P*' measure leaves out of reckoning the area *OML* as well as the area *LMNK* and corresponds to the area *OMN* divided by the area *OST*.

In its modified form, '*P*' measure if poverty is given by:

$$P = \frac{2}{(q+1)nZ} \sum_{i=1}^{q} (Z - Y_i)(q + 1 - i)$$

Where '*P*' is the measure of poverty, '*n*' the population size, Y_i is the income or expenditure of the ith individual arranged in the ascending order of magnitude; *q* is the number of people below the poverty line, *Z* is the cut-off point and *i* is the rank of the ith person.

Thus while most other measures are merely concerned with the problem of identifying the poor among the total population in terms of poverty line, Sen's '*P*' measure makes use of all the information available on the poor. Thus compared to other measures, it is not only analytically more sound, but also a more comprehensive and an efficient index of poverty.

Recently some modifications[21] have been suggested to Sen's '*P*' measure. However, since we are dealing with ungrouped data in the present study, Sen's 1976 modified version has been made use of, to estimate the '*P*' measure from the net household income of our sample households. The proportion of persons below the poverty line (Rs. 833.80 in Punjab and Rs. 811.49 in Bihar at 1980-81 prices), their average per capita annual income and the value of '*P*' measure for different sample villages and for all villages of Punjab and Bihar are presented in Table 6.10. This table highlights the following important facts.

Firstly, the proportion of population subsisting below the poverty line in Punjab (nearly 24.0%) is much lower than in Bihar (about 91.0%). Secondly, the average per capita income of labour households below the poverty line is much greater in Punjab than in Bihar. The per capita income level of a typically poor household in Punjab (Rs. 681.07) is roughly 43.0 per cent higher than that of a poor household in Bihar (Rs. 475.72 only). Thirdly '*P*' measure works out to be much lower in Punjab (0.059) than in Bihar (0.473). It is thus beyond doubt that the magnitude of absolute poverty is terribly higher in Bihar than in Punjab.

If we compare nearly equally distanced pair of Punjab and Bihar villages, we observe that the incidence of poverty is much higher in Bihar villages, compared with their counterparts in Punjab. Again, per capita income of persons below the poverty line is much higher in Punjab villages than in Bihar villages suggesting thereby that the poor of Punjab are much less poor than those of Bihar. Similarly, the value of *'P'* measure at varying distances from the focal town is much higher in Bihar villages than in Punjab villages. This again signifies that gains of agricultural modernisation have accrued relatively more to the poor labour households in Punjab than in Bihar. It is more so in the extremely remote villages from the focal town.

It can, therefore, be inferred that Punjab model of economic transformation since the late sixties has helped the households in the State to benefit from highly remunerative and gainful employment opportunities both in the on-and non-farm sectors. In contrast, it is, indeed, distressing that Bihar model has thrown up nothing but acute deprivation and poverty for a preponderant majority of its rural labour households. It is a grim situation that in Bihar nearly 88.0 per cent of the rural labour households continue to live below the poverty line. Even in villages near the urban focal town, the incidence of poverty among such households is extremely high, and, as we move into the interior of the countryside, the Bihar scenario seems to reveal a situation of precarious existence.

There is yet another way of looking at the economic situation of the poor households in the study areas of Punjab and Bihar. Besides computing the per capita income of the various layers of the poor households, we develop some rough idea of the additional income needed for such households to cross the crucial mark of poverty level earnings. Table 6.11 invites a few observations.

Firstly, per capita income level of the poor households in Punjab (Rs. 681.07) considered as a whole is approximately 43.0 per cent higher than the per capita income level of poor household in Bihar (Rs. 475.72). Secondly, while all the poor labour households of Punjab in our sample would need roughly 22.0 per cent additional income in order to flip over the poverty line, in Bihar, no less than 71.0 per cent more would be needed for this purpose. The degree of abject poverty among the sample households of Bihar is adequately conveyed through this measure for the total of sample households,

TABLE 6.10: Sen's '*P*' Measure Calculated for Per Capita Net Household Income of Labour Households in Punjab and Bihar

Sl. No.	Description	State	Village								All
			V1	V2	V3	V4	V5	V6	V7	V8	
1	2	3	4	5	6	7	8	9	10	11	12
1.	Proportion of Persons Below Poverty Line	PJB	18.85	18.99	21.38	10.87	19.08	24.13	42.93	28.47	24.08
		BHR	79.47	74.63	78.08	95.28	92.39	98.80	100.00	95.58	91.48
2.	Per Capita Income of the Persons Below the Poverty Line	PJB	656.49	719.83	724.83	756.42	731.58	658.08	624.19	675.48	681.07
		BHR	520.51	570.53	592.94	520.08	548.47	444.25	421.79	416.96	475.72
		di	26.12	26.17	22.24	45.44	33.39	48.13	47.99	62.00	43.17
3.	Poverty Measure '*P*'	PJB	0.050	0.031	0.039	0.010	0.027	0.063	0.142	0.064	0.059
		BHR	0.35	0.307	0.273	0.423	0.372	0.535	0.559	0.547	0.473

Note: 1. PJB = Punjab
2. BHR = Bihar
3. $di = \frac{PJBi - BHRi}{BHRi}$
4. *i* is the Per Capita Net Household Income of the Poor Household in ith Village.

TABLE 6.11: Average Per Capita Net Household Income of the Rural Labour Households Below the Poverty Line (Rs. 833.80 per capita per annum in Punjab and Rs. 811.49 per capita per annum in Bihar at 1980-81 Prices)

(Mean Value in Rs.)

Sl. No.	Poor Households	PUNJAB		BIHAR		Differential (di)
		X	Y	X	Y	
1.	Bottom 20.00 per cent	546.79	287.01 (52.49)	290.23	521.26 (179.60)	88.40
2.	Next 20.00 per cent	646.72	187.08 (28.93)	401.49	410.00 (102.12)	61.08
3.	Next 20.00 per cent	700.39	133.41 (19.05)	476.71	334.78 (70.23)	46.92
4.	Next 20.00 per cent	747.38	86.42 (11.56)	560.80	250.69 (44.70)	33.27
5.	Next 20.00 per cent	787.89	45.91 (5.83)	712.85	98.64 (13.84)	10.53
6.	All Poor Households	681.07	152.73 (22.43)	475.72	335.77 (70.58)	43.17

Note: 1. X = Per Capita Income (Rs.)
2. Y = Additional Income needed to Cross Over the Poverty Line.
3. Figures in the parentheses indicate the additional income as percentage of per capita income to cross over the poverty line.
4. di = Differential between per capita income of Punjab and Bihar i.e.

$$\frac{XPJB - XBHR}{XBHR}$$

yet the real misery can be pinpointed if we look into the additional income requirement of the bottom 40.0 or 20.0 per cent of these households. The bottom 20.0 per cent of our sample households in Bihar would need as much as 180.0 per cent more of income if they have to cease to be poor; in contrast, the bottom 20.0 households in the Punjab sample suggest supplementation to the tune of about 52.0 per cent. Similarly, while the top 20.0 per cent of our sample households in Bihar would need as much as 14.0 per cent additional income to cross over the poverty line, in contrast, the top 20.0 per cent poor households in Punjab are already veering around the poverty line itself, since they just need only 6.0 per cent additional income to move above the poverty line. Again as is evident at different steps of the distribution, the percentage share of additional income needed by the poor labour households to cross over the poverty line is roughly 3-4 fold higher in Bihar compared with that in Punjab. These figures are thus good enough to convey a situation of utter destitution under which the labour households live in rural

Bihar. These are also suggestive of the formidable institutional and other interventions needed to improve upon their sub-human existence.

Our data, therefore, dispels the belief that the gains of rapid economic growth in general and agricultural transformation in particular, wherever achieved, have not percolated to the poor. On the other hand, Punjab-Bihar contrast clearly reveals that such gains have been shared by different strata of the rural population in Punjab because the State has had a happy experience of fast and sustained growth, and such gains have largely bypassed the lower strata of rural population in Bihar because growth here has not only been very low, but unsteady as well. Consequently, there has not been much to filter down the ladder of rural hierarchy.

NOTES

1. It is mainly because of smaller number (i.e. 48) households in PNLH group in Bihar compared with 137 in Punjab out of a total of 300 sample households in each of the study ares of Punjab and Bihar.
2. R. Radhakrishna and S.A.R. Sastry (1979), "Rural Poverty: A Historical Perspective", *Productivity,* Vol. XIX, No. 4, January-March, pp. 531-543.
3. Ranjit Sau, (1978), "Growth, Employment and Removal of Poverty", *Economic and Political Weekly,* Vol. XIII, No. 31-33, Special Number, August, p. 1280; and G. Parthasarthy (1979), "Inter-State Variation in Unemployment and Growth of Agriculture", *The Indian Journal of Labour Economics,* Vol. XXII, Nos. 1-2, April-July, pp. 45-50.
4. D.T. Lakdawala, (1978), "Growth, Unemployment and Poverty," *The Indian Journal of Labour Economics,* Vol. XXI, No. 1, 2, April-July p. 1-30; and J.N. Sinha (1978), "Rural Employment Planning: Dimensions and Constraints," *Economic and Political Weekly,* Vol. XIII, No. 6-7, Annual Number , pp. 295-313.
5. For a detailed and comprehensive survey, see, S.A.R. Sastry (1980), "A Survey of Literature in Poverty, Income Distribution and Development", *Artha Vijnana,* Vol. XXII, No. 1, March, pp. 62-88; ——— (1980), "Poverty, Concepts and Measurement", *The Indian Journal of Economics,* Vol. LXI, No. 241, October, pp. 147-160; and Amitabh Kundu (1981), "Measurement of Poverty: Some Conceptual issues", *Anvesak,* Vol XI, No. 1-2, June-December, pp. 80-96.
6. B.S. Minhas (1970), "Rural Poverty, Land Redistribution and Development Strategy: Facts and Policy", *Indian Economic Review,* Vol. V, (New Series), April, pp. 97-128; P.K. Bardhan (1973). "On the Incidence of Poverty in Rural India of the Sixties", *Economic and Political Weekly,* Vol. VIII, Nos. 4-6, Annual Number, February, pp. 245-54; V.M. Dandekar and Nilkantha Rath, (1971) *Poverty in India*-1 : Dimensions and Trends" *Economic and Political Weekly,* Vol. VI, No. 1, January 2, pp. 25-48; ————— "Poverty in India-II : Policies and Programme", *Economic and Political Weekly,* Vol. VI, No. 2, January 9, pp. 106-146 ; A. Vaidynathan (1974), "Some Aspects of Inequalities in Living Standards in Rural India", in T.N. Srinivasan and P.K. Bardhan (ed), *Poverty and Income Distribution in India,* Statistical Publishing House, Calcutta, pp. 215-241; I.Z. Bhatty (1974), "Inequality and Poverty in

Rural India", in Srinivasan and Bardhan (ed), *Op. Cit,* pp. 291-316; Montek S. Ahluwalia (1978), "Rural Poverty and Agricultural Performance in India", *The Journal of Development Studies,* Vol. XIV, No. III, April, pp. 298-323; and ———— (1986), "Rural Poverty, Agricultural Production and Prices: A Reexamination", in John W. Mellor and Gunvant M. Desai (ed), *Agricultural Change and Rural Poverty: Variations on a Theme by Dharm Narain,* Oxford University Press, New Delhi, pp. 59-75.

7. I.Z. Bhatty, (1974) *op. cit.*
8. B.S. Minhas, (1970), *op. cit;* and A. Vaidyanathan, (1974), *op. cit.*
9. V.M. Dandekar and Nilkantha Rath (1971) *op. cit;* and P.K. Bardhan (1973), *op. cit.*
10. Indira Rajaraman, (1974), *"Constructing the Poverty Line: Rural Punjab 1960-61,* Woodrow Wilson School of Public and International Affairs, Princeton, New Jersy.
11. ————(1975), "Poverty, Inequality and Economic Growth: Rural Punjab, 1960-61-1970-71", *Journal of Development Studies,* Vol XI, No. 4, July, pp. 278-290.
12. This expert committee consisted of distinguished scholars such as Prof. D.R. Gadgil, Prof. V.K.R.V. Rao, Dr. P.S. Lokanathan, Dr. B.N. Ganguli, Mr. Ashok Mehta, Mr. M.R. Masani, Mr. Shriman Narayan, Mr. Anna Sahib Sahasrabudhe and Mr. Pitambar Pant.
13. P.K. Bardhan (1973) *op. cit.*
14. See for example, G.S. Bhalla and G.K. Chadha (1983), *Green Revolution and The Small Peasant: A Study of Income Distribution Among Punjab Cultivators,* Concept Publishing Co. Delhi, p 153, and Harbans Singh (1986), *Employment Income and Consumption of Rural Labour Households in a Green Revolution Region: A Case Study of Punjab and Haryana,* Ph.D. Thesis, Jawaharlal Nehru University, New Delhi, p. 118.
15. V.M. Dandekar and Nilkantha Rath, (1971), *op. cit,*; Ashok Rudra (1974), "Minimum Level of Living- A Statistical Examination", in T.N. Srinivasan and P.K. Bardhan (ed),*op. cit*, pp 281-290; P.V. Sukhatme (1978) : "Assessment of Adequacy of Diets of Different Income Levels," *Economic and Political Weekly,* Vol. No. XIII, Nos. 31-33, Special Number, August, pp. 1373-1384, and P.G.K. Panikar (1980) *Inter-regional Variations in Colorie Intake,* Working Paper No. 111, Centre for Development Studies, Trivandrum. These calorie estimates for defining the poverty line have differed between 2100 to 2400 calories per person per day.
16. B.S. Minhas, (1970) *op. cit.*
17. P.K. Bardhan, (1973), *op. cit,* and A. Vaidyanathan, (1974) *op. cit.*
18. For instance, recently in May 1988, a Committee has been constituted under the chairmanship of Prof. D.T. Lakdawala to suggest measures regarding the collection of more reliable data on poverty. By implications, it means that the official data gathered so far on poverty are less reliable.
19. P.K. Bardhan, (1973) *op. cit,* p. 247. Incidentally Bardhan and Dandekar and Rath have arrived at the same figure i.e. Rs. 15.00 P.M. at 1960-61, All India prices, for determining the cut-off point.
20. Amartya Sen, "Poverty: An Ordinal Approach to Measurement", *Econometrica,* Vol. 44, No. 2, March 1976, pp. 219-231.
21. For example, several scholars such as I.Z. Bhatty (1974), F. Seastrand and R. Diwan (1975), M. Alamgir (1976), N. Kakawani (1977), S. Anand (1977) and K. Hamada and N. Takayama (1977), have proposed several modifications to Sen's measure of poverty.

7

EMPLOYMENT/EARNING PATTERN OF THE MIGRANT LABOUR IN RURAL PUNJAB

In the previous chapter, we have analysed the pattern of total yearly employment and earnings of the resident labour households of Punjab and Bihar. It has been observed that there are significant differences in the pattern of employment/earnings as also in the incidence and intensity of poverty between the labour households of Punjab and Bihar. The present chapter is devoted to analyse another important phenomenon of Punjab agriculture, namely the phenomenon of migrant labour. To be more specific, the basic objective here is to analyse the pattern of employment and the corresponding level of earnings accruing to this category of farm labour in Punjab.

Migration of agricultural labourers into Punjab agriculture from the rural areas of Bihar and eastern Uttar Pradesh is a recent but significant phenomenon. The huge influx of migrant labour has mainly occurred in the wake of the Green Revolution in Punjab. Though it is commonly believed that this migration has made an impact of far reaching consequence on the local economy of Punjab, yet not many attempts have been made so far to study this important aspect of Punjab agriculture [see footnote 38, Chapter 1, of the present study]. As such, there exists an important research gap. A modest attempt is made in the present chapter to fill this void.

In this context, we address ourselves to a number of questions such as what are the socio-economic characteristics of the migrants? What are the areas of their outmigration? What is the pattern of their employment and earnings? What proportion of year round employment and earnings in agriculture is enjoyed separately by the resident labour and the migrant labour in rural Punjab? And finally, what are the pull and push factors responsible for inmigration/ outmigration? To answer these questions, we propose to examine the following hypotheses:

1. It is from relatively backward areas of Bihar that the migrant labour outflows into Punjab.
2. The share of the migrant labour in total yearly wage-paid on-farm employment/earnings is inversely related to distance from the focal town.

Before we seek empirical answers to these hypotheses and the other problems enumerated above, it is important to look at the scheme of analysis proposed in the present chapter. The chapter is divided into four sections. Section I highlights the phenomenon of the migrant labour. Section II deals with the socio-economic characteristics of migrant labour as also the identification of areas of its outmigration. Section III is concerned with the employment pattern and earning levels of this category of labour on the basis of our sample data. Finally, Section IV, besides attempting to locate factors responsible for inmigration/outmigration, also presents the broad conclusions emerging from our analysis.

SECTION I

The Emergence of Migrant Labour

As noted earlier in this chapter, an important phenomenon of migrant labour into Punjab agriculture, from the rural areas of Bihar and eastern Uttar Pradesh, has taken place in the wake of the Green Revolution in Punjab. Broadly speaking, this large scale migration has had effects which highlight simultaneously the important aspects of development failures in areas of outmigration (i.e. Bihar and eastern Uttar Pradesh) as also the problems of attained economic development in the areas of inmigration (i.e. Punjab).

The Green Revolution in Punjab since the late sixties has opened up many productive and highly remunerative avenues of wage-paid on-farm employment. Besides, the developmental activity that has been taking place simultaneously has also generated considerable demand for manual labour in many non-farm activities such as construction, rickshaw pulling, earth work on roads and railway tracks, industrial work, *paledari* (loading and unloading of grains in the grain markets), etc. Consequently, under the pressure of rising demand for labour, huge influx of migrant labour into Punjab ensued since early 1970s both in the rural and urban and sub-urban areas.

To put the record straight, the migrant labour into the State of Punjab is attracted to higher employment opportunities in the rural as well as urban areas of the State. In general, the destination is defined before departure so that the migrants heading for seasonal rural employment stay in the villages, and those expecting to work in urban-industrial centres do not generally combine urban with rural employment. That is why, all the 150 respondent migrant labourers in our case reported rural, and only rural, employment.

The farm sector in Punjab absorbs labour force not only from its own rural areas, but also from the rural areas of Bihar and eastern Uttar Pradesh which have lot of surplus labour. The bulk of the migrants are seasonal farm labourers. They are generally employed for harvesting of wheat/paddy and transplantation of paddy, etc.

It needs to be underlined here that the inmigration into Punjab has taken place mainly because of increased demand for labour. The pattern of agricultural development in Punjab since the emergence of Green Revolution offers the most convincing explanation for the emergence of this important phenomenon. On account of radical shifts in the cropping pattern especially after the introduction of 'rice revolution' in the early seventies, the tendency over the years in agriculture has been towards an increase in demand for farm labour. The cultivation of paddy, which is considered to be a labour-intensive crop started on a very large scale in Punjab only a decade ago and has witnessed phenomenal expansion since then. Given a strong irrigation base, it has proved to be relatively more profitable commercial crop. At present, it constitutes one of the two major crops of the area, the other being wheat. Paddy cultivation in Punjab very heavily depends upon the availability of the 'migrant labour' as, for this crop, it is considered to be relatively more skilled than the resident labour.

Over the years, a large number of industrial units have also come up in the urban and sub-urban areas of Punjab. These have absorbed a large chunk of resident labour force from the rural areas of Punjab. Besides, the demand for wage-paid non-farm labour has also increased on account of the launching of various programmes by central and State governments such as construction of storage facilities, godowns, expansion of drainage and water supply facilities, etc. All such factors have contributed substantially to the growth of migrant labour in Punjab.

Migrant Labourers in Punjab

The migrant labourers in rural Punjab usually travel and work in groups. The lodging arrangements for the group are made by the farmer employers on tubewells/farm houses. Sometimes, the migrants reside in rented accommodations also. However, the practice of rented accommodation is not quite common as yet. Food arrangements are made by the migrants themselves out of the kind earnings received by them from their farmer employers in Punjab. Cash purchases, whenever required, are also made from petty shopkeepers in the village.

Petty Contract System and the Mode of Wage Payment

In our survey, a migrant group may consist up to 25 members. Every group of migrant labourers (or for that matter in any other part of rural Punjab) is headed by a person who is more knowledgeable, more articulate and better informed about local life and people. This person is commonly known as a '*Jamadar*' or a '*Thekedar*'. He is not necessarily the seniormost member of the group. The head of the migrant group finds employment for the group members, settles the terms and conditions of the contract, at best supervises but very rarely does the manual work himself. By doing so, he, therefore, acts as a link between the Punjabi farmer on the one hand, and, '*bhaiya* labourer' on the other. In a way, his job is that of a petty contractor between the two parties. Although the power of this petty contractor has waned substantially over the years due to the emergence of direct and independent contacts developed by the regular migrants with the Punjabi farmer, yet he still wields enough power to maintain his supremacy over the group. It is mainly because of the fact that owing to his previous contacts with the farmer employers in Punjab, he can manage employment for the group members within the shortest possible span of time. Needless to say, for the migrant labourers, time is of great essence.

As regards the mode of wage payment, it was discovered during our survey that employment on daily basis is not the only mode employing the migrant labour. This labour generally undertakes work on a piecemeal basis, popularly known as the 'contract system' or 'theka system' in the study area of Punjab. As said earlier, the terms of 'contract' are finalised between the head of the migrant group and the farmer employer in Punjab.

SECTION II

Socio-economic Characteristics of the Migrants

It might be a good idea to look at the socio-economic characteristics of the migrants, as emerge in our sample data. Besides, it may also be interesting to identify the areas of out-migration of the migrant labour in Punjab. Table 7.1 depicts a few important socio-economic characteristics of the migrant labour.

To begin with, we observe that out of the total sample of 150 migrants in Punjab, more than three-fourths of them hailed from Bihar only. A large majority of the remaining belonged to Uttar Pradesh (about 21.0%). As far as land status of the migrants is concerned, nearly 61.0 per cent of them were found to be cultivating some piece of land and the average size of the land owned and cultivated was 0.93 ares. The financial position of the migrants is, therefore, conditioned by the income derived from small pieces of land (both owned + leased-in) and wage earnings. By implication, uneconomic owned or leased-in holdings are only a meagre source of household income. Besides, the level of wages was invariably reported to be extremely low in areas of outmigration compared with that in the study area of Punjab. It is, therefore, the exigency arising out of mass poverty and economic destitution which forces the labourers to outmigrate to Punjab with the expectation of getting more remunerative avenues of on-farm employment. Secondly, the caste composition of the migrants reflects that a preponderant majority (nearly 83.0%) of the total migrants belong either to the scheduled castes or to the backward classes. Thirdly, a look at the literacy level shows that more than three-fourth of the total migrants are illiterate; only about 17.0 per cent of them are educated below primary level. Again, while about 3.0 per cent are below middle, only 1.0 per cent of them were found to be middle and above. Fourthly, on an average, the family size of migrant is 7.1 which is higher than that of the resident labour either in Bihar (5.7) or in Punjab (5.5) [Table

2.12, Chapter 2, of the present study]. It can perhaps be argued that besides other economic factors, demographic pressure may also be responsible for pushing some people out in pursuance of additional employment/earning, *albeit* small or occasional. The seasonal demand from Punjab goes well to meet their urge for supplementation. Fifthly and more importantly, while 17.0 per cent of

TABLE 7.1: Socio-Economic Characteristics of the Migrant Labour in Punjab

Sl. No.	Indicator	Total Number	Percentage of the Total
1	2	3	4
1.	Total Number of Migrants in the Sample	150	100.00
2.	Area of Outmigration:		
	(a) Bihar	117	78.00
	(b) Uttar Pradesh	32	21.33
	(c) Bengal	1	0.67
3.	Land Status:		
	(a) With Land	91	60.67
	(b) Without Land	59	39.33
4.	Average Area Owned (Acres)	0.93	
5.	Caste Composition:		
	(a) Scheduled Castes	59	39.33
	(b) Backward Classes	65	43.33
	(c) Others	26	17.34
6.	Literacy Level:		
	(a) Illiterate	118	78.67
	(b) Literate but Below Primary	25	16.67
	(c) Primary but Below Middle	5	3.33
	(d) Middle and Above	2	1.33
7.	Average Family Size	7.08	–
8.	Age Composition (Years):		
	(a) Below 15	0	0.00
	(b) 15 – 20	26	17.33
	(c) 21 – 25	48	32.00
	(d) 26 – 40	67	44.67
	(e) 40 Years and above	9	6.00
9.	Inception of Migration:		
	(a) Before 1970-71	0	0.00
	(b) Between 1970-71 – 1975-76	28	18.67
	(c) Between 1975-76 – 1980-81	122	81.33
	(d) All Migrants	150.00	100.00

the total migrants are in the age group of 15 – 20 years, nearly 77.0 per cent of them are in the age group of 21 – 40 years. It is important to note that in spite of the fact that there has been large scale inmigration into Punjab, there is no evidence as yet of the migration of child labour (i.e. 0 to 14 years age group). This is also indicative of another fact that a vast majority of the migrants belong to young and middle age groups who alone can undertake the strain of long journeys followed by hard manual labour on Punjab farms, invariably expected to be accomplished in short spells of time. Longer working hours per day are a well accepted norm. Lastly, as regards the inception of migration, we observe that none of our sample migrants reported to be coming to Punjab for wage-paid agricultural employment before 1970-71. Further, while 19.0 per cent also reported to be coming between 1970-71 and 1975-76, an overwhelming majority of them (nearly 81.0%) reported to be coming between 1975-76 and 1980-81. This lends substance to our view that migration of farm labourers has occurred only in the wake of rice revolution commencing in the early 1970s.

Land Status

Table 7.2 presents the distribution of migrant labourers on the basis of land holding size which their families cultivate back home.

Table 7.2 reveals that while 39.0 per cent of the total migrants do not have any title to land and as such are only landless labourers, nearly 23.0 per cent were found to be cultivating less than 1.0 acre of land. Another 23.0 per cent were found to be cultivating between 1.00 – 1.49 acres and only 14.0 per cent cultivating 2 acres and above. This suggests that most of the migrants are either landless or are cultivating only small pieces of land.

Areas of Outmigration

The basic objective behind identifying the areas of out migration is to know if indeed it is from the relatively backward areas of Bihar and easter Uttar Pradesh that the outmigration of labour takes place. If so, then it can be argued that it is the lack of development in the areas of outmigration which is largely responsible for outmigration of farm labourers. Specifically, we propose to test the hypothesis that "it is from relatively backward areas of Bihar that the migrant labour outflows in to Punjab".

TABLE 7.2: Distribution of Migrant Agricultural Labourers as Per Holding Size

Sl. No.	Size Class of the Operational Holding (Acres)	Number of Migrants	Percentage of the Total
1	2	3	4
1.	— 0.00	59	39.33
2.	0.01 — 0.99	35	23.33
3.	1.00 — 1.49	20	13.34
4.	1.50 — 1.99	15	10.00
5.	2.00 and above	21	14.00
	All Migrants	150	100.00

To test this hypothesis we present the distribution of migrants according to the areas of outmigration. Then by pressing into service our districtwise composite index (Table 2.4 in Chapter 2 of the present study) based on 1975-76 data, we can either confirm or reject our hypothesis. Table 7.3 presents the essential details in this regard.

It is important to note that 78.0 per cent of the total number of migrants in our sample were from Bihar, about 21.0 per cent from Uttar Pradesh and just one migrant from West Dinajpur district of West Bengal. Further, while 62.0 per cent of the total sample respondents hailed from Champaran (east and west) and Sitamarhi districts of Bihar, the remaining districts of the State just accounted for only 16.0 per cent of them. Again, among the migrants from Uttar Pradesh, nearly 18.0 per cent reported to be coming from Gorakhpur district and the remaining from Basti district. Interestingly, none of the migrants surveyed by us in the study areas of Punjab reported to be coming from the study area of Bihar. Similarly, none of the sample households in Bihar reported outmigration in Punjab. On the other hand, out of the total migrants coming from Bihar, nearly 80.0 per cent were from the two districts of Champaran (east and west) and Sitamarhi districts. In an much as these districts rank fairly low[1] in the agricultural development hierarchy of Bihar, it is obvious that the exigency of outmigrating to a destination of higher and assured earning per day of work done operates more acutely in these backward pockets. In comparison, Bhojpur — our chosen study area in Bihar, is among the top 2 to 3 districts of Bihar in the matter of agricultural development. This, in turn, offers relatively better avenues of on-farm employment compared with other districts of Bihar.

TABLE 7.3: Identification of Areas of Outmigration in Bihar, Uttar Pradesh and West Bengal

Sl. No.	Name of the District	Number of Migrants	Percentage of the Total (150)	Percentage of the Total Migrants in Each State
1	2	3	4	5
	BIHAR			
1.	Champaran (E & W)	54	36.00	46.15
2.	Sitamarhi	39	26.00	33.33
3.	Muzaffarpur	6	4.00	5.13
4.	Vaishali	1	0.67	0.86
5.	Darbhanga	7	4.67	5.98
6.	Gopalganj	2	1.33	1.71
7.	Purnea	3	2.00	2.57
8.	Saharsa	5	3.33	4.27
A.	Total Bihar	117	78.00	100.00
	UTTAR PRADESH			
9.	Gorakhpur	27	18.00	84.37
10.	Basti	5	3.33	15.63
B.	Total Uttar Pradesh	32	21.33	100.00
	WEST BENGAL			
C.	West Dinajpur	1	0.67	100.00
	Total (A+B+C)	150.00	100.00	

Note: 1. E = East 2. W = West

It is also sometimes said that socio-cultural milieu in certain areas of Bihar keep people bound to their ancestral lands, although they subsist at very low level of living. This may partly be responsible for keeping the spate of migration from many other districts of Bihar on a very low keel (Table 7.3). In a nutshell, our sample data confirms the hypothesis that it is from the relatively backward areas of Bihar that the migrant labour outflows into Punjab.

SECTION III

Employment/Earning Pattern

In this section, we propose to examine the impact of rural-urban distance on the employment/earning pattern of the migrant labour in Punjab as also the distribution of wage-paid on-farm employment/earnings between the migrant labour and the resident labour. In this regard, we propose to test our second hypothesis which envisages an inverse relationship between the share of the migrant labour in total yearly wage-paid on-farm employment/earnings and rural-urban distance. As regards the distribution of employment time and earnings between the migrant labour and the resident labour, percentage shares of these variables have been compared. Besides, the blowing up technique (as explained earlier in Chapter 4) has also been pressed in to service to make the analysis more convincing.

To begin with, Table 7.4 contains the mean values of overall and componentwise employment/earnings accruing to the migrant labour in rural Punjab. It is relevant to point out that all the 150 respondents in our sample were seasonal migrants only and none of them had availed of urban employment of any kind. In other words, the entire earning of each migrant labourer included in our sample accrued from rural employment, partly from on-farm and partly from non-farm avenues.

Table 7.4 throws up a few notable points. Firstly, on average, a migrant labourer in rural Punjab gets nearly 133.0 mandays of total employment and earns Rs. 1,301.74 in a year. Consequently, per day earning is Rs. 9.76. Secondly, since our basic concern is with the employment/earnings of migrant labour in rural Punjab, it is not surprising that on-farm employment/earnings account for nearly 97.0 per cent of total mandays of employment/earnings per migrant labourer. By implication, very negligible non-farm employment/earnings accrue to this labour and that too only occasionally.

If we look in terms of distance from the focal town, we observe that per migrant mandays of employment and the consequent level of earnings as also the per day earning tend to decline as we move into the interior of the countryside. The same pattern holds for on-farm employment, which is quite understandable since more than 97.0 per cent of their employment is on agricultural activities. It is, however, a different matter that the mandays of employment available to a

TABLE 7.4: Pattern of Rural Employment and Earnings of the Migrant Labour in Punjab

(Mean Value, Per Annum)

Sl. No.	Employment/ Earning Source	Variable	Village V1	V2	V3	V4	V5	V6	V7	V8	Average	Regression Equation $Yi = \alpha + \beta Dj$	No. of Observations (N)
1	2	3	4	5	6	7	8	9	10	11	12	13	14
1.	On-Farm Employment	Emp	153.75	144.60	124.40	135.89	123.90	125.04	120.14	131.78	129.86	Yi = 141.63 - 1.34**D	150
			(96.75)	(100.00)	(96.07)	(95.17)	(100.00)	(95.45)	(98.56)	(98.51)	(97.35)	[1.70]	
		Ern	1607.26	1518.11	1268.27	1306.20	1214.86	1168.67	1104.64	1165.64	1274.28	Yi = 1512.40 -27.10*D	150
			(97.48)	(100.00)	(96.88)	(96.17)	(100.00)	(96.28)	(98.82)	(98.73)	(97.89)	[3.63]	
		Epd	10.45	10.50	10.20	9.61	9.81	9.35	9.19	8.85	9.81	Yi = 10.70 - 0.10*D	150
												[7.17]	
		PPR	100.00	100.00	100.00	100.00	100.00	100.00	100.00	100.00	100.00		
2.	Non-Farm Employment	Emp	5.17	–	5.09	6.89	–	5.96	1.75	2.00	3.53	Yi = 29.93 - 0.06D	18
			(3.25)	(–)	(3.93)	(4.83)	(–)	(4.55)	(1.44)	(1.49)	(2.65)	[0.05]	
		Ern	41.59	–	40.82	51.96	–	45.09	13.21	15.00	27.45	Yi = 243.58 - 1.74D	18
			(2.52)	(–)	(3.12)	(3.83)	(–)	(3.72)	(1.18)	(1.27)	(2.11)	[0.19]	
		Epd	8.05	–	8.02	7.54	–	7.56	7.55	7.50	7.77	Yi = 7.98 - 0.03*D	18
												[2.19]	
		PPR	25.00	–	11.43	44.44	–	14.81	7.14	11.11	12.00		

Contd.

TABLE 7.4 *Contd.*

1	2	3	4	5	6	7	8	9	10	11	12	13	14	
3.	Total Yearly	Emp	158.92 (100.00)	144.60 (100.00)	129.49 (100.00)	142.78 (100.00)	123.90 (100.00)	131.00 (100.00)	121.89 (100.00)	133.78 (100.00)	133.39 (100.00)	Yi =	145.57 - 1.39**D [1.65]	150
		Ern	1648.85 (100.00)	1518.11 (100.00)	1309.09 (100.00)	1358.16 (100.00)	1214.86 (100.00)	1213.76 (100.00)	1117.85 (100.00)	1180.64 (100.00)	1301.74 (100.00)	Yi =	1544.24 -27.60 D [3.50]	150
		Epd	10.38	10.50	10.11	9.51	9.81	9.27	9.17	8.83	9.76	Yi =	10.67 - 0.10*D [7.19]	150
		PPR	(100.00)	(100.00)	(100.00)	(100.00)	(100.00)	(100.00)	(100.00)	(100.00)	(100.00)			

Note: 1. Notations Emp., Ern., Epd. and PPR are explained in Table 4.1.
2. Figures in the parentheses represent percentages of the total yearly employment/earnings.
3. Figures in [ ] are the 't' values.
* shows the significance of 't' values at 0.05 level.
** shows the significance of 't' values at 0.10 level.

migrant labourer from on-farm sources keep on declining as the rural-urban distance increases. In other words, to a migrant labourer, the remoter villages offer lower employment time. This could not ordinarily be otherwise because resident labour in the extremely remote villages participates in wage-paid on-farm employment on a big scale. It seems that the rate of substitution of local labour by migrant labour keeps on declining as we move away from the focal town. There is a natural tendency for the local labour living in the nearby villages to commute to urban focal town in order to avail of more gainful wage-paid non-farm urban employment and thus leaving a bigger scope for migrant labour to attend to agricultural operations. As the distance from the focal town increases, the commutability of local labour starts declining, mandays of employment in agricultural operations increase for them, and consequently the migrant labour got slightly lower mandays of on-farm employment compared with those enjoyed by their migrating brethren in villages near the town. The declining trend of the quantum of on-farm employment and earning, in relation to rural-urban distance, is thus explained by the above discussion.

Let us now look into the relative shares of the migrant labour and the resident labour in the total yearly wage-paid on-farm employment/earnings on overall as also on daily basis. In this regard, we work out the total mandays of wage-paid on-farm employment and earnings through the blowing up technique and compare the same with the corresponding figures for the migrant labour, for each of the sample village and for all villages taken together. This would show how the migrant labourer competes with the resident labour force. Naturally, this competition would have differing intensity as we move from the villages near the urban town to those into the interior of the countryside. Table 7.5 sets out the picture of this competition in a fairly broad sense. A few comments are in order.

Firstly, the share of resident labour in overall wage-paid on-farm employment/earnings in Punjab (nearly 70.0%) is much higher than that of the migrant labour (nearly 30.0%). The higher share of employment/earnings of the resident labour may be due to the fact that while migrant labour works and earns only on per day basis and that also in peak seasons, the employment/earnings of the resident labour consist of attached and daily based components. Secondly, if we look in terms of distance from the focal town, we observe that the share of resident labour in total yearly wage-paid on-farm employment is higher than that of the migrant labour both in villages near the town as well as away from it. Thirdly, while the share of the resident labour in the total wage-paid agricultural employment/earnings tends to increase with increase in rural-urban distance; the share of migrant labour on the other hand, records a declining pattern. This lends further substance to our view that with increase in rural-urban distance, the dependence of the resident labour on wage-paid agricultural employment also increases. As a result of this, the migrant labour has to face increasing competition from the resident labour of Punjab in the remote areas of the countryside. It is, therefore, obvious that the share of migrant labour in the overall wage-paid on-farm employment/earnings becomes smaller in the remote villages than in villages near the focal town/urban or sub-urban areas.

An analysis of the share of the migrant labour *vis-a-vis* that of the resident labour of Punjab in the wage-paid on-farm employment on daily basis also lends further credence to our view mentioned above. To begin with, we observe that on daily basis also, the share of resident labour (approximately 56.0%) in the total yearly wage-paid on-farm employment is much higher compared with that of the migrant labour (roughly 44.0% only). The lower share of the migrant labour is due to the fact that migration is only a seasonal phenomenon and that too mainly for specific field crop operations such as paddy transplantation and harvesting and wheat harvesting and threshing etc. Next, if we look in terms of distance from the focal town, we find that in villages near the town wage-paid on-farm employment on daily basis is very largely sustained by the migrant labour; its share in employment/earnings is over 60.0 per cent compared with less than 40.0 per cent for the resident labour households. On the other hand, in the extremely remote village of the countryside in Punjab, the share of the local labour in employment/earnings from wage-paid on-farm employment on daily basis is between 2 to 3 times larger than that of the migrant labour.

The above conclusion can be reinforced by assessing the respective position of the local and the migrant labour yet in another way. We work out labour use and level of earnings per acre of gross cropped area separately for the migrant labour and the resident labour on overall as well as daily basis. Table 7.5 present the essentials in this regard.

TABLE 7.5: Villagewise Distribution of Wage-Paid On-Farm Employment/Earnings between the Migrant and Resident Labour in Punjab

Sl. No.	Village/s	Overall Wage-Paid On-Farm Employment						Daily Wage-Paid On-Farm Employment					
		Employment (Mandays)			Earnings (in Rs.)			Employment (Mandays)			Earnings (in Rs.)		
		MGRT	RSDT	Total	MGRT	RSDT	Total	MGRT	RSDT	Total	MGRT	RSDT	Total
1	2	3	4	5	6	7	8	9	10	11	12	13	14
1.	V1	49.00	51.00	100.00	51.49	48.51	100.00	61.88	38.12	100.00	62.79	37.21	100.00
		(18.86)	(19.63)	(38.49)	(197.36)	(185.95)	(383.31)	(18.86)	(11.62)	(30.48)	(197.36)	(116.94)	(314.30)
2.	V2	33.66	66.34	100.00	36.90	63.10	100.00	55.67	44.33	100.00	57.21	42.79	100.00
		(6.48)	(12.77)	(19.25)	(67.91)	(116.15)	(184.06)	(6.48)	(5.16)	(11.64)	(67.92)	(50.81)	(118.73)
3.	V3	29.56	70.44	100.00	31.76	68.24	100.00	48.67	51.33	100.00	48.31	51.69	100.00
		(6.05)	(14.42)	(20.47)	(61.68)	(132.52)	(194.20)	(6.05)	(6.38)	(12.43)	(61.68)	(66.00)	(127.68)
4.	V4	49.24	50.76	100.00	51.34	48.66	100.00	66.19	33.81	100.00	64.61	35.39	100.00
		(9.69)	(9.99)	(19.68)	(93.12)	(88.25)	(181.37)	(9.69)	(4.95)	(14.64)	(93.12)	(51.00)	(144.12)
5.	V5	25.95	74.05	100.00	27.22	72.78	100.00	38.08	61.92	100.00	36.79	63.21	100.00
		(7.03)	(20.06)	(27.09)	(68.97)	(184.44)	(253.41)	(7.03)	(11.43)	(18.46)	(68.97)	(118.52)	(187.49)
6.	V6	20.97	79.03	100.00	21.47	78.53	100.00	36.38	63.62	100.00	34.57	65.43	100.00
		(5.05)	(19.03)	(24.08)	(47.18)	(172.61)	(219.79)	(5.05)	(8.83)	(13.88)	(47.18)	(89.29)	(136.47)
7.	V7	28.50	71.50	100.00	30.23	69.77	100.00	40.07	59.93	100.00	40.12	59.88	100.00
		(4.46)	(11.19)	(15.65)	(41.32)	(95.36)	(136.68)	(4.46)	(6.67)	(11.13)	(41.32)	(61.68)	(103.00)
8.	V8	15.77	84.23	100.00	16.23	83.77	100.00	26.79	73.21	100.00	26.02	73.98	100.00
		(3.45)	(18.43)	(21.88)	(30.52)	(157.48)	(188.00)	(3.45)	(9.43)	(12.88)	(30.52)	(86.78)	(117.30)
	All	27.97	72.03	100.00	29.84	70.16	100.00	43.94	56.06	100.00	43.79	56.21	100.00
		(5.87)	(15.12)	(20.99)	(57.59)	(135.43)	(193.02)	(5.87)	(7.49)	(13.36)	(57.59)	(73.92)	(131.51)

Note: 1. MGRT : Migrant Labour 2. RSDT : Resident Labour.
4. Figures in the parentheses under the relevant headings represent the Mean Values Per Acre of Gross Cropped Area

It can be observed from Table 7.5 that on overall basis per acre employment time and the level of earnings for the migrant labour decreases from nearly one-half in the first village to just 16.0 per cent in the extremely remote village, while that of the resident labour becomes as high as 84.0 per cent in the last village compared with 50.0 per cent in the village in close proximity to the focal town.

If we carry out this comparison on daily based employment/ earnings, assuming for the time being the absence of employment/ earnings accruing to attached farm servants, we observe that while the share of the resident labour force nearly doubles (about 74.0%) in the extremely remote village of the countryside compared with that in the immediate vicinity of the urban focal town (about 37.0%); the share of the migrant labour per acre of gross cropped area declines from nearly 62.0 per cent in the first village to about 26.0 per cent in the last village from the focal town. This is equally true both of labour use as well as earnings raised per acre of gross cropped area. An important fact, however, needs to be underlined that the overall share of the resident labour in employment/earnings of per acre of gross cropped area is higher compared with that of the migrant labour both on total employment basis as well as on daily wage-paid employment basis. Thus, the hypothesis that in the Punjab, the share of migrant labour in wage-paid on-farm employment, whether observed on the basis of time criterion or per acre of gross cropped area, goes on declining as we move to villages away from the town gets confirmation in our sample data.

Operationwise On-farm Employment/Earnings

It is important to look into the operationwise composition of agricultural employment/earnings of the migrant labour. Table 7.6 presents the necessary details in this regard.

It is obvious that the total on-farm employment time of the migrant labour is fairly unevenly distributed among the various crop operations. Participation of each migrant labour in harvesting is must; 88.0 per cent of them work for weeding: nearly three-fourths of them for sowing, and so on. However, except for sowing (which includes the operation of rice transplantation), the location of a particular village does not seem to affect the degree of participation by migrant labour in different operations. For sowing, as the rural-urban distance increases, a smaller proportion of migrant labour works for this operation, perhaps for the reason that local labour also becomes increasingly available in remoter villages.

TABLE 7.6: Village-wise Pattern of On-Farm Employment/Earnings of the Migrant Labour in Punjab on Daily Basis

(*Mean Value, Per Annum*)

Sl. No.	Operation	Variable	Village V1	V2	V3	V4	V5	V6	V7	V8	Average	Regression Equation $Yi = a + b\,Dj$	No. of Observations (*N*)
1	2	3	4	5	6	7	8	9	10	11	12	13	14
1.	Sowing and Transplantation	Emp	32.25 (20.98)	30.45 (21.06)	30.46 (24.49)	21.11 (15.53)	17.50 (14.13)	17.96 (14.36)	18.50 (15.40)	14.89 (11.30)	23.76 (18.30)	$Yi = 37.37 - 0.66^{*}D$ [3.66]	111
		Ern	348.34 (21.67)	334.53 (22.04)	329.23 (25.96)	218.40 (16.72)	182.15 (14.99)	182.60 (15.62)	181.41 (16.42)	139.49 (11.97)	249.64 (19.60)	$Yi = 416.72 - 9.90^{*}D$ [6.05]	111
		Epd	10.80	10.99	10.81	10.35	10.41	10.17	9.81	9.37	10.51	$Yi = 11.29 - 0.08^{*}D$ [3.35]	111
		PPR	83.33	85.00	88.57	77.78	60.00	66.67	64.29	44.44	74.00		
2.	Weeding	Emp	47.42 (30.84)	37.71 (26.07)	25.05 (20.14)	40.45 (29.77)	29.40 (23.72)	39.59 (31.67)	35.00 (29.13)	38.67 (29.34)	35.03 (26.98)	$Yi = 38.61 + 0.14D$ [0.30]	132
		Ern	398.86 (24.82)	311.73 (20.53)	200.91 (15.84)	312.73 (23.94)	224.84 (18.51)	303.38 (25.96)	253.68 (22.96)	277.27 (23.79)	272.70 (21.42)	$Yi = 329.32 - 2.20D$ [0.60]	132
		Epd	8.41	8.27	8.02	7.73	7.65	7.66	7.25	7.17	7.78	$Yi = 8.45 - 0.08^{*}D$ [9.39]	132
		PPR	100.00	85.00	82.86	100.00	80.00	85.19	96.43	77.78	88.00		
3.	Harvesting and Threshing	Emp	61.83 (40.21)	64.00 (44.26)	53.54 (43.04)	57.22 (42.11)	61.90 (49.96)	55.30 (44.23)	56.21 (46.79)	62.78 (47.64)	57.75 (44.47)	$Yi = 59.16 - 0.16D$ [0.45]	150
		Ern	740.32 (46.06)	752.06 (49.54)	597.65 (47.12)	618.61 (47.36)	677.98 (55.81)	580.81 (49.36)	580.23 (52.53)	626.19 (53.72)	631.64 (49.60)	$Yi = 707.39 - 8.62^{*}D$ [2.06]	150
		Epd	11.97	11.75	11.16	10.81	10.95	10.50	10.32	9.97	10.94	$Yi = 11.74 - 0.10^{*}D$ [4.78]	150
		PPR	100.00	100.00	100.00	100.00	100.00	100.00	100.00	100.00	100.00		

Contd.

TABLE 7.6 *Contd.*

1	2	3	4	5	6	7	8	9	10	11	12	13	14
4	Other Agricultural Operations such as Watering, Manuring, etc.	Emp	12.25 (7.97)	12.45 (8.61)	15.34 (12.33)	17.11 (12.59)	15.10 (12.19)	12.19 (9.74)	10.43 (18.68)	15.44 (11.72)	13.32 (10.25)	*Yi* = 14.93 + 0.64**D* [4.04]	100
		Ern	119.74 (7.45)	119.79 (7.89)	140.53 (11.08)	156.46 (11.98)	129.89 (10.69)	105.89 (9.06)	89.32 (8.09)	122.70 (10.52)	119.48 (9.38)	*Yi* = 150.11 + 3.72**D* [3.06]	100
		Epd	9.78	9.62	9.16	9.14	8.60	8.69	8.57	7.94	8.97	*Yi* = 9.87 - 0.09**D* [4.77]	100
		PPR	75.00	75.00	77.14	88.89	90.00	59.26	42.86	44.44	66.67		
5.	Total On-Farm Employment on Daily Basis	Emp	153.75 (100.0)	144.60 (100.0)	124.40 (100.0)	135.89 (100.0)	123.90 (100.0)	125.04 (100.0)	120.14 (100.0)	131.78 (100.0)	129.86 (100.0)	*Yi* = 141.63 - 1.34***D* [1.70]	150
		Ern	1607.26 (100.0)	1518.11 (100.0)	1268.27 (100.0)	1306.20 (100.0)	1214.86 (100.0)	1168.67 (100.0)	1104.64 (100.0)	1165.64 (100.0)	1274.28 (100.0)	*Yi* = 1512.40 - 27.10**D* [3.63]	150
		Epd	10.45	10.50	10.20	9.61	9.81	9.35	9.19	8.85	9.81	*Yi* = 10.70 - 0.10**D* [7.17]	150
		PPR	100.00	100.00	100.00	100.00	100.00	100.00	100.00	100.00	100.00		

Note: 1. Notations Emp, Epd, and PPR are explained in Table 4.1.
2. Figures in the parentheses represent percentages of the total yearly employment/earnings.
3. Figures in [ ] are the 't' values.
* Shows the significance of 't' values at 0.05 level.
** Shows the significance of 't' values at 0.10 level.

As regards the division of migrant labour's time and earnings among different operations, harvesting alone accounts for nearly 45.0 per cent of the total time and about 50.0 per cent of the total earnings from on-farm employment. The next important crop operation is weeding which provides 27.0 per cent of employment-time and 21.0 per cent of on-farm earnings. The third place goes to sowing, an so on.

If we look into the relative importance of each crop operation for villages at varying distances from the focal town, it is fairly evident that the location of a particular village does not affect the distribution of employment-time and earnings among the individual crop operations. In other words, practically for each village, harvesting occupies the first place, weeding the second and sowing the third, as regards the share of employment-time and earning. It is thus clear that the migrant labour's employment in Punjab's agriculture has a well-defined pattern, perhaps in conformity with their skills on the one hand, and, the crop-specific necessity of substituting outside labour for local labour on the other.

It may be useful to compare per day earning of the migrant labour with that of local labour, in respect of different crop operations. Table 7.6 may be read with Table 4.7 (Chapter 4) for this comparison. It is interesting to see that except for sowing, for all other operations, the local labour commands a relatively higher per day earning; for sowing, the migrant labour has a slight edge. The migrant labour is generally believed to be more specialised in handling the operation of sowing (which in our case includes rice transplantation); hence, a slightly higher wage rate to the migrant labour for this operation, or more expressly for rice transplantation. More important, however, is the fact that per day earning for most other operations does not differ much between the local and the migrant labour. It seems, the availability of migrant labour has tended to depress the wage rates that would have otherwise accrued to the local labour. In a broad sense, the labour market is opened up beyond the State frontiers and the demand for labour for Punjab agriculture is being matched by supply both from inside and outside. Perhaps, it may be wrong to say that the national labour market determines the level of wage rate in the agriculture of Punjab. Very surely, we have no reason to subscribe to the view that in the agriculture of Punjab, the migrant labour is being exploited or discriminated against, *inter alia*, as far as daily wage rates are concerned. Such assertions do not seem to hold. On the contrary, if indeed a grouse is flashed, it lies more with the resident labour in the sense that the huge influx of migratory labour has prevented the local wage rate to rise. Some degree of antagonism between the two types of labour is, therefore, quite understandable. However, the total pinch is not so glaring in as much as the local labour has other avenues of employment to fall back upon.

SECTION IV

Why Migrate?

Why does large scale inmigration occur every year into the farm sector of Punjab? A meaningful answer to this question is to be expected from the migrants themselves. Their perception about the process and the reasons for migration must be fully relied upon. In the present section, this is precisely what we do. In most of what follows, only qualitative answers, as given by our respondents, are summarised; it would not have been possible to formulate precise quantitative figures.

Broadly speaking, the growth of migration owes itself partly to the problems concerning the failure of development programmes in areas of outmigration and partly to those related with attained economic development in areas of inmigration. More Specifically, two types of factors were listed almost by each of the migrant labourer figuring in our sample. These factors are 'economic and social factors' and 'seasonal differences'. A word about them:

(i) Under 'economic and social' factors, reference is generally made to 'pull factors' and 'push factors'. While 'pull factors' operate in the areas of inmigration; 'push factors', on the other hand, work in the areas of outmigration. Further, while 'pull factors' include high wage rate, better working conditions, comparatively free labour market and freedom from social oppression and economic exploitation; factors such as mass unemployment and underemployment, low level of earnings, prevalence of abject poverty and existence of social oppression on a very large scale can be placed under 'push factors'. It is, in fact, the simultaneous interaction between these 'pull and push' factors which causes inmigration/outmigration.

(ii) Seasonal differences between Punjab and Bihar/eastern Uttar

Pradesh farm sectors may be listed as other factors responsible for migration. The demand for labour in agriculture is subject to seasonal fluctuations over the production year; while demand for wage-paid farm labour is very high during the peak seasons of sowing, transplantation and harvesting, it is fairly low for other crop operations. Generally, labour shortage is felt during the peak season while a great degree of underemployment/unemployment exists during the slack season. Thanks to a great deal of seasonal and climatic variation across regions of a country, especially for as big a country as India, peak agricultural season in one part does not exactly coincide with peak season in another. This readily facilitates short-term seasonal migration from one region to the other. In our case, crops mature earlier in Bihar and eastern Uttar Pradesh. Consequently, post-harvest slack season in these areas coincides with the period of wheat harvesting and paddy transplantation in Punjab. Since the migrant labour is needed in Punjab summarily for these crop operations, there is thus a nice synchronisation of slack season in Bihar with peak season in Punjab and vice versa. It works to the benefit of both areas; on the one hand, agriculture in Punjab is sustained on ready availability of migrant labour, and, on the other, it adds to the total duration of gainful employment and earning levels of the migrant labour.

The foregoing analysis shows that it is the adoption of new agricultural technology, intensification of cultivation, shift in the cropping pattern in Punjab, rising commercialisation of agriculture and undertaking of various development programmes in the non-farm sector, that the demand for labour has been rising steadily in Punjab. The increase in demand for labour over the years has had the effect of pushing up the earning levels in various wage-paid activities. The growth of migrant labour in Punjab, in fact, has arrested the upward tendency in wage rates in various on-farm activities in the rural areas in Punjab. The resident labour, though grudgingly cohabitates with the migrants, also prefers more remunerative avenues of non-farm employment. It has also been observed that because of increase in rural-urban distances in Punjab, there are some important variations in the employment/earning pattern of those migrant labourers who are working in villages near the town than those who work in the villages relatively away from the urban focal town. Finally, although seasonal variations in the pattern of labour demand between the areas of inmigration and outmigration exert considerable influence on migration, yet it is essentially an economic phenomenon. In fact, the propensity to migrate emanates from the simultaneous working of the various pull and push factors, as mentioned earlier. To be more precise, it is the glaring wage differentials in the areas of inmigration and outmigration which exert the primary influence on migration.

NOTE

1. It is important to note that in the matter of agricultural development, the districts of west and east Champaran rank respectively 18th and 19th and the district of Sitamarhi ranks 21st in our composite index. In contrast, Bhojpur district ranks 2nd in the matter of agricultural development. For further details, please see Table 2.4, Chapter 2, of the present study.

8

CONSUMPTION PATTERN IN PUNJAB AND BIHAR

The contrast between the rural labour households of Punjab with those of Bihar would not be complete unless we look into their consumption standards also. The present chapter deals with the consumption pattern of our sample households. For an analytical discussion of the issues involved, the following estimates are obtained from our sample data:

(1) the commodity-wise per capita consumption expenditure to highlight the variations between the Punjab and the Bihar situations;
(2) the percentage share of each item of consumption in the total per capita domestic expenditure to study the relative importance of different items of consumption;
(3) the variations in the cash component of consumption expenditure of such households to focus our attention on the employer-employee relationship between the two study areas;
(4) the distribution of consumption expenditure to study variations in the consumption pattern of different strata of sample households within as also between the two study areas; and
(5) the expenditure elasticities of different commodities bearing implications for the consumption standards of the labour households in the two study areas.

The discussion runs into 2 sections. Section I reviews critically some of the major methodological developments regarding the measurement of consumption standards, especially in the estimation of Engel elasticities. Section II attempts to analyse the consumption pattern of the sample households in terms of averages, percentages, expenditure elasticities, etc.

SECTION I

Consumer Behaviour: Empirical Approaches

The studies on the economics of consumption are deservedly popular due to the fact that consumption is considered to be the be-all and end-all of all economic activity. In economic literature, one comes across two main approaches for the analysis of consumption pattern. The first approach, popularly known as the 'time-series approach' involves the choice of an appropriate mathematical form expressing the quantities consumed as function of income and relative prices. Further, by making use of the method of multiple regression, its parameters are estimated from the time series data. Whether the use of this approach is suitable, depends upon the availability of time-series data on the one hand, and on the precise objectives of the inquiry, on the other. But the use of this approach is questioned on the ground that many of the relationships, originally assumed to be stable, may undergo considerable changes over time. The second empirical approach is based upon the income and consumption expenditure of a cross-section of households. This approach is developed in the mould of *ceteris paribus* clause. While making use of this approach, a plethora of family-budget studies[1] have been conducted in several countries from time to time. It needs to be pointed out here that all such investigations regarding consumer behaviour were made in countries outside India. In India, the availability of nationwide N.S.S. data on household consumption, inception of planning in 1951 and the compulsions emerging out of the planning process and publication of some reports[2] seem to have stimulated much empirical interest in studies on consumer behaviour. Consequently, a large number of research workers[3] and some research institutes[4] have come out with some interesting and revealing findings regarding consumer behaviour. Some leading journals[5] have also contributed substantially in this regard.

Admittedly, it is beyond the purview of the present study to critically evaluate the efficacy of each empirical approach, yet it may not be out of place to underline a few important features of such studies.

Firstly, the Indian studies on consumption encompass a wide array of regional experiences covering different time periods and thus reflecting the effect of different development situations.

Secondly, the Indian studies on consumption reveal a rich variety of functional specifications but a more or less uniform estimational procedure. The classical least squares estimating technique has really ruled the roost. Thirdly, while scholars like Rudra have made use of linear expenditure system developed originally by Richard Stone, there are others who have examined the impact of grouping of observations on co-efficient of determination in the Engel-curve formulations. Lastly, most studies, based as they are on N.S.S. consumption data, work out expenditure elasticities rather than income elasticities; ordinarily, income figures at the household level are just not available in published reports.

To sum up, studies conducted in India cover different periods of time. They have followed a variety of techniques for the estimation of Engel elasticities. Also that a number of explanations for variations in household expenditure in different regions (or States) have been offered. If only these studies had considered the disproportionate effects of household size on its consumption, perhaps their conclusions regarding regional variations would have been different. Baldota's study bears ample testimony to this assertion. It is, therefore, obvious that although consumption has been of a nebulous character in modern economics, yet it has always been at its very centre. Consequently, empirical research in the field of consumption has been controversial but thrilling experience for the economists.

SECTION II

Consumption Pattern: Punjab-Bihar Contrasts

In the preceding section, we have examined the empirical approaches on consumption pattern. In the present section, it is proposed to probe if there exist significant variations in the consumption pattern of the two States. Inasmuch as the two States represent sharp economic contrasts, the observed differences in the consumption pattern would tend to reflect the responses of the rural labour households to rising income levels and better standard of living in areas of fast economic growth compared with those in the less growing areas. The percolation effects of high growth must reflect themselves in better living conditions of the rural people if indeed the growth process does not become too restricted or too sterile.

We deem it necessary to point out some features emerging from the consumption data gathered by us. While most of the food-items such as cereals, gram and pulses, salt and spices are regularly consumed and so reported, practically by each household, there are other items such as clothing and bedding, footwear, etc., which are not regularly purchased and hence the number of positive respondents in their case is markedly less than the total sample households. Similarly, expenditure on marriage and other social ceremonies is not incurred as regularly as on food items. These expenditures are encountered much less commonly in Bihar than in Punjab, and for obvious reasons, their inclusion in total per capita expenditures distort the picture of poverty. We discuss these details later.

For the computation of household expenditure, we have had to follow a procedure slightly different from the one usually followed in N.S.S. surveys. In our case, while information on consumption expenditure for food-items was gathered on monthly basis, the one pertaining to non-food items such as clothing and bedding, and footwear could be obtained meaningfully only on three-monthly basis. Again, information about expenditure on marriage and social ceremonies was gathered on half yearly basis. It may also be clarified that items such as *pan*, tobacco, and other intoxicants have been covered in food-items and placed alongwith processed food such as beverages, refreshments etc., since most of our respondents could not provide separate expenditure figures for such individual components. It is interesting to note that both in Punjab and Bihar, the percentage of positive respondents for individual items of consumption is very high for some commodity groups and markedly low for others. For example, while this percentage is very high in both the States for items such as cereals, gram and pulses, edible oils, fuel and light, etc.; it is very low for other commodities most notably, meat eggs and fish, consumer durables, etc. Mean values for the latter may be considered as indicative of qualitative variations and not quantitative ones. Again, the percentage of households reporting consumption of certain items such as milk and milk products, vegetables and fruits, *gur* and sugar, processed food and beverages, etc., varies widely between the two States. Such variations in the positive responses can also be discovered in non-food items such as footwear, education, conveyance and conveyance services, medicine and health and miscellaneous goods and services.

To begin with, we would like to see total household expenditure against total household income for the sample villages of Punjab and Bihar. Table 8.1 shows a very important contrast between the two States. For every village in Punjab, we discover that, on an average, the rural labour households are saving a part of their annual income. The reality of net savings is indeed a redeeming feature, especially because we are dealing with people belonging to the lower echelons of the rural society. The possibility of slight underestimation of consumption expenditure cannot be ruled out, especially because some items or a portion of some items of consumption is earned through kind wages or else is provided free of cost to the labourers at peak hours of work, etc. Such accruals in consumption may be missed by respondents with the result that consumption figures get slightly underplayed. It is as well possible that consumption of milk and milk products is also under-reported primarily because there is a tendency to underplay gains on production side. In many cases, investment in dairying is institutionally financed and the borrowers would almost always under-report the production and sale of milk. Unluckily, we have no firm data to go into these details or work out the degree of under-estimation. In any case, the moot point still remains and the possibility of real savings even among the rural labour households of Punjab need not be ruled out. On the other hand, the average picture in most of the Bihar villages is quite depressing; the annual consumption expenditure overshoots the annual household income, and as a consequence, negative savings accrue.

It may be more satisfying to see savings in Punjab and dissavings in Bihar in relation to the level of income. The complement of average propensity to save is the average propensity to consume (hereafter a.p.c.). We work out a.p.c., as in Table 8.1.

A well-received proposition in the literature on consumer behaviour is that the higher-income households generally save larger proportion of their income. Following this proposition, we should expect, (i) the average propensity to consume (a.p.c.) of Punjab households to be lower than that of Bihar households (ii) within each State, a.p.c. of households in villages located near the town to be lower compared to those belonging to the distantly located villages; and (iii) a.p.c. of Bihar households to be relatively higher than that of Punjab households at all conceivable distances from the focal town.

Table 8.1 provides some empirical answers in this regard. First, the overall a.p.c. of Punjab households works out to be less than unity (.81) compared with above-unity in Bihar (1.02). Secondly, in both the States, the a.p.c. reveals a tendency to increase as we move into the interior of the countryside. Lastly, the a.p.c. of Punjab households is lower than that of Bihar households at all comparable distances from the focal towns.

TABLE 8.1: Average Propensity to Consume of Labour Households in Punjab and Bihar

(Mean Value, Per Annum)

Sl. No.	Village/s	Punjab				Bihar			
		$\bar{Y}$	$\bar{C}$	$\bar{S}$	a.p.c. ($\bar{C}/\bar{Y}$)	$\bar{Y}$	$\bar{C}$	$\bar{S}$	a.p.c. ($\bar{C}/\bar{Y}$)
1	2	3	4	5	6	7	8	9	10
1.	V1	6876.53	5494.44	1382.09	0.80	3403.93	3345.11	58.82	0.98
2.	V2	6280.73	5002.94	1277.79	0.80	3758.13	3297.09	461.04	0.88
3.	V3	6454.64	5018.84	1435.80	0.78	3626.36	3321.09	305.27	0.92
4.	V4	7621.18	6099.97	1521.21	0.80	2692.10	2795.42	-103.32	1.04
5.	V5	7243.94	5779.19	1464.75	0.80	3384.60	3326.40	58.20	0.98
6.	V6	6184.84	5060.55	1124.29	0.82	2529.02	2771.44	-242.42	1.10
7.	V7	5253.67	4536.47	717.20	0.86	2360.64	2720.56	-359.92	1.15
8.	V8	5245.12	4704.31	540.81	0.90	2354.48	2555.32	-200.84	1.09
	All	6243.06	5058.38	1184.68	0.81	2854.15	2919.14	-64.99	1.02

Note: 1. $\bar{Y}$ = Average Income Level
2. $\bar{C}$ = Average Consumption Expenditure
3. $\bar{S}$ = Average Saving Level
4. a.p.c. = Average Propensity to Consume ($\bar{C}/\bar{Y}$)

Thus a distinct pattern of a.p.c. as observed above confirms all our hypotheses set out a little earlier. These features of a.p.c. highlight the following important points:

First, over a wide range of Bihar villages, more surely, for those located far away into the interior of the countryside, there is the unmistakable phenomenon of negative savings. In some villages, the negative savings are as high as 15.0 per cent. In contrast, the rural labour households in every village of Punjab are showing net savings over their annual consumption expenditure. The rate of savings varies between 10.0 to 22.0 per cent, the overall figure is nearly 19.0 per cent which is fairly respectable.

The accrual of savings in Punjab is directly attributable to higher income which has been made possible due to better employment opportunities in the farm as well as non-farm sectors. This, in turn, seems to have set into motion two major developments witnessed in Punjab *over the years*. On the one hand, it has led to the building of productive assets especially dairying in the form of milch cattle, while on the other, it has led to investments in household assets namely residential dwellings, electricity installation in these dwellings, etc. It is as well a fact that household investments in status based assets such as ratio, watch, fan, other consumer durables, etc, commenced much earlier in the case of Punjab while such items are perhaps catching up in Bihar only in recent years. It should not be a surprise that in Punjab we discovered items such as radio/transistor, watch, fan etc. in a preponderant majority of our sample households, while in Bihar not more than 10 households reported possession of such items. Second, the greater-than-unity a.p.c. of Bihar households implies that such households do not earn sufficient income to finance their household expenditure and are incurring deficit as a consequence. There are studies to show that such deficit households are invariably obliged to under-take petty consumption loans which, in turn, tend to keep them under feudal and semi-feudal stranglehold. The phenomenon of perpetual indebtedness is a natural fall-out of recurring consumption deficits. That is how, the semi-feudal production relations in the agriculture of Bihar are variously explained through consumption-credit-employment nexus.[6]

A contrasting consumption scenario in Punjab in relation to that in Bihar would pose a natural question. Do the labour households in Punjab observe a different set of consumption priorities compared with their less fortunate brethren in Bihar? A comparison of percentage share of expenditure under each commodity group may provide reliable clues in this regard. The figures in parentheses in Table 8.2 are such percentage shares and may, therefore, be taken as indicator of such priorities across villages in Punjab and Bihar.

It is evident that in Punjab, the sample households incur about 72.0 per cent of their total per capita expenditure on food items compared with a relatively higher figure of nearly 78.0 per cent in Bihar. While non-food items account for about 28.0 per cent in Punjab, their share is relatively low at about 22.0 per cent in Bihar. If a detailed examination of food-items is made, it is obvious that in Punjab, cereals, milk and milk products, gur and sugar are the items of high priorities. In contrast, expenditure on cereals alone occupies a little more than 55.0 per cent of the total per capita expenditure in

TABLE 8.2: Villagewise and Commoditywise Per Capita Annual Consumption Expenditure in Punjab and Bihar

(*Mean Value in Rs.*)

Sl. No.	Commodity	State	Village								Regression		No. of Observations
			V1	V2	V3	V4	V5	V6	V7	V8	Average	$Yi = \alpha + \beta D_j$	
1	2	3	4	5	6	7	8	9	10	11	12	13	14
1.	Cereals and Cereal Products	PJB	244.26	277.12	290.19	314.41	298.07	310.12	330.32	334.06	298.76	$Yi = 260.96 + 4.43^* D$	300
			(24.58)	(26.70)	(29.21)	(34.67)	(31.25)	(31.79)	(38.69)	(36.09)	(30.82)	[4.31]	
		PPR	100.00	100.00	100.00	100.00	100.00	100.00	100.00	100.00	100.00		
		BHR	321.35	310.90	332.79	328.67	308.17	278.85	278.58	280.57	296.38	$Yi = 327.80 - 3.14^* D$	300
			(50.52)	(50.80)	(54.39)	(55.38)	(54.96)	(56.40)	(58.03)	(58.91)	(55.23)	[4.26]	
		PPR	100.00	100.00	100.00	100.00	100.00	100.00	100.00	100.00	100.00		
2.	Gram and Pulses	PJB	30.19	32.56	36.61	36.72	36.79	39.83	45.04	45.67	37.99	$Yi = 31.10 + 0.83^* D$	298
			(3.04)	(3.14)	(3.69)	(4.05)	(3.85)	(4.08)	(5.28)	(4.93)	(3.92)	[5.39]	
		PPR	100.00	95.74	100.00	100.00	100.00	100.00	100.00	100.00	99.33		
		BHR	37.39	30.84	38.38	35.97	33.16	33.26	30.37	31.35	33.25	$Yi = 37.77 - 0.37^* D$	293
			(5.88)	(5.04)	(6.27)	(6.06)	(5.91)	(6.73)	(6.33)	(6.58)	(6.20)	[3.15]	
		PPR	100.00	91.89	96.15	100.00	100.00	97.65	97.37	100.00	97.67		
3.	Edible Oils	PJB	40.61	44.20	43.31	43.73	42.55	44.22	43.17	44.56	43.50	$Yi = 42.55 + 0.13 D$	299
			(4.08)	(4.26)	(4.36)	(4.82)	(4.46)	(4.53)	(5.06)	(4.81)	(4.49)	[0.63]	
		PPR	100.00	100.00	100.00	100.00	100.00	100.00	100.00	96.15	99.67		
		BHR	31.77	25.40	29.48	25.41	24.18	23.46	21.39	22.03	24.60	$Yi = 29.49 - 0.48^* D$	300
			(4.99)	(4.15)	(4.82)	(4.28)	(4.31)	(4.75)	(4.46)	(4.63)	(4.58)	[5.10]	
		PPR	100.00	100.00	100.00	100.00	100.00	100.00	100.00	100.00	100.00		

Contd.

TABLE 8.2 *Contd.*

1	2	3	4	5	6	7	8	9	10	11	12	13	14
4.	Milk and Milk Products	PJB	120.64	123.29	134.02	111.74	118.92	115.16	93.34	103.26	118.35	$Yi = 136.29 - 2.10^{*} D$	300
			(12.14)	(11.88)	(13.49)	(12.32)	(12.46)	(11.81)	(10.93)	(11.16)	(12.21)	[3.76]	
		PPR	100.00	100.00	100.00	100.00	100.00	100.00	100.00	100.00	100.00		
		BHR	21.28	31.29	10.05	15.61	19.27	15.57	4.96	6.70	14.83	$Yi = 84.09 + 0.19 D$	52
			(3.34)	(5.11)	(1.64)	(2.63)	(3.44)	(3.15)	(1.03)	(1.41)	(2.76)	[0.13]	
		PPR	30.77	35.14	7.69	14.29	20.00	20.00	7.89	5.77	17.33		
5.	Meat, Eggs and Fish	PJB	7.51	4.04	3.31	—	3.60	1.50	1.99	0.71	2.91	$Yi = 21.07 - 0.43^{**} D$	48
			(0.76)	(0.39)	(0.33)	(–)	(0.38)	(0.15)	(0.23)	(0.08)	(0.30)	[1.71]	
		PPR	42.86	19.15	16.67	—	21.74	7.94	14.29	7.69	16.00		
		BHR	2.30	2.81	0.53	1.06	0.74	1.31	1.02	0.26	1.25	$Yi = 12.53 - 0.150$	33
			(0.36)	(0.46)	(0.09)	(0.18)	(0.13)	(0.26)	(0.21)	(0.06)	(0.03)	[0.87]	
		PPR	23.08	18.92	7.69	9.52	13.13	9.41	10.53	3.85	11.00		
6.	Vegetables and Fruits	PJB	55.63	61.25	51.21	48.25	48.43	44.96	39.57	43.01	49.23	$Yi = 60.08 - 1.21^{*} D$	298
			(5.60)	(5.90)	(5.16)	(5.32)	(5.08)	(4.61)	(4.63)	(4.65)	(5.08)	[4.86]	
		PPR	100.00	100.00	98.72	100.00	100.00	100.00	97.14	100.00	99.33		
		BHR	17.85	13.98	11.32	8.54	7.99	9.05	5.08	5.35	9.39	$Yi = 21.16 - 0.54^{*} D$	173
			(2.81)	(2.29)	(1.85)	(1.44)	(1.42)	(1.83)	(1.06)	(1.12)	(1.75)	[5.41]	
		PPR	30.77	78.38	53.85	52.38	53.33	61.18	42.11	42.31	57.67		
7.	Gur and Sugar	PJB	55.34	74.50	69.03	54.52	60.95	64.80	56.88	53.67	65.03	$Yi = 74.26 - 1.08^{*} D$	300
			(6.57)	(7.18)	(6.95)	(6.01)	(6.39)	(6.64)	(6.66)	(5.80)	(6.71)	[4.74]	
		PPR	100.00	100.00	100.00	100.00	100.00	100.00	100.00	100.00	100.00		
		BHR	4.14	4.24	5.61	3.74	2.46	3.11	2.58	2.97	3.48	$Yi = 11.20 - 0.22^{*} D$	115
			(0.65)	(0.69)	(0.92)	(0.63)	(0.44)	(0.63)	(0.54)	(0.62)	(0.65)	[3.73]	
		PPR	38.46	45.95	42.31	42.86	26.67	35.29	36.84	38.46	38.33		

Contd.

TABLE 8.2 *Contd.*

1	2	3	4	5	6	7	8	9	10	11	12	13	14
8.	Salt and Spices	PJB	28.83	31.53	30.45	31.37	28.42	32.77	33.95	36.72	31.81	$Yi = 28.82 + 0.35^{*} D$	300
			(2.90)	(3.04)	(3.07)	(3.46)	(2.98)	(3.36)	(3.98)	(3.97)	(3.29)	[2.35]	
		PPR	100.00	100.00	100.00	100.00	100.00	100.00	100.00	100.00	100.00		
		BHR	22.95	20.16	21.68	19.01	19.10	19.73	17.48	18.07	19.58	$Yi = 21.98 - 0.24^{*} D$	300
			(3.61)	(3.29)	(3.55)	(3.21)	(3.41)	(3.99)	(3.64)	(3.79)	(3.65)	[3.36]	
		PPR	100.00	100.00	100.00	100.00	100.00	100.00	100.00	100.00	100.00		
9.	Processed Food, Beverages, Pan, Tobacco, etc.	PJB	79.54	78.33	58.44	35.05	47.39	44.72	32.61	32.15	53.47	$Yi = 83.43 - 3.34^{*} D$	300
			(8.00)	(7.55)	(5.88)	(3.86)	(4.97)	(4.59)	(3.82)	(3.47)	(5.52)	[2.54]	
		PPR	100.00	100.00	100.00	100.00	100.00	100.00	100.00	100.00	100.00		
		BHR	24.32	21.70	13.34	9.12	10.99	14.03	13.45	10.37	14.60.	$Yi = 26.30 - 0.65^{*} D$	219
			(3.82)	(3.55)	(2.18)	(1.54)	(1.96)	(2.84)	(2.80)	(2.18)	(2.72)	[4.34]	
		PPR	84.62	75.68	76.92	61.90	73.33	72.94	76.32	65.38	73.00		
A.	All food Items	PJB	672.55	725.81	716.58	675.79	685.12	698.09	676.88	693.79	701.25	$Yi = 718.38 - 2.01 D$	300
			(67.67)	(70.04)	(72.14)	(74.51)	(71.82)	(71.56)	(79.28)	(74.96)	(72.34)	[0.95]	
		PPR	100.00	100.00	100.00	100.00	100.00	100.00	100.00	100.00	100.00		
		BHR	483.34	461.31	463.18	447.13	624.06	398.38	374.91	377.67	417.35	$Yi = 642.78 - 10.60^{*} D$	300
			(75.98)	(75.37)	(75.71)	(75.34)	(75.98)	(80.58)	(78.10)	(79.30)	(77.77)	[6.23]	
		PPR	100.00	100.00	100.00	100.00	100.00	100.00	100.00	100.00	100.00		
10.	Fuel and Light	PJB	48.98	52.92	50.23	43.52	48.28	49.93	47.05	48.77	49.69	$Yi = 51.58 - 0.22 D$	300
			(4.93)	(5.10)	(5.06)	(4.80)	(5.06)	(5.12)	(5.51)	(5.27)	(5.13)	[1.23]	
		PPR	100.00	100.00	100.00	100.00	100.00	100.00	100.00	100.00	100.00		
		BHR	23.80	23.27	23.76	23.03	20.60	21.01	20.69	20.05	21.68	$Yi = 24.12 - 0.24^{*} D$	300
			(3.74)	(3.18)	(3.88)	(3.88)	(3.67)	(4.25)	(4.31)	(4.21)	(4.04)	[3.95]	
		PPR	100.00	100.00	100.00	100.00	100.00	100.00	100.00	100.00	100.00		

Contd.

TABLE 8.2 *Contd.*

1	2	3	4	5	6	7	8	9	10	11	12	13	14
11.	Clothing and Bedding	EJB	38.36	64.70	47.35	45.67	33.17	56.39	41.75	37.08	50.10	*Yi* = 118.59 - 0.78 *D*	134
			(5.92)	(6.23)	(4.77)	(5.04)	(3.48)	(5.78)	(4.89)	(4.01)	(5.17)	[0.81]	
		EPR	47.62	55.32	43.59	42.86	34.78	44.44	40.00	42.31	44.67		
		BHR	41.78	28.28	29.89	28.24	29.91	21.64	22.36	18.23	25.30	*Yi* = 71.18 - 1.26* *D*	128
			(6.57)	(4.62)	(4.88)	(4.76)	(5.33)	(4.38)	(4.66)	(3.82)	(4.72)	[2.10]	
		EPR	30.00	43.24	50.00	47.62	66.67	38.82	36.84	36.54	42.67		
12.	Footwear	EJB	9.91	10.07	7.65	7.59	5.38	7.42	5.98	5.73	7.60	*Yi* = 27.76 - 0.66* *D*	103
			(1.00)	(0.97)	(0.77)	(0.84)	(0.56)	(0.76)	(0.70)	(0.62)	(0.78)	[1.98]	
		EPR	38.09	36.17	32.05	42.86	30.43	36.51	31.43	34.62	34.33		
		BHR	4.13	1.39	1.96	1.54	1.45	1.50	0.62	0.95	1.55	*Yi* = 10.04 - 0.25 *D*	59
			(0.65)	(0.23)	(0.32)	(0.26)	(0.26)	(0.30)	(0.13)	(0.20)	(0.29)	[1.70]	
		EPR	30.77	16.22	34.62	19.05	33.33	17.65	7.89	17.31	19.67		
13.	Education	EJB	11.94	7.23	9.64	10.21	11.74	9.30	7.16	8.80	9.16	*Yi* = 18.76 - 0.06 *D*	143
			(1.20)	(0.70)	(0.97)	(1.13)	(1.23)	(0.96)	(0.84)	(0.95)	(0.94)	[0.19]	
		EPR	66.67	48.94	43.59	57.14	52.17	46.03	42.86	46.15	47.67		
		BHR	5.30	2.18	0.28	3.22	2.80	0.92	0.85	0.84	1.63	*Yi* = 13.43 - 0.40* *D*	49
			(0.83)	(0.36)	(0.05)	(0.54)	(0.50)	(0.19)	(0.18)	(0.18)	(0.30)	[2.70]	
		EPR	34.62	21.62	7.69	23.81	26.67	11.76	13.16	11.54	16.33		
14.	Conveyance and Conveyance Services	EJB	8.71	11.07	8.86	7.15	11.03	9.18	6.19	5.67	8.80	*Yi* = 23.47 - 0.34* *D*	128
			(0.38)	(1.07)	(0.89)	(0.79)	(1.16)	(0.94)	(0.72)	(0.61)	(0.91)	[2.30]	
		EPR	38.10	44.68	43.59	42.86	60.87	42.86	37.14	30.77	42.67		
		BHR	2.60	1.74	2.58	1.16	2.80	1.52	1.30	1.01	1.66	*Yi* = 8.14 - 0.10*D*	69
			(0.14)	(0.28)	(0.42)	(0.19)	(0.50)	(0.31)	(0.27)	(0.21)	(0.31)	[1.76]	
		EPR	30.77	24.32	30.77	14.29	40.00	23.53	18.42	15.38	23.00		

Contd.

TABLE 8.2 *Contd.*

1	2	3	4	5	6	7	8	9	10	11	12	13	14
15.	Medicine and Health	PJB	37.19	27.11	22.57	24.79	26.10	23.30	20.11	18.86	24.15	*Yi* = 46.20 - 0.99* *D*	192
			(3.74)	(2.60)	(2.27)	(2.73)	(2.74)	(2.39)	(2.36)	(2.04)	(2.49)	[4.56]	
		PPR	80.95	55.32	58.97	85.71	78.26	65.08	65.71	57.69	64.00		
		BHR	11.34	8.76	8.05	7.45	7.16	6.49	5.31	5.71	7.14	*Yi* = 19.31 - 0.17** *D*	121
			(1.78)	(1.43)	(1.32)	(1.26)	(1.28)	(1.31)	(1.10)	(1.20)	(1.33)	[1.83]	
		PPR	53.85	45.95	46.15	47.62	46.67	36.47	34.21	32.69	40.33		
16.	Consumer Durables	PJB	17.12	11.50	12.40	18.18	29.09	11.14	10.51	5.04	12.88	*Yi* = 60.87 - 0.06 *D*	63
			(1.72)	(1.11)	(1.25)	(2.00)	(3.05)	(1.14)	(1.23)	(0.54)	(1.33)	[0.05]	
		PPR	28.57	19.15	23.08	42.86	30.43	15.87	17.14	15.38	21.00		
		BHR	3.67	1.76	3.66	0.99	1.37	1.80	1.16	0.99	1.82	*Yi* = 9.86 - 0.17 *D*	65
			(0.58)	(0.29)	(0.60)	(0.17)	(0.24)	(0.36)	(0.24)	(0.21)	(0.34)	[0.92]	
		PPR	38.46	24.32	23.08	23.80	26.67	21.18	15.79	13.46	21.67		
17.	Miscellaneous Goods and Services	PJB	30.20	31.73	28.95	19.17	25.32	26.72	23.75	23.58	27.43	*Yi* = 31.74 - 0.51* *D*	300
			(30.4)	(3.06)	(2.91)	(2.11)	(2.65)	(2.74)	(2.78)	(2.55)	(2.83)	[2.33]	
		PPR	100.00	100.00	100.00	100.00	100.00	100.00	100.00	100.00	100.00		
		BHR	7.81	8.10	9.73	8.10	9.39	7.84	5.17	5.68	7.42	*Yi* = 12.11 - 0.14* *D*	206
			(1.23)	(1.32)	(1.59)	(1.36)	(1.67)	(1.59)	(1.08)	(1.19)	(1.38)	[2.33]	
		PPR	73.08	72.97	76.92	71.43	80.00	70.59	55.26	61.54	68.67		
18.	Total Non-FooD Items	PJB	222.93	216.21	187.65	176.28	190.12	193.40	162.50	153.52	189.83	*Yi* = 217.66 - 3.26* *D*	300
			(22.43)	(20.84)	(18.89)	(19.44)	(19.93)	(19.83)	(19.03)	(16.59)	(19.58)	[2.48]	
		PPR	100.00	100.00	100.00	100.00	100.00	100.00	100.00	100.00	100.00		
		BHR	100.43	75.48	79.91	73.72	75.48	62.72	57.45	53.46	68.19	*Yi* = 89.87 - 2.16* *D*	300
			(15.79)	(12.33)	(13.06)	(12.42)	(13.46)	(12.69)	(11.97)	(11.22)	(12.71)	[4.99]	
		PPR	100.00	100.00	100.00	100.00	100.00	100.00	100.00	100.00	100.00		

Contd.

TABLE 8.2 *Contd.*

1	2	3	4	5	6	7	8	9	10	11	12	13	14
19.	Marriage and Social Ceremonies	PJB	98.38	94.68	89.06	54.90	78.65	84.02	14.41	78.20	78.29	*Yi* = 201.83 - 3.61*D*	136
			(9.90)	(9.12)	(8.97)	(6.05)	(8.25)	(8.61)	(1.69)	(8.45)	(8.08)	[0.72]	
		PPR	52.38	51.06	48.72	71.43	34.78	39.68	34.29	50.00	45.33		
		BHR	52.33	75.24	68.73	72.60	59.23	33.27	47.67	45.13	51.10	*Yi* = 116.66 - 1.38*D*	149
			(8.23)	(12.29)	(11.23)	(12.23)	(10.56)	(6.73)	(9.93)	(9.48)	(9.52)	[0.89]	
		PPR	53.85	67.57	53.85	52.38	46.67	38.82	55.26	44.23	49.33		
20.	Total Yearly Expenditure	PJB	993.86	1037.70	993.29	906.97	953.88	975.50	853.79	925.51	969.37	*Yi* = 1040.98 - 8.40* *D*	300
			100.00	100.00	100.00	100.00	100.00	100.00	100.00	100.00	100.00	[2.06]	
		BHR	636.10	612.03	611.82	593.45	560.77	494.37	480.03	476.26	536.64	*Yi* = 642.78 - 10.60* *D*	300
			100.00	100.00	100.00	100.00	100.00	100.00	100.00	100.00	100.00	[6.23]	
21.	Per Capita Monthly Expenditure (at 1980-81 prices)	PJB	82.82	86.48	82.77	75.58	79.49	81.29	71.15	77.13	80.78		
		BHR	52.01	51.00	50.99	49.45	46.73	41.20	40.00	39.69	44.72		
22.	Per Capita Monthly Income (at 1980-81 prices)	PJB	95.89	104.49	100.41	97.82	91.65	95.02	77.74	84.93	95.04		
		BHR	51.76	57.09	54.64	45.06	47.88	37.64	35.12	36.81	43.21		

Figures in [ ] under column 13 are the respective 't' values.

Note: * denotes significance of 't' values at 0.05 level.

** denotes significance of 't' values at 0.10 level.

Bihar in sharp contrast to only 31.0 per cent in Punjab. The Punjab households are obviously 'adequately' fed as far as items for basic human existence are concerned; their Bihar brethren have still to earmark more than half of their total expenditure on assuring sheer existence to themselves.

It is also evident from Table 8.2 that irrespective of distance from the focal town, the relative shares of different commodity groups mentioned above register more or less a similar pattern in both the States. It is interesting to note that with the exception of cereals, gram and pulses and salt and spices, the percentage shares of all other commodity groups in the total per capita expenditure, are higher for Punjab households compared with Bihar households in villages near as well as away from the focal town. Further, while the percentage share of cereals increases with increase in rural-urban distance from the focal town in the two States, the shares of meat, eggs, and fish, vegetables and fruits, etc. tend to display a declining pattern. This may be considered as an indicator of slightly more nutritious food enjoyed by households in nearby villages on account of the more pronounced impact of urbanisation on the one hand, and relatively higher income levels, on the other.

Among the non-food items, clothing and bedding, fuel and light, miscellaneous goods and services (cinema and other amusements, sundry articles such as soap etc., barber charges, cosmetics, tax paid on consumer durables), medicine and health account for a major proportion (nearly 16.0 per cent in Punjab and 11.00 per cent in Bihar) of the total per capita annual consumption expenditure. Also, since the respective percentage figures for such items are relatively higher in Punjab villages than those in the corresponding Bihar villages, it reflects improved living standards for the former. Put in another way, it shows that Punjab households being relatively free of the worry to arrange a square meal, are bringing in more and more of non-food items; in particular, allocation of higher proportions of expenditure to items such as clothing and bedding, medicine and health, fuel and light, etc. by Punjab households compared with those in Bihar, signifies the consumption reorientations ushered in by the expanding levels of households incomes in Punjab. The desperate picture of Bihar households, as far as important components of non-food items are concerned, stands out more starkly if indeed we look at the abysmally low per capita figures for most of the items (Table 8.2).

In brief, it is clear that the absolute level of per capita expenditure on all items of consumption is fairly higher for the rural labour households of Punjab compared with those of Bihar, in the overall sense as also in each pairwise comparison among the villages of the two States. In particular, the consumption basket in Bihar reveals a more pronounced cereal orientation and thus inferior in content while the same in Punjab reveals a relatively more diversified combination with a rising stress on non-food items. Nevertheless, more or less, the same set of priorities are observed in both the areas. In this sense, consumption habits do not seem to have led to drastic inter-commodity substitutions; a big component of expenditure goes to food; in the food basket cereals and other items are consumed according to a more or less fixed degree of necessity; nearly all non-food items occur in the consumption basket of both the States, again in the same order of importance. The most crucial feature is wide variation in the actual level of consumption between the two areas.

Cash Component of Expenditure

It has been brought out in a quite a number of studies[7] that consumption ties play a very crucial role in determining the employer-employee relationship in certain parts of Indian agriculture for the type of households we are dealing with. It implies that besides market purchases, such households are heavily dependent on their respective employers for meeting their consumption requirements in more than one way. For instance, even though cultivation of owned or leased-in tiny pieces of land also contributes, to some extent, in their total consumption basket, yet it is the wages received in kind for operations such as wheat and paddy harvesting, other perquisites (meals, tea, etc.) shared by the working members from employer's kitchen and above all the cultivation of wage-received land by the attached farm servants in Bihar, which constitute a very significant proportion of total consumption expenditure of such households. Moreover, the practice of contracting occasional consumption loans (both cash and kind), from the employer-farmer, is another method for creating and sustaining dependence of such households on their concerned employers.

In view of the facts mentioned above, it is, important to examine the ratio of two components of consumption (cash and the other reflecting dependence on the employer). Such an exercise is also expected to be useful in knowing, if the cash component of expenditure reveals any distinct pattern between Punjab and Bihar in terms of distance form the focal town. For this purpose, we have estimated the percentage of cash component out of the total expenditure made on the individual items of consumption. In this regard, Table 8.3 provides the following meaningful information.

First, for items such as salt and spices and processed food (including beverages, *pan*, tobacco and other intoxicants, etc.) among the food items, and education, conveyance and conveyance services, medicine and health, miscellaneous goods and services, consumer durables among the non-food items as also on marriage and other social ceremonies, the entire expenditure is in cash, both in Punjab and Bihar. Secondly, on commodities such as gur and sugar, edible oils, vegetables and fruits, meat, eggs and fish, gram and pulses among the food items and clothing and bedding, footwear, etc., among the non-food items, cash expenditure makes up a very high proportion of total expenditure incurred on them, both in Punjab and Bihar.

However, such broad similarities notwithstanding, there are some important differences between Punjab and Bihar. For instance, at the aggregate level, the proportion of cash component in the total consumption expenditure of the rural labour households is higher in Punjab (nearly 66.0%) against about 48.0 per cent in Bihar. Again the share of market purchases for all food-times is nearly 57.0 per cent in Punjab against only 39.0 per cent in Bihar. Similarly, approximately 45.0 per cent of cereal requirements in Punjab and just 26.0 per cent in Bihar are met through market purchases. In other words, roughly 55.0 per cent of the cereal requirements in Punjab and nearly 74.0 per cent in Bihar are met largely from employers coffers through wages in kind and other perquisites received by working members and petty consumption loans obtained from employers. Viewed in this sense, our study shows that consumption ties between employer-employee relations are relatively stronger in Bihar than in Punjab where wage payment in cash has emerged on a wide scale after the onset of the Green Revolution, especially after rice cultivation started on a big scale in early 1970s. Moreover in most other items of consumption, share of cash component in the total expenditure is higher in Punjab than in Bihar. In this context, two important points emerge from our analysis. The

TABLE 8.3: Cash Expenditure as Percentage of Total Expenditure on an Item in Punjab and Bihar.

Sl. No.	Item	State	Village								All House-holds
			V1	V2	V3	V4	V5	V6	V7	V8	
1	2	3	4	5	6	7	8	9	10	11	12
1.	Cereals and Cereal Products	PJB	61.03	61.01	46.40	37.46	39.41	42.83	37.32	32.33	45.14
		BHR	35.71	49.55	21.59	12.82	17.31	28.51	17.67	14.80	25.90
2.	Gram and Pulses	PJB	77.05	71.26	68.55	62.11	66.52	63.85	59.89	56.32	65.64
		BHR	64.39	68.68	51.56	38.84	42.65	68.56	58.44	59.03	60.39
3.	Edible Oils	PJB	78.86	71.38	69.24	60.65	66.62	64.24	58.57	56.81	66.41
		BHR	79.60	81.34	66.21	71.85	66.29	80.43	81.29	86.23	78.65
4.	Milk and Milk Products	PJB	37.27	39.77	21.16	14.08	13.69	33.57	33.71	30.16	28.60
		BHR	35.33	12.61	0.00	13.32	0.00	11.86	12.73	0.00	12.56
5.	Meat, Eggs and Fish	PJB	100.00	100.00	81.50	n.r.	59.68	81.24	88.05	100.00	88.53
		BHR	68.95	75.10	0.00	100.00	45.09	58.15	30.88	0.00	54.82
6.	Vegetables, Fruits, etc.	PJB	73.38	66.54	70.41	60.55	68.19	64.74	57.86	56.27	66.11
		BHR	82.31	85.59	66.48	69.73	70.88	80.23	80.68	82.37	79.23
7.	*Gur* and Sugar	PJB	94.60	100.00	95.02	100.00	91.77	98.22	100.00	93.44	96.73
		BHR	78.00	82.23	59.77	74.28	77.49	81.14	76.67	85.50	77.73
8.	Salt and Spices	PJB	100.00	100.00	100.00	100.00	100.00	100.00	100.00	100.00	100.00
		BHR	100.00	100.00	100.00	100.00	100.00	100.00	100.00	100.00	100.00
9.	Processed Food, Beverages, *Pan*, Tobacco, etc.	PJB	100.00	100.00	100.00	100.00	100.00	100.00	100.00	100.00	100.00
		BHR	100.00	100.00	100.00	100.00	100.00	100.00	100.00	100.00	100.00
A.	All Food-items	PJB	68.89	68.46	56.76	48.78	50.07	56.26	52.10	48.01	57.24
		BHR	48.78	56.19	33.77	26.20	28.29	41.71	32.93	30.28	38.98
10.	Fuel and Light	PJB	45.76	55.36	44.41	38.57	22.39	40.33	37.39	27.70	41.21
		BHR	48.74	41.09	39.44	33.59	28.11	37.48	34.81	32.89	37.36

Contd.

TABLE 8.3 *Contd.*

1	2	3	4	5	6	7	8	9	10	11	12
11.	Clothing and Bedding	PJB	100.00	100.00	98.57	100.00	100.00	98.37	99.25	99.15	99.21
		BHR	99.31	97.06	94.85	98.10	95.35	98.86	100.00	98.32	97.99
12.	Footwear	PJB	100.00	100.00	98.42	100.00	100.00	97.56	98.03	98.36	98.86
		BHR	98.36	95.30	77.07	89.25	70.62	95.87	100.00	92.85	92.42
13.	Education	PJB	100.00	100.00	100.00	100.00	100.00	100.00	100.00	100.00	100.00
		BHR	100.00	100.00	100.00	100.00	100.00	100.00	100.00	100.00	100.00
14.	Conveyance and Conveyance Services	PJB	100.00	100.00	100.00	100.00	100.00	100.00	100.00	100.00	100.00
		BHR	100.00	100.00	100.00	100.00	100.00	100.00	100.00	100.00	100.00
15.	Medicine and Health	PJB	100.00	100.00	100.00	100.00	100.00	100.00	100.00	100.00	100.00
		BHR	100.00	100.00	100.00	100.00	100.00	100.00	100.00	100.00	100.00
16.	Consumer Durables	PJB	100.00	100.00	100.00	100.00	100.00	100.00	100.00	100.00	100.00
		BHR	100.00	100.00	100.00	100.00	100.00	100.00	100.00	100.00	100.00
17.	Miscellaneous Goods and Services	PJB	100.00	100.00	100.00	100.00	100.00	100.00	100.00	100.00	100.00
		BHR	100.00	100.00	100.00	100.00	100.00	100.00	100.00	100.00	100.00
B.	All Non-food items	PJB	88.56	89.21	84.04	85.86	80.99	83.80	81.71	78.52	84.42
		BHR	88.38	82.08	80.03	79.92	78.86	78.79	77.03	75.24	80.01
C.	Total Food + Non-fooD items	PJB	73.82	73.11	62.09	56.46	56.70	61.99	57.68	53.68	62.87
		BHR	56.02	60.10	40.50	34.34	36.22	46.70	38.77	36.06	44.88
D.	Marriage and Social Ceremonies	PJB	100.00	100.00	100.00	100.00	100.00	100.00	100.00	100.00	100.00
		BHR	100.00	100.00	100.00	100.00	100.00	100.00	100.00	100.00	100.00
E.	Total HouseholD Expenditure	PJB	76.00	75.48	65.61	59.72	60.50	65.76	58.43	58.02	65.98
		BHR	59.46	64.72	46.61	41.34	42.03	49.93	44.67	41.70	48.16

Note: (i) PJB : Punjab
(ii) BHR : Bihar
(iii) n.r. : Expenditure not reported by any sample household.

Punjab labour households owing to their greater dependence on market purchases, are comparatively more prone to inflationary pressures than their counterparts in Bihar. On the other hand, it is fairly evident that the employment of agricultural labour in Bihar is very highly on kind-wage basis; on cereals, only about 26.0 per cent of cash expenditure is involved. It follows that the employer-employee relations in Bihar are much different than in Punjab; informal contracts including consumption ties seem to prevail in large measure in Bihar. The exploitative nature of such ties follows as a consequence. There is perhaps some truth in what is generally believed about employment-credit-consumption interlockings prevailing in the semi-feudal agrarian structure of Bihar.

If a comparison is made between the consumption pattern of Punjab and Bihar labour households in terms of distance from the focal town, we observe that cash component as proportion of total expenditure tends to decline from about 76.0 per cent to nearly 58.0 per cent in Punjab and from nearly 59.0 per cent to about 42.0 per cent in Bihar as we move away from the focal town. Again, in the case of all food-items, the proportion of cash expenditure declines from nearly 69.0 per cent to about 48.0 per cent in Punjab, and from about 49.0 per cent to about 30.0 per cent in Bihar. Similarly, the share of cash expenditure on cereals declines from approximately 61.0 per cent to about 32.0 per cent in Punjab and from nearly 36.0 per cent to just 15.0 per cent in Bihar from a village located in the immediate vicinity of the focal town to the extremely remote village. Even in other food and non-food items, the shares of cash component are higher in villages near the town compared to those located away from it. This is true both in Punjab and Bihar. Finally, if a village-to-village comparison is made between Punjab and Bihar, we observe that the cash component of total household expenditure as also of all food-items and cereals is much higher in Punjab than in Bihar. It is equally true in the case of non-food items as well. Such findings lend further substance to our contention that Punjab households although enjoying a uniformly higher per capita consumption practically for each commodity, yet are more prone to inflationary pressures *vis-a-vis* their counterparts in Bihar, and, that the latter are depending, to a very large extent, on wages in kind for running their kitchen. Whatever exploitative contents of wages in kind can be visualized for an agrarian economy characterised by semi-feudal land relations, are presumably operating in Bihar. The dependence on kind-wages tends to increase as we move away from the urban focal town; in the last village of Bihar (approximately 18 km away from Buxar), only 15.0 per cent cash expenditure is involved on cereal consumption. It can perhaps be concluded that the 'ills' of wages in kind, whatever be their nature, operate more intensively in the villages in the interior of the countryside in Bihar.

Distribution of Consumption Expenditure

In the preceding section, we have observed that the absolute level of per capita consumption expenditure of an average household in Punjab is significantly higher than that of its counterpart in Bihar. Since variations in consumption may exist among the sample households, both within Punjab and Bihar, it may be useful to analyse the distribution of consumption expenditure among the various strata of sample households. For this objective, the households have been arranged into decile groups, in ascending order of their net household income.[8] The percentage share of each decile in the total as well as individual commodity expenditure has been worked out. This rearrangement has been done to facilitate comparison between the employment-income-consumption nexus of the labour households in the two States.

Table 8.4 shows that the total consumption expenditure is unevenly distributed among the various decile groups. For example, the bottom-most decile has only 7.0 per cent share of consumption expenditure in Punjab and a little more than 6.0 per cent in Bihar. On the other extreme, the top-most decile has nearly 17.0 per cent share both in Punjab and Bihar. Although in terms of decile-wise shares or the value of Gini-ratio, the distribution of total consumption expenditure is strikingly similar in both the States, yet in absolute terms, each decile of Punjab is much better off than its counterpart in Bihar. For example, a 10.0 per cent share for a decile group in Punjab is quantitatively much superior to a 10.0 per cent share in Bihar. The only good point of Table 8.4 is that in the distribution of a much smaller consumption expenditure, the Bihar situation observes the same pattern as in Punjab.

The commoditywise distribution of consumption expenditure reveals a few further insights (Appendix Table A-8.1). For example, the Gini-ratios for cereals, gram and pulses, edible oils, salt and spices, all food items, fuel and light, etc. are extremely low in both the study areas and it can be maintained that the distribution for these commodity groups has practically no skewness. Then Bihar reveals a slightly more skewed distributional pattern as regards expenditure on milk and milk products, meat, eggs and fish, vegetables aand fruits, gur and sugar and processed food among the food items, and medicine and health, consumer durables, etc. among the non-food items. Bihar's skewness in the case of milk and milk products needs to be underlined in particular. The unevenness in the distribution of expenditure on marriage and social ceremonies is relatively more pronounced in the case of Punjab compared with Bihar. This suggests that those among the rural labour households of Punjab which are relatively better off would like to spend relatively more on these items, at least for its demonstrative effect and status value. Such 'luxury' expenditure are incurred by Bihar households as well, but on a much lower scale; perhaps more balanced on proportionate basis. Hence, the Gini-ratio is smaller for Bihar compared with that for Punjab. Lastly, in the consumption of nutritious items such as milk and milk products on the food side, and, footwear on the non-food side, as also in marriage and other social ceremonies, the poorest among the rural labour households of Bihar are either totally bereft of these items or account for only an insignificant proportion.

TABLE 8.4: Distribution of Total Consumption Expenditure in Punjab and Bihar

Sl. No.	Percentage of Households	Percentage of Consumption	
		Punjab	Bihar
1	2	3	4
1	10.00	6.91	6.32
2	20.00	14.28	13.82
3	30.00	21.74	21.48
4	40.00	29.35	29.29
5	50.00	38.14	37.79
6	60.00	47.57	47.44
7	70.00	57.92	58.35
8	80.00	69.41	70.60
9	90.00	83.30	83.53
10	100.00	100.00	100.00
Consumption Concentration ratio or Gini-Co-efficient.		0.163	0.163

Expenditure Elasticities[9]

Table 8.5 gives commoditywise expenditure elasticity '*e*' and other related estimates. For a number of commodity groups, the same functional form fits well both for Punjab and Bihar, although, as is expected, the values of elasticity differ strikingly between the two areas. If may be noted in passing that in Bihar none of the functional forms gives acceptable fits on the basis of standard statistical criteria in respect of commodity groups such as milk and milk products, gur and sugar, conveyance and conveyance services, consumer durables and miscellaneous non-food items.

Some broad features are as follows. First, for all food-items, expenditure, elasticity is fairly high in both the States. However, if a detailed examination is made of expenditure elasticities for different food items, there are some important differences between the two States. For example, expenditure elasticities for cereals, meat, eggs and fish, vegetables and fruits, and processed food and beverages, (including pan, tobacco and other intoxicants) are much higher in Punjab than in Bihar. The reverse is true in the case of gram and pulses. The higher expenditure elasticities for Punjab households *vis-a-vis* those of their counterparts in Bihar in most food-items but lower in gram and pulses clearly convey that consumption-basket of the former is qualitatively far superior compared with the latter. The low expenditure elasticity in the case of gram and pulses for Punjab households than that of their counterparts in Bihar can be attributed to its substitution by more nutritious commodity namely vegetables and fruits, which has been made possible due to higher earning levels in Punjab.

Second, for non-food items as a whole, expenditure elasticity is much higher in Punjab compared with that in Bihar. The same is true in the case of other non-food items such as fuel and light, clothing and bedding, footwear and medicine and health. This shows that Punjab labour households maintain an edge over their counterparts in Bihar as regards non-food items as well.

Third, the expenditure elasticity for marriage and social ceremonies is fairly high and greater than unity in both the areas. However, Bihar figure is higher than that of Punjab. It is due to the fact that expenditure on this term is governed by social taboos than by per capita total expenditure.

TABLE 8.5: Plausible Engel Functions in Punjab and Bihar

Sl. No.	Commodity Group	Punjab			Bihar		
		Functional Form	Exp.Elasticity(e)	$R^2/\bar{R}^{-2}$	Functional Form	Exp.Elasticity(e)	$R^2/\bar{R}^{-2}$
1.	Cereals and Cereal Products	2	0.782	0.985	2	0.618	0.990
2.	Gram and Pulses	7	0.617	0.927	7	0.697	0.884
3.	Edible Oils	5	0.371	0.992	5	0.312	0.890
4.	Milk and Milk Products	4	1.288	0.780	—	—	—
5.	Meat, Eggs and Fish	1	1.954	0.891	5	0.787	0.432
6.	Vegetables, Fruits, etc.	2	0.955	0.927	5	0.465	0.599
7.	*Gur* and Sugar	7	0.507	0.902	—	—	—
8.	Salt and Spices	5	0.333	0.939	5	0.293	0.900
9.	Processed food, Beverages, *Pan*, Tobacco, etc.	3	0.904	0.806	5	0.318	0.439
A.	All Food-items	2	0.781	0.987	2	0.757	0.983
10.	Fuel and Light	7	0.486	0.870	7	0.199	0.831
11.	Clothing and Bedding	3	2.065	0.824	3	1.848	0.868
12.	Footwear	5	1.279	0.778	5	0.516	0.246
13.	Conveyance & Conveyance Services	5	0.584	0.690	—	—	—
14.	Medicine and Health	3	0.692	0.545	3	0.554	0.247
15.	Consumer Durables	5	0.923	0.738	—	—	—
16.	Miscellaneous Non-food items	1	0.832	0.776	—	—	—
17.	Marriage and Social Ceremonies	5	1.609	0.888	5	1.928	0.950
B.	All Non-fooD items	2	1.384	0.955	5	0.448	0.900

Functional Form :

1. Linear 2. Quadratic 3. Hyperbolic 4. Semi-log 5. Log-inverse 7. Log-linear R^2 = Co efficient of Determination. $\bar{R}^{-2}$ = Adjusted Co-efficient of Determination

The preceding analysis shows that there are significant differences between the consumption pattern of Punjab and Bihar labour households. Not only that Punjab households are enjoying a higher level of living compared with their counterparts in Bihar, but also their propensity to spend out of every incremental income is higher than that of the latter.

NOTES

1. Some outstanding earlier contributions in the field of family-budget studies are by R.G.D. Allen and A.L. Bowley (1935); *Family Expenditures: A Study of its Variations,* London; Henry Schultz (1938); *Theory and Measurement of Demand,* University of Chicago Press, Chicago (1972 edn); H. Wold and L. Jureen (1953); *Demand Analysis : A Study in Econometrics,* John Wiley and Sons Inc. New York; H.S. Houthakker (1953); "Compensated Changes in Quantities and Qualities Consumed" *Review of Economic Studies,* Vol. XIX (3), No. 5, pp. 55-64; ———— and S.J. Prais (1955); *An Analysis of Family Budgets,* Cambridge University Press, Cambridge; Richard Stone (1954); *The Measurement of Consumer Expenditure and Behaviour in the United Kingdom. 1920-38,* Cambridge University Press, Cambridge, Vol. I; and Stigler, G.J. (1954); "The Early History of Empirical Studies on Consumption Behaviour in the United Kingdom 1920-38" *Journal of Political Economy,* Vol. LXII, No. 2, April, pp. 95-113.
2. Some of these reports are: *Agricultural Labour Enquiry Reports,. All Indian Rural Credit Survey, Enquires into the Family Budgets of Middle Class Employees of the Central Government and Various reports published by N.S.S.O.*
3. See for example, Ravi Verma (1959); "Income Elasticity of Demand for Foodgrains: A Regional Approach", *Artha Vijnana,* Vol. I, No. 4, pp. 271-281; S.N. Baldota (1964); "Bias in Income Elasticity Estimates Derived from Expenditure per Family Data—A Note", *Arthan Vijnana,* Vol. 6, No. 1 pp. 37-43; N. Sreenivasa, Iyengar (1967); "Some Estimates of Engel Elasticities Based on N.S.S. Data", *Journal of Royal Statistical Society,* Series A (General), Vol. 130, pp. 84-97; Balvir Singh (1968); *Consumption Functions in India,* Ph.D. Thesis (Unpublished) University of Delhi; Devendra B. Gupta (1963); *Consumption Patterns in India — A Study of Inter — Regional Variations,* Tata McGraw Hill Publishing Co., Bombay, New Delhi; R. Radha Krishna (1977); "Approximate Determination of Indifference Surface from Family Budget Data", *Artha Vijnana,* Vol. XIX, No. 3, pp. 247-258; and B.M. Mahajan and H. Mahajan (1981); "Effects of Grouping of Observations on Co-efficient of Determination in Engel Curve Analysis", *Artha Vijnana,* Vol. XXIII, No. 4, pp. 352-365.
4. For example, Indian Statistical Institute (I.S.I.), Calcutta has published a magnificent collection of papers on the subject by its research workers. Similarly, National Council of Applied Economic Research (N.C.A.E.R.), New Delhi has also published a very important document entitled, *"Long Term*

Projections of Demand and Supply of Selected Agricultural Commodities, 1960-61 to 1975-76".

5. In Particular, mention may be made of the following: *Anvesak, Artha Vijnana, Econometrica, Indian Economic Journal, Economic and Political Weekly,* and *Journal of Royal Statistical Society,* etc.
6. For a detailed meaningful discussion on the subject please see, Pradhan H. Prasad (1973); "Production Relations : Achilles' Heel of Indian Planning", *Economic and Political Weekly,* Vol. VIII, No. 19 Special Article, May 12, pp. 869-872; —— (1974); "Reactionary Role of Usurer's Capital in Rural India", *Economic and Political Weekly,* Vol. IX, Nos. 32-34, Special Number, August, pp. 1305-1308; and Amit Bhaduri (1973); "A Study in Agricultural Backwardness under Semi-Feudalism", *The Economic Journal,* Vol. 83, March, pp. 120-137.
7. Pradhan H. Prasad (1973 and 1974); *Ibid.* p. 870 and p. 1305 Amit Bhaduri (1973); *Ibid.,* p. 122.
8. Generally, in consumption studies, especially those based on N.S.S. data, total expenditure is used for classifying various strata of households primarily because total household income figures are not available. Since we have the advantage of knowing income figures, we prefer to evolve decile groups with income rather than expenditure levels.
9. Procedural details for the estimation of expenditure elasticities are given in Chapter 3.

9

CONCLUSION AND POLICY RECOMMENDATIONS

The nuances of the recent Indian growth experience suggest that Indian agriculture has experienced highly impressive advances with the onset of the Green Revolution since the mid-sixties. These nuances further reveal that under the impact of the new farm technology, the socio-economic scene in the countryside has undergone formidable changes. A striking feature of our above-mentioned growth experience has, however, been its differential character, presumably because depending upon factor endowments, institutional set-up and infrastructural facilities, the new farm technology has been shared unevenly in different areas. Marked differences are also discernible with respect to its labour absorptive capacity[1] across different regions. Consequently, the socio-economic transformation which has occurred in the countryside in the wake of the Green Revolution represents two contrasting situations. While areas such as Punjab and Haryana seem to have experienced a profound impact of the dynamics of rural transformation; those like Bihar, Orissa and Madhya Pradesh, seem to have had only a limited impact.

To put the record straight, different views are prevalent among the scholars regarding the percolation effect of the economic growth in general and that of agricultural transformation in particular as witnessed in the Indian countryside since the mid-sixties. Some scholars are of the view that the gains of recent economic modernisation as brought about by the rapid agricultural growth in the wake of the Green Revolution, have tended to trickle-down to the rural poor. There are others who have argued the other way round and have squarely blamed it for the growing immiserization of the working class.

The main objective of the present study has been to understand the dynamics of rural transformation by examining, in depth, the changing structure of employment and the corresponding levels of income and consumption standards of the rural labour households in two contrasting growth scenarios of Punjab and Bihar. It would help us to ascertain the economic base of the two States of the Indian union which have experienced contrasting growth in the matter of their respective agricultural development. The said objective is sought to be achieved by analysing the detailed and comprehensive household level data gathered from 300 sample households in 8 unidirectionally located villages from the designated focal towns (i.e. Khanna in the case of district Ludhiana of Punjab and Buxar in the case of district Bhojpur of Bihar) in each of the two States and another 150 migrant agricultural labourers in the sample villages of the former. The data pertain to the agricultural year 1980-81.

The methodology used in the present study has been devised to seek empirical answers to various questions as have been outlined in the preface of this study. To meet the various objectives of the study as highlighted in Chapter 1, the quantitative as well as qualitative differences regarding the employment-income-consumption nexus of the rural labour households in the two States have been examined through arithmetic averages, percentages and simple regressions. The empirical findings of the study hover around the various estimated coefficients.

Our study throws up a number of interesting conclusions regarding the household economy of the labour households in the two areas characterised by similarity and contrast. Some such conclusions which offer many useful insights into the issues under consideration are:

To being with, our results reveal that agriculture and allied activities continue to be the mainstay for a majority of the rural labour households both in Punjab and Bihar. Despite this similarity, one cannot, however, obliterate the fact that the Punjab model of economic transformation has made a splendid contribution in establishing the hegemony of its rural labour households in all correlates of overall employment/earnings over their counterparts in Bihar. Little wonder, therefore, that the total yearly employment/earnings in Punjab are not only structurally more diversed, but also are more remunerative than in Bihar.

An important conclusion that emerges from our findings is that sheer labour effort does not matter much in the modern system of agricultural production; the level of technology-in-use, coupled with the effective functioning of the rural institutions have their own role to play in augmenting or/and diversifying employment/earning opportunities for the rural labour households. It is borne out by the fact that employment/earnings through dairying and poultry activities has emerged to be a much more lucrative proposition for the rural labour households in Punjab (roughly 25.0 per cent share in total on-farm employment and earnings) than for those of Bihar (just 13.0 per cent of total on farm employment and only 5.0 per cent of total on-farm earnings). Thus, there is every reason to believe that by mollifying the severity of overall income distribution in rural Punjab, employment and earnings through such activities have tended to diversify and strengthen the household economy of the rural labour households to a far greater extent in Punjab, compared with those in rural Bihar.

Another significant development which draws our special attention with respect to Punjab model of economic transformation is that a stable and consistently growing commercial agriculture in the State has been capable of generating many new and expanding avenues of non-farm employment and incomes for the economically weaker sections of the rural society. Such non-farm avenues of employment and earnings have opened up for the rural labour households both in the rural as well as in the nearby urban and semi-urban industrial centres mainly because the agricultural sector in its own growth process has tended to forge and strengthen many demand and supply inter-sectoral linkages. It is worthwhile to point out here that these inter-sectoral linkages have mainly emerged in the wake of the Green Revolution in the State and have been largely facilitated by a widespread network of village link roads. Consequently, non-farm urban wage employment has played a decisive role in offering over 4 times more remunerative employment in the State of Punjab compared with Bihar. Bihar, in fact, is too far behind in this regard.

As in the overall sense, we observe that the superiority of Punjab labour households over their counterparts in Bihar also gets reflected in an alternative way. For instance, in terms of distance from the urban focal town, an average labour household in Punjab at about 17 km is far better placed than the one in Bihar at a distance of 2 or 3 km in all manifestations of their respective household economics. Moreover, in each pair of nearly equally distanced Punjab and Bihar villages, there are marked differences in favour of Punjab households over their counterparts in Bihar. This shows that the strong economic base of rural Punjab, giving rise to higher wage paid rural non-farm employment together with expanding industrial and other economic activities in the urban areas, generates lots of wage-paid urban employment for its rural labour households. In sharp contrast, Bihar scenario reflects weakness both at the village level and in terms of extremely poor rural-urban linkages.

It is further interesting to observe that both in Punjab and Bihar, the rural labour households in general and agricultural labour households in particular are drifting away from attached jobs and attached obligations. To put it otherwise, the incidence of seeking employment on daily basis is very high in both the study areas. Many possible explanations can be advanced for the emergence of this phenomenon. Firstly, this is probably due to the fact that for economic considerations, rural labour households in Punjab want to keep their employment options open. Secondly, due to huge influx of migrant labour during the peak seasons in Punjab, the demand for attached farm servants has considerably declined. In Bihar, on the other hand such developments are rather conspicuous by their absence; in any case their degree is fairly low. In this connection, it is important to note that in Bihar, low labour demand in agriculture, coupled with increasing supply of labour owing to high population pressures, keeps the wage rate low. Consequently, in Bihar farmers prefer to employ labour in daily basis.

Punjab-Bihar differentials on the issues under consideration, thus, clearly signify what the growing agriculture of Punjab has brought to its rural labour households and what has yet to happen in the case of Bihar on any significant scale. Our findings on Punjab scenario are suggestive of the fact that a fast growing agriculture has bestowed many productive employment opportunities not only on those households which are largely dependent on wage-paid on-farm employment, but also on those which have a more diversed employment structure. Furthermore, farm employment is fairly competitive with non-farm employment in Punjab and those households which are primarily dependent on the former do not have to suffer an undue disadvantage. This remunerative aspects of Punjab agriculture assumes additional significance in view of the huge pace of farm mechanication as also the intervening effects of migrant labour which characterise the Punjab model of rural transformation.

A disaggregated analysis of the per capita net household income of the rural labour households in the two States reveals that according to the established norms, about 22.0 per cent of the rural labour households in the Punjab sample and nearly as high as 88.0 in the Bihar sample are subsisting below the poverty line. Furthermore, our results also indicate that the poor households in Punjab are far less poor as compared to those of Bihar. It is obvious from the fact that while all the poor households of Punjab in our sample would require roughly 22.0 per cent additional income to cross above the poverty line mark; in Bihar on the other hand, they need no less than 71.0 per cent for this purpose. Thus, the prevalence of widespread poverty among the rural labour households of Bihar and its low incidence in Punjab shows that while the Punjab model of economic transformation has helped the rural labour households in the State to benefit from the highly remunerative and gainful employment opportunities both in the on- and non-farm sectors; the Bihar model, in comparison, has thrown up acute economic destitution and poverty for a preponderant majority of its rural labour households. Our empirical findings, therefore, clearly maintain that the gains of rapid economic growth do indeed tend to trickle-down to all strata of the rural society provided growth is high and sustained as has been the case in Punjab. Thus, in contrast to a popular belief that agricultural growth leads to immiserization of the working class, our results clearly establish a positive association between the level of economic development and level of per capita income of even the lowliest among the rural labour households. In rural Bihar, on the other hand, enough growth does not seem to have taken place to filter down to those who constitute the lowest rung of social and economic hierarchy. The extremely grim situation in Bihar, in fact, poses a serious challenge to the policy makers to devise appropriate strategies to improve upon the sub-human existence of the rural labour households in that State.

Our study also brings out a number of interesting facts about the phenomenon of migrant labour in rural Punjab as witnessed in the wake of the Green Revolution. Firstly, it is essentially an economic phenomenon summarised by glaring wage differentials in areas of in-an out-migration. Secondly, the incidence of outmigration by farm labourers is much higher from areas of more backward agriculture in Bihar. Third, the share of migrant labour vis-a-vis the resident labour in Punjab in total yearly on-farm employment/earning tends to decline as we move away from the focal town into the interior of the countryside. This is probably due to the fact that has to face higher degree of competition from the resident labour mainly because the employment options for the latter become limited. Finally, and perhaps more importantly, although the presence of migrant labour in rural Punjab has tended to depress the money wage rates for the rural labour, yet there does not seem to be any cogent reason to believe that the migrant labour is being exploited or discriminated against, *inter alia*, as far as daily wage rates are concerned.

Some important differences are also noticeable regarding the consumption behaviour and the levels of living of the rural labour households in the two study areas. In this regard, less than unity a.p.c (average propensity to consume) of Punjab labour households compared with above unity for those of their counterparts in Bihar needs to be underlined, in particular. Our analysis of the a.p.c. in the two States clearly signifies the accrual of net savings in Punjab and the working of the unmistakable phenomenon of negative savings in Bihar. This implies two things. Firstly, the labour households in Punjab seem to be utilising these savings for productive as well as non-productive uses. Some such uses are the purchase of livestock and poultry, construction of residential dwellings, purchase of need and/or other status based assets such as radios, watches, bicycles, etc. and on demonstrative expenditure on marriage and other social ceremonies. Secondly and perhaps more importantly, being deficit households, the labour households in Bihar, are invariably obliged to undertaken petty consumption loans, which, in turn, might be responsible for keeping them under feudal and semi-feudal stranglehold. Such a view gains further empirical ground when we look at the cash component of consumption in the total expenditure on an item of consumption. For example, while labour households in Punjab purchase nearly two-thirds of their total consumption expenditure from the market, their counterparts in Bihar, spend a little less than one-half of their total households expenditure on market purchases. Further, while in Bihar, nearly three-fourths of their annual cereal requirements are met largely from employers' coffers through wages in kind and other perquisites received by working members and petty consumption loans obtained from employers; the corresponding figure in Punjab is roughly 55.0 per cent. It implies two things. Firstly, Punjab labour households, owing to their greater dependence on market purchases, are more prone to inflationary pressures than their counterparts in Bihar. Secondly and possibly more importantly, employer-employee relations are much more different in Punjab, compared with those in Bihar. Informal contracts including consumption ties thus seem to prevail in a large measure in Bihar than in Punjab. The natural fall out in Bihar is the presence of employment-credit-consumption interlockings with all their exploitative contents affecting the rural labour there.

Some interesting facts emerge from our data regarding the composition of the consumption basket of the Punjab and Bihar labour households. It is indeed a healthy development to note that not only the consumption basket of the rural labour households in Punjab is far superior than that of their counterparts in Bihar, but also the former seem to be bringing-in more and more items of nutritious food and other non-food items in their consumption basket compared with the latter. Relatively higher expenditure (about 27.0%), incurred by Punjab labour households on items such as vegetables and fruits, meat, fish, eggs, clothing, footwear, medicine and health and education against just 11.0 per cent by Bihar households on such items, is a clear demonstration of the evidence on consumption reorientations, which the expanding levels of household income have sought to usher-in in Punjab and their absence in Bihar.

Distribution of consumption expenditure in various deciles further establishes the supremacy of Punjab labour households over their counterparts in Bihar. While commodity groups such as cereals and cereal products, gram and pulses, edible oils, salt and spices, all food-items, fuel and light evince practically no skewness in either of the two States; slightly more skewed distributional pattern is discernible in Bihar in the case of numerous commodity groups such as milk and milk products, meat, fish, fruit and vegetables, gur and sugar, processed food, medicine and health and consumer durables. What is important to note here is that in the case of milk and milk products and footwear, the poorest among the rural labour households in Bihar are either totally deprived of or these items account for only an insignificant proportion. Again a higher skewness in the distribution of consumption expenditure on marriage and other social ceremonies in Punjab than in Bihar may be on account of higher degree of demonstration effect and other status-value considerations.

Finally, it is equally interesting to observe that consumption elasticities in the case of many food and non-food items are higher for Punjab labour households than for those of Bihar households. In a sense, our data tend to maintain the quantitative as well as qualitative superiority of the consumption basket of the labour households in the progressive region of Punjab than in backward Bihar. In this regard, our results indicate that not only the labour households of Punjab are enjoying a higher level of living compared with those of Bihar, their propensity to expend out of every incremental income is also higher, compared to that of the latter.

POLICY RECOMMENDATIONS

An important implication of our findings concerning the employment-income-consumption differentials between rural labour households of Punjab and Bihar is a clear manifestation of the fact that while the Punjab model of rural economic transformation has succeeded in making a decisive impact on the magnitude of rural poverty, that of Bihar on the other hand, has not. This is most certainly due to the fact that growth itself has eluded the State so far. Whatever growth has taken place, particularly in the agricultural sector, has been punctuated by periodic ups and downs, often by big margins and till today the State has not succeeded in insulating itself from such instabilities. Keeping apart the extremely archaic agrarian structure typical of the rural Bihar, the lack of adequate and sustained growth process has contributed to the low level of earnings against equally arduous human labour put in by rural labour households. Can the Punjab model of transformation of rural economy be transferred to Bihar is, therefore, a natural question to be answered by this study. Before answering this question, it is worthwhile to briefly recapitulate some striking features of Punjab and Bihar agriculture. For example rising commercialisation of agriculture, assured and fairly equitable distribution of irrigation facilities, well developed network of village link roads and power facilities, growing and dynamic rural institutions, fairly high level of farm mechanisation, progressive State patronage etc., are some of the outstanding features of Punjab model of economic transformation. In comparison, feudal and semi-feudal rural institutions, poor irrigation base in one part of the State and devastating floods in the other, poor infrastructural facilities, growth resisting institutional set up, low level of farm mechanisation, caste ridden social set-up, perfunctory and uncommitted role played by the State, underline the inherent weaknesses of Bihar agriculture. However, in view of the continuing and expectedly high dependence of the vast majority of rural labour households on agricultural employment, a lasting solution to the problem of poverty has to be sought by synchronizing the development efforts in the farm as well as the non-farm sectors. In the farm sector itself, there is tremendous scope for diversification. Extreme dependence on crop production alone can never be the answer for low levels of gainful employment. Supplementary activities such as dairying and poultry must be encouraged and institutionally supported on a big scale. Perhaps, the political economy of the prevailing agrarian realities may not come in the way of such a strategy. This does not, however, negate the possibilities of creating additional productive employment in crop production. To remind ourselves, a very striking feature of Punjab model of rural transformation has been its assured and fairly equitable irrigation base brought about by many institutional packages. This strong irrigation base, coupled with the availability of rural infrastructural facilities is, in fact, considered to be the sheet-anchor of agricultural development in Punjab. It can, therefore, be argued that for promoting wage-paid on-farm employment/ earnings in rural Bihar (and other backward States), the additional productive and gainful employment can be created through multiple cropping by means of proper water management, power and transport (or road) facilities for rural use, strengthening institutional credit institutions, and so on. It also requires the search for short duration, quick-maturing, photosensitive H.Y.V. seeds. The multiple cropping will not only increase the demand for labour but also push up the level of earnings which, in turn, may reduce the severity of the problem of poverty of such households. This strategy to promote wage-paid on-farm employment through water management alongwith the provision of H.Y.V. seeds, fertilizers and credit expansion, shall work simultaneously, on two points. On the one hand, the would-be outmigrants should avail themselves of more avenues of productive employment in their own areas, and on the other, it will add up to the employment and earning levels of the labour households in the areas of inmigration (i.e. Punjab in our case).

The awkward situation of Bihar labourers working nearly for the same number of days in a year but deriving half, or even less, the income compared with Punjab will be rectified through the above policy actions. In one word, the expansion of agricultural productivity alone is a necessary condition for raising per day on-farm earnings of the labour households.

As suggested above, it is essential to promote self-employment among the rural poor. In this direction, subsidiary occupations such as dairying, poultry and piggery may be developed in a big way. It can be achieved by means of providing subsidized inputs, credit liberalisation and providing market facilities for the products of such activities. These are expected to be helpful in mollifying the severity of the problem of poverty. Moreover, in the absence of these crucial requirements and infra-structural facilities, other non-farm employment promotion programmes such as rural industrialisation and development of cottage and small scale industries may fail to generate additional employment on any significant scale. Further, for promoting gainful employment through various rural development programmes among the rural poor, well co-ordinated policy packages are needed. It is, therefore, desired that the choice among alternative programmes for using public and private resources to promote avenues of gainful employment for the rural poor is evaluated against the social objectives. Therefore, only such massive programmes of rural works need to be launched as may aim at expanding the efficiency of rural infra-structural facilities on the one hand, and, improving the earning position of the rural poor, on the other.

Thanks to a much less rigid caste structure, and the availability of diverse avenues of non-farm employment, the Punjab has been witnessing a great degree of inter-generational (and perhaps, intra-generational) occupational mobility. The Bihar scenario is a sharp contrast. Here, the caste rigidities have acquired proverbial notoriety. The economic situation is governed largely by semi-feudal production relations. These structural weaknesses of the rural Bihar have tended to strengthen further the socio-economic and political hold of the rural oligarchy over the rural labour households. It is not, therefore, surprising and as is testified by some studies,[2] that the public funds for the development of infrastructural facilities and additional funds for alleviation of poverty have been appropriated by the rural rich in connivance with the corrupt Indian bureaucracy. To put the record straight, in the given structural milieu, policy interventions of the poverty alleviation type as embodied in the various 'target group programmes' in the name of the poor have very largely tended to benefit the non-poor. Consequently, dominant classes in rural India in general and backward areas in particular, have come to wield enormous social, economic and political control over the mostly illiterate, socially downtrodden and economically weak rural labour households which, in turn, has further tended to strengthen the feudal and semi-feudal rural institutions. There is enough empirical evidence that suggests that the existing power structure, instead of being serious about the desired structural change, is doing its utmost to dodge such a change. As such there are no sweeping hopes anywhere in sight in the near future in this regard. In our opinion, the limited options, therefore, are the development of agriculture in the backward areas, increased diversification of the rural economy through promoting dairying/poultry enterprises, increasing the rural-urban contact by developing rural infrastructure and a carefully planned process of rapid agro-industrialisation.

NOTES

1. For outstanding contributions on labour absorption in Asian and Indian Agriculture respectively, please see S. Ishikawa, (1978); *"Labour Absorption in Asian Agriculture"*, International Labour Organisation, Bangkok; and International Labour Organisation (1978); *Labour Absorption in Indian Agriculture: Some Exploratory Investigations*, Bangkok.
2. Pradhan H. Prasad (1985); "Poverty and Agricultural Development", *Economic and Political Weekly*, Vol. XX, No. 50, December 14, pp. 2221-2224; and M.L. Dantwala (1987); "Growth and Equity in Agriculture", *Indian Journal of Agricultural Economics*, Vol. 42, No. 2, April-June, pp. 149-159.

APPENDIX-1 A

Wages of Agricultural Labourers : Empirical Evidence

In the wake of the Green Revolution in India, attempts have been made to study the wage rates of hired agricultural labourers. Some research workers have attempted to examine the seasonal variations of the wage rates and/or its relation to unemployment in agriculture. The general conclusion that emerges from their findings is that there exist seasonal fluctuations in the wage rates between various agricultural operations but such differences between agricultural months are not so important.[1] Some scholars, while attempting to examine the factors affecting the wage rates for agricultural labourers conclude that irrigation or multiple cropping do generate a positive response not only in the wage income but also in the daily wage rates for agricultural labourers.[2] A few research workers have also undertaken to make a comparison of the wage rates for different category of workers, viz., pure wage earners and wage-earners-cum-small farmers. It has been observed that earning per day for those who worked as employees on others' farms was higher for pure wage earners than for wage earners-cum-small farmers.[3] In some studies, an attempt has been made to study wage rates for attached and casual labourers. It has been argued that on account of differences in seasonal demand for labour, social and economic deprivation of attached labourers and uncertainty of employment of the casual labourers in general, wage rate for the casual labourers is higher, compared with their attached counterparts.[4] In addition to the above, a number of studies on the trend[5] in money and real wage rates for agricultural labourers have appeared over the years. It needs to be pointed out that on account of differences in coverage of time and area, data base, methodology, etc., the results of different studies on the trend in money and real wages are not strictly comparable. This limitation apart, these studies provide some interesting insights into the issue of trend in agricultural wages especially after the onset of the Green Revolution. For instance, in most such studies, it has been observed that under the impact of new farm technology, money wages of agricultural labourers have increased. There has, however, been a conflicting evidence in so far as real wages are concerned.

Some studies point out that the Green Revolution or agricultural development in general has not been significantly helpful in raising the wage rates in real terms.[6] It has been observed that even though agricultural production has significantly increased under the impact of the new farm technology, yet real wages of agricultural labourers have either remained stagnant[7] or slightly declined,[8] instead of increasing.

In his well-known attempts[9] based on data for agricultural labourers, Bardhan has tried to demonstrate his point by comparing the changes in money and real wage rates in Punjab and Kerala. In his earlier attempt[10] he maintained that between Punjab and Kerala money wage rates for agricultural labour increased faster in Kerala than in Punjab during the period 1956-57 to 1964-65. This development assumes significance in view of the fact that production growth was faster in Punjab than in Kerala and cost of living was of the same order in the two. In his later attempt[11] by extending the period of his earlier attempt to 1970-71, he observed that the initial decline in the real wage rates in Punjab was only a temporary phenomenon and an increase was noticeable in real wage rates since mid-sixties: Again, what is interesting is the fact that compared with Punjab, in States such as Kerala where new farm technology has not made as perceptible a dent as in the former, real wage rates have gone up much faster. This rapid increase in the real wage rates of farm labour in Kerala over Punjab has occurred, maintains Bardhan, owing to the powerful and efficient organisation of agricultural labourers. Some other studies with different data[12] base have also come out with conclusions as are consistent with that of Bardhan's findings. However, some studies point out that even if it is conceded that wage rates have registered some increase as some of the scholars make us believe, the share of such wages in the total agricultural income has declined due to the fact that growth rate of overall agricultural production has far outpaced the increase in real wages.[13]

While refuting this pessimistic view, some studies strike an optimistic note by observing that there has taken place a significant increase in real wages in the Green Revolution area as a result of the introduction of new farm technology. The trend has been so at least in the later years of the Green Revolution. Consequently, it has been argued that there exists a positive association between real wage rates and the impact of new farm technology.[14] Still further if labour is assumed to include family as well as hired labour, then factor share of labour in the total agricultural income has also gone up.[15]

Though the afore-mentioned studies provide some useful insights into the issue pertaining to real wages, yet their operational significance is handicapped due to certain limitations. First, as said earlier, these studies have different database, cover different areas, relate to different periods of time and follow different methodologies. As such, their results are not strictly comparable. Second, apart from methodological errors, in most such studies, an attempt has not been made to differentiate between the daily wage and yearly wage. A higher daily wage may not be inconsistent with low yearly wage, if the introduction of the new agricultural technology causes displacement of human labour. It has been observed that such differences are there between Punjab — the throbbing heartland of the Green Revolution and other areas and even within Punjab between the pre-and post Green Revolution periods. Third, generalisations regarding the trend in real wages cannot be made from these studies alone since the observations made in most[16] studies pertain to the very early years of the Green Revolution. And last, what is important is not the trend in real wages alone but also the trend in the levels of living of agricultural labourers. In this regard, it is important to note that no only the extent of increase or decrease in the consumption standards of agricultural labourers in the wake of the Green Revolution has been inadequately probed, the available evidence has also remained largely inconclusive. In other words, some studies venturing on the temporal relationship between the incidence of rural poverty and agricultural growth have come out with two divergent views regarding the trend in the incidence of rural poverty, their methodological constraints however notwithstanding. While some studies have maintained that the incidence of rural poverty has increased over time,[17] there are others which have argued that poverty and agricultural development are related the other way round.[18]

The preceding discussion shows that the trend in real wages as also in the incidence of rural poverty in the wake of agricultural transformation in India, have remained debatable issues. Though the debate has not fully settled as yet, the available evidence largely supports inverse association between agricultural growth and rural poverty. In this context, a comparison of per day and overall earning/income levels as undertaken in the present study, assumes added significance in more than one respects. First, we can test the validity of trickle-down of gains (both in terms of per day/yearly earnings and incidence of poverty), accruing from agricultural transformation in areas representing sharp contrast. Second, our concern is mainly with those households who are commonly designated as poor. And finally, our choice of a later year i.e. 1980-81 is also useful in a way that it incorporates the possibility of agricultural transformation having consolidated itself more solidly, compared with the earlier years.

NOTES

1. Nilkantha Rath and R.V. Joshi (1966), "Relative Movements of Agricultural Wage Rates and Cereal Prices: Some Indian Evidence", *Artha Vijnana,* Vol. 8, No.2, June, pp. 115-132; N. Krishnaji (1971), "Wages of Agricultural Labour", *Economic and Political Weekly,* Vol. VI, No. 39, Reviews of Agriculture, September 25, pp. A148-A151; Robert W. Herdt and Edward A. Baker (1972), "Agricultural Wages, Production and the High-Yielding-Varieties", *Economic and Political Weekly,* Vol. VII, No. 13, Review of Agriculture, March, 25, pp. A23-A30; S.V. Sethuraman (1972), "Seasonal Variations in Unemployment and Wage Rate: Implications for Rural Employment Programme", *Economic and Political Weekly,* Vol. VII, No. 24, June, 10, pp. 1149-1155; and, S.S. Grewal and H.S. Bal (1974), "Impact of Green Revolution on Agricultural Wages in Punjab", *Indian Journal of Agricultural Economics,* Vol. XXIX, No. 3, Conference Number, July-September, pp. 40-47.
2. Kalpna Bardhan (1973), "Factors Affecting Wage Rats for Agricultural Labour", *Economic and Political Weekly,* Vol. VIII, No. 26, Review of Agriculture, June 30, pp. A56-A64; S.S. Grewal and H.S. Bal (1974), "*Op. Cit,* p. 43; V.N. Mishra and S.B. Lal Gupta (1974), "Productivity, Wages and its Determinants in Gujarat Agriculture; An Inter-District Analysis", *Indian Journal of Agricultural Economics,* Vol. XXIX, No. 3, Conference Number, July-September, pp. 22-34; and D.P. Singh (1980), "The Impact of the Green Revolution on the Poor", *Agricultural Situation in India,* Vol. XXXV, No. 5, pp. 317-325.
3. P.K. Bardhan (1973), "Variations in Agricultural Wages A Note", *Economic and Political Weekly,* Vol. VIII, No. 21, May 26, pp. 947-950.
4. Rakesh Basant (1984), "Attached and Casual Labour Wage Rates", *Economic and Political Weekly,* Vol. XIX, No. 9, March 3, pp. 390-396.
5. P.K. Bardhan (1970), "Green Revolution and Agricultural Labourers in India", *Economic and Political Weekly,* Vol. V, No. 29-31, Special Number, July, pp. 1239-1246; ——— (1973), *Op. Cit,* N. Krishnaji (1971), *Op. Cit,* A.V. Jose,

(1974), "Trends in Real Wage Rats of Agricultural Labourers", *Economic and Political Weekly,* Vol. IX, No. 13, Review of Agriculture, March 30, pp. A25-A30; ——— (1988), "Agricultural Wages in India", *Economic and Political Weekly,* Vol. XXIII, No. 26, Review of Agriculture, June 25, pp. A46-A58; Deepak Lal (1976), "Agricultural Growth, Real Wages and the Rural Poor in India", *Economic and Political Weekly,* Vol. XI, No. 26, Review of Agriculture, June 26, pp. A47-A61; Sheila Bhalla (1979), "Real Wage Rates of Agricultural Labourers in Punjab 1961 — 77: A Preliminary Analysis", *Economic and Political Weekly,* Vol. XIV, No. 26, Review of Agriculture, June 30, pp. A57-A68; and G. Parthasarathy and K. Adiseshu (1982), "Real Wages of Agricultural Labourers in Andhra Pradesh : Two Decades of Stagnation", *Economic and Political Weekly,* Vol. XVII, No. 31, July, 31, pp. 1245-1248.

6. P.K. Bardhan (1970), *Op. Cit.* p. 1240; and N. Krishnaji (1971), *Op. Cit.* p. A151.
7. G. Parthasarthy and K. Adiseshu (1982), *Op. Cit.* p. 1248.
8. P.K. Bardhan (1974), *Green Revolution and Agricultural Labourers,* Rural Development for Weaker Sections, Indian Society of Agricultural Economics and Indian Institute of Management, Ahmedabad, Seminar Series, XII; and C.T. Kurien (1980), "Dynamics of Rural Transformation: A Case Study of Tamil Nadu," *Economic and Political Weekly,* Vol. XV, Nos. 5-7, Annual Number, February, pp. 365-390.
9. P.K. Bardhan (1970 and 1973), *Op. Cit.*
10. P.K. Bardhan (1970), *Op. Cit.*
11. P.K. Bardhan (1973), *Op. Cit.*
12. For example, A.V. Jose while using Agricultural Wages in India (AWI) data and covering 1956-57 — 1971-72 period came out with conclusions as are consistent with those of Bardhan's based on N.S.S. data. For further details, please see, A.V. Jose (1974), *Op. Cit.,* However, regarding the reliability of AWI data; please see, V.M. Rao (1972), "Agricultural Wages in India — A Reliability Analysis", *Indian Journal of Agricultural Economics,* Vol. XXVII, No. 3, July-Sept., pp. 38-57.
13. John W. Mellor, and Uma J. Lee (1973), "Growth Linkages of the New Foodgrain Technologies", *Indian Journal of Agricultural Economics,* Vol. XXVIII, No. 1, pp. 35-55; G. Parthasarthy and D.S. Prasad (1974), "Response to and Impact of H.Y.V. Rice according to Land Size and Tenure in a Delta Village", *Developing Economies,* Vol. XII, No. 2, pp. 182-198; and C.H. Hanumantha Rao (1975), *"Technological Change and Distribution of Gains in Indian Agriculture",* The Macmillan Company of India Ltd., Delhi.
14. James, W. Gough (1971), "Agricultural Wages in Punjab and Haryana: A Note", *Economic and Political Weekly,* Vol. VI, No. 13, Review of Agriculture, March 27, pp. A19-A20; H. Laxminarayan (1973), *The Social and Economic Implications of the large Scale Introduction of High Yielding Varieties of Wheat in Haryana,* Agro Economic Research Centre, Delhi, (Part I & II); ——— (1977), "Changing Conditions of Agricultural Labourers", *Economic and Political Weekly,* Vol. XII, No. 43, October 22, pp. 1817-1820; and, Biswanath Santra (1974), "Trends in Agricultural Wages: Some Indian Evidence", *Indian Journal of Agricultural Economics* Vol. XXIX, No. 3, Conference Number, July September, pp. 1-16.
15. Dayanath, Jha (1974), "Agricultural Growth, Technology and Equality", *Indian*

Journal of Agricultural Economics, Vol. XXIX, No. 3, Conference Number, July-September, pp. 207-216; and, G.C. Mandal (1983), "Share of Agricultural Labour in National Agricultural Product : An Exercise", *Economic and Political Weekly,* Vol. XVIII, Nos. 52-53, Review of Agriculture, December 24-31, pp. A151-A155.

16. In needs to be pointed out here that studies by Bhalla and Parthasarthy and Adiseshu are exceptions here in as much as they cover some later years as well. However, as Bhalla's study deals with Punjab i.e. one of the areas for the present study, it deserves some comments. Bhalla, while examining the strength of the Green Revolution in raising farm productivity and huge influx of the migrant labour into agricultural labour force into Punjab,has made some interesting observations for the period 1961-77. She observes that while agricultural output fell short of 1961 levels only in 1963, real wages have fallen short in several years due to presence of inflationary pressures. Further, while agricultural output increased by approximately two and half times during the period compared with 1961 levels, real wages of agricultural labourers registered a meagre increase of only 15.0 per cent. She further demonstrates that operationwise difference in real wages can be largely explained by farm output growth.
17. P.K. Bardhan (1973), "On the Incidence of Rural Poverty in India of the Sixties", *Economic and Political Weekly,* Vol. VIII, Nos. 4-6, Annual Number, February, pp. 245-254; Indira Rajaraman (1975), "Poverty, Inequality and Economic Growth: Rural Punjab 1960-61 — 1970-71", *Journal of Development Studies,* Vol. XI, No. 4, pp. 278-290; C.T. Kurien (1980), *Op. Cit.;* Joan P. Mencher (1974), "Conflicts and Contradictions in the Green Revolution", *Economic and Political Weekly,* Vol. IX, Nos. 6-8, Annual Number, February, pp. 309-323. ———— (1980), "The Lessons and Non-Lessons of Kerala: Agricultural Labourers and Poverty", *Economic and Political Weekly,* Vol. XV, Nos. 41-43, Special Number, October, pp. 1718-1802; and Ashwani Saith (1981), "Production, Prices and Poverty in Rural India", *Journal of Development Studies,* Vol. XVII, No. 2, January, pp. 196-213, see especially, p. 206.
18. C.H. Hanumantha Rao (1977), "Agricultural Growth and Rural Poverty: Some Lessons from Past Experience", *Economic and Political Weekly,* Vol. XII, Nos. 33 & 34, Special Number, August, pp. 1369-1374: Montek S. Ahluwalia (1978), "Rural Poverty and Agricultural Performance in India", *Journal of Development Studies,* Vol. XIV, No. 3, April, pp. 298-323; ———— (1986), "Rural Poverty, Agricultural Production and Prices: A Reexamination", in John W. Mellor and Gunvant M. Desai (ed), *Agricultural Change and Rural Poverty: Variations on a theme by Dharm Narayan,* Oxford University Press, New Delhi, p. 73; K.N. Nivair (1981), "Agricultural Labourers and Poverty: A Comment", *Economic and Political Weekly,* Vol. XVI, No. 38, September, pp. 1549-1552; J.N. Sinha (1981), "Full Employment and Anti-Poverty Plan: The Missing Link", *Economic and Political Weekly,* Vol. XVI, No. 50, December 12, pp. 2043-2052; Pradhan H. Prasad (1985), "Poverty and Agricultural Development", *Economic and Political Weekly,* Vol. XX, No. 50, December, pp. 2221-2224; and G.K. Chadha (1986), *"The State and Rural Economic Transformation: The Case of Punjab 1950-85",* Sage Publications India Pvt. Ltd., New Delhi.

APPENDIX-1 B

Studies on Rural Unemployment/Underemployment

Owing to its far-reaching socio-economic implications, the problem of unemployment/underemployment is now universally acknowledged as a major economic challenge confronting most of the over-populated predominantly agriculture economies. Much useful thought has been given to the understanding of this vital issue.[1] Of late, concepts of rural unemployment/underemployment have grown not only in terms of number or variety, but in terms of analytical sophistication as well.[2] While it is not possible to make an appraisal of all the studies conducted so far on the issue under consideration, but a brief review of some major developments is expected to pave the way for a more useful analysis.

The Surplus Labour: Estimations Dichotomy

That there exists considerable surplus work-force in the farm sector of most of the predominantly agricultural underdeveloped economies, is a well known fact. Following the lead given by Nurkse, the issue of surplus work force has fascinated a great deal of attention over the years. Consequently, it has come to be realised that this surplus labour force, if withdrawn from the farm sector and engaged in the alternative non-farm work, is bound to play a crucial role in the economic betterment of these countries characterised by mass poverty. But can this surplus labour force be withdrawn without affecting adversely the production in the farm sector? This issue has been a subject of heated controversy. Broadly speaking, two diametrically divergent views have emerged on the subject. One view is that this redundant surplus labour force can be withdrawn without introducing important changes in agricultural reorganisation or suffering production losses in the farm sector.[3] The second view[4] runs contrary to it.

It needs to be stressed here that the controversy as mentioned above, has mainly centred around the definition and methods of estimation of unemployment/underemployment on the one hand, and, the generalisations about the phenomenon for the country as a whole on the basis of a single objective reality, on the other. In a sense, most of the controversy about the definitions of unemployment has arisen largely because of a strong urge to seek, defend or use a single criterion which may be useful for all purposes. But this urge is evidently irrational and unnecessary.[5]

Although the decennial census and the National Sample Surveys provide countrywide data on employment and unemployment in India, yet such data are not strictly comparable due to the fact that the concepts of unemployment/underemployment and the methods of arriving at such estimates are not the same in the two sources referred to above. For instance, for being qualified as employed, a person should put-in some regular work of more than one hour a day throughout the greater part of the working season for seasonal occupations and an employment for 15 days preceding the day of visiting the household (or date of enquiry) in non-seasonal occupations.[6] Compared with this, a person according to the N.S.S. can be qualified as employed if he or she had worked on any day in the reference week.[7] It is not out of place to mention that while the former source includes only those labourers in the labour force as are seeking work; the latter source includes both those who are seeking work or are available for work. Both these sources in general and the latter in particular, follow a labour force approach. Further while taking into account the recognition aspect, it combines time, income and willingness criteria for qualifying a person as employed/ unemployed. Accordingly, a person can be treated as unemployed under the two following conditions:

(i) the person must be in need of employment which he overtly or covertly recognises, i.e. he must seek a job or he must be available for one; and
(ii) the person must be without employment involuntarily.

It is important to note that different research workers have advanced different criteria for the estimation of unemployment/ underemployment. For instance, Sen has put forward as many as three such criteria for the estimation of unemployment/underemployment. These three criteria are popularly known as production or 'productivity criterion', the 'income criterion' and the 'recognition criterion',[8] in the economic literature. In a pioneering attempt Raj Krishna[9] has added yet another criterion viz., the 'time criterion' for the measurement of unemployment/underemployment. It is again important to note that while making use of one or more criteria, various research workers in India have come out with varying estimates of unemployment/underemployment.[10] The latest attempt, which invites some comments in this regard, is by Harbans Singh[11] who has employed time criterion for estimating unemployment/ underemployment among the rural labour households of Punjab and Haryana. Though the study offers some interesting insights into the rate of participation of males and females, determination of wage rate as also the extent of their unemployment/underemployment, yet it suffers from two main limitations. First, it deals with the early phase of the Green Revolution based as it is on 1975-76 data; and, second mandays of employment have not been standardised. In regard to using day as unit of time, Singh argues, "that generally wages are paid in rural areas in terms of number of days worked and not according to the number of hours worked".[12] This argument does not hold everywhere. First, in areas such as Bihar and some other parts of rural India, where beck-and-call system is in operation, the attached farm servants (though employed on yearly or six monthly basis) have the option of working outside as and when there is no work on employers' fields. Second and more important is the fact that in most part of the country in general and Green Revolution areas in particular, wages have come to be paid according to the quantum of work (Contractual Wage Payment) and not according to number of days worked, as Singh argues. It has come to be so at least in peak season operations such as wheat harvesting, paddy transplantation/harvesting and even in operations like weeding and cotton picking etc., in the wake of the Green Revolution in Punjab. Moreover, in peak seasons, driven by sole economic considerations, the workers normally work between 12 to 14 hours a day. Under such circumstances, to treat a day of 12 to 14 hours and a day of 9 to 10 hours in normal on-farm work and a day of 8 hours of non-farm work on the same plane is not justified.

If viewed carefully, Indian studies on unemployment/under-employment suffer from a number of limitations. First, most employment surveys conducted over the years do not take into account the impact of seasonality on the overall incidence of unemployment/underemployment, concerned as they are usually with a very small reference period i.e. a week, a fortnight or a month. Second, in backward areas, agriculture is largely practised as a way of life instead of a commercial activity. It is especially so in the case of small, marginal and sub-marginal farmers. Third, possibility of seeking meaningful answers becomes even more remote, unless the questions to already employed are specifically asked with reference to job opportunity with a known wage, type of work involved, conditions and location of work. Indian studies, by and large, have ignored this aspect. Consequently, highly erratic[13] answers have been obtained from the respondents when asked to State if they were willing to work more so that the extent of their underemployment could be determined. Fourth, because of the existence of self-employment, it has not been possible to have a correct estimate of unemployment/underemployment. Fifthly, most of the empirical studies conducted so far on the estimation of surplus labour have not distinguished between static and dynamic concepts of surplus labour.[14] On account of these limitations, the findings of most of the studies provide only an ambiguous picture of unemployment/ underemployment and leave much scope for guess-work and confusion.[15]

In the light of the above-mentioned discussion, it is pertinent to point out that even though several improvements have been made to the methods of measuring unemployment/underemployment and various types of data are available, but their interpretation and use have posed a number of problems. Further, controversies over refinements of secondary importance or of no great significance in the Indian context have also tended to overshadow the essentials and obscure the useful insights which could otherwise be gained from the material collected over the years. Also, because of these conceptual and other problems, the concept of unemployment or underemployment as the term is generally understood, was not applicable in rural areas. . .the information so derived was of no use for policy purpose. In order to get a meaningful analysis of employment situations in the rural sector, studies have to be conducted within the framework of the rural sector.[16] The present study, therefore, focusses on the employment pattern and income levels of non-cultivating rural labour households in terms of labour-time utilisation and level of earnings raised.

NOTES

1. M.L. Dantwala (1953), "Notes on Some Aspects of Rural Unemployment", in *Indian Journal of Agricultural Economics 1940—64: Selected Readings*, the Indian Society of Agricultural Economics, Bombay, 1965, pp. 273-286; and ——— (1976), "Rural Employment: Facts and Issues", *The Indian Journal of Labour Economics*, Vol. XXII, No. 1 and 2, pp. 1-24.
2. K.N. Raj (1976), "Trends in Rural Unemployment: An Analysis with Reference to Conceptual and Measurement Problems", *Economic and Political Weekly*, Vol. XI, Nos. 31-33, Special Number, pp. 1281-1293.
3. Ragnar Nurkse (1953), *"Problems of Capital Formation in Underdeveloped Countries"*, Oxford University Press, Delhi, P. 35; W. Arthur Lewis (1954), "Economic Development with Unlimited supplies of Labour", Reprinted in A.N. Aggarwala and S.P. Singh ed. (1958), *"The Economics of Underdevelopment"*, Oxford University Press, Delhi, pp. 400-449; John W. Mellor and Robert D. Stevens (1956), "The Average and Marginal Product of Farm Labour in Underdeveloped Economies", *Journal of Farm Economics*, Vol. XXXVIII, August, pp.780-791; P.N. Rosenstein Rodan (1957), "Disguised Unemployment and Underemployment in Agriculture", *Monthly Bulletin of Agricultural Economics and Statistics*, Vol. 6, August, pp. 1-7; Dipak Mazumdar (1959), "The Marginal Productivity Theory of Wages and Disguised Unemployment", *Review of Economic Studies*, Vol. 26, June, pp. 190-197; J.P. Bhattacharjee (1961), "Underemployment Among Indian Farmers: Analysis of the Nature and Extent Based on Data for Bihar", *Artha Vijnana*, Vol. 3 No. 3, reprinted in A.M. Khusro (ed.) (1968), *"Readings in Agricultural Development"*, Allied Publishers Bombay, pp. 488-526; N.A. Mazumdar (1961), *"Some Problems of Underemployment"*, Popular Book Depot, Bombay, 1961; A.K. Sen, (1966), "Peasants and Dualism with or without Surplus Labour", *Journal of Political Economy*, Vol. 74, No. 5, October, pp. 425-448; ———, (1975), *"Employment, Technology and Development"*, Clarendon Press, Oxford, London; Shakuntla Mehra (1966), "Surplus Labour in Indian Agriculture", *Indian Economic Review*, Vol. 1, No. 1 (New Series), pp. 111-129; Tarlok Singh (1969), *"Poverty and Social Changes With A Reappraisal"*, Orient Longmans, Bombay; S.King Seth, abridged (1972), *Gunnar Myrdal's Asian Drama-An Inquiry into the Poverty of Nations"*, Allen Lane, The Penguin Press, see especially Chapters 15, 16, and 18; Ashok Rudra (1973), "Direct Estimation of Surplus Labour in Agriculture", *Economic and Political Weekly*, Vol. III, No. 4-6, Annual Number, February, pp. 277-280; Kanta Ahuja (1978), *"Idle Labour in Village India"*, Manohar Publications, New Delhi; and Harbans Singh (1986), *"Employment Income and Consumption of Rural Labour Households in a Green Revolution Region: A Case Study of Punjab and Haryana"*, Ph.D. Thesis, Jawaharlal Nehru University, New Delhi.
4. Doreen Warriner (1955), *Land Reforms and Economic Development*, Fiftieth Anniversary Commemoration Lectures, National Bank of Egypt, Cairo; Jacob Viner (1957), "Some Reflections on the Concept of Disguised Unemployment", *The Indian Journal of Economics*, Vol. 38, No. 148, July, pp. 17-23; Harry T. Oshima (1958), "Underemployment in Backward Economies: An Empirical Comment", *Journal of Political Economy*, Vol. 66, pp 259-264; Theodore W.

Schultz (1964), "*Transforming Traditional Agriculture*", Lyall Book Depot, Ludhiana, p. 70; and M. Paglin (1965), "Surplus Agricultural Labour and Development: Facts and Figures", *The American Economic Review*, Vol. LV, No. 4, September, pp. 815-834.

5. Raj Krishna (1973), "Unemployment in India", *Economic and Political Weekly*, Vol. VIII, No. 9, March 3, pp. 478-484.
6. Govt. of India, *Census of India*, p. 35. It needs to be pointed out that the underlying instruction was that, "if on the check or the revision round such a person is found to be unemployed, no change in the original entry should be made" and that "a person who is working but was absent from his work during the fifteen days preceding the day on which enumerated or even exceeding the period of fifteen days due to illness or other causes, should be treated as worker".
7. It is worthwhile pointing out that the criteria for a person to be qualified as employed/unemployed as adopted by the NSS has not been consistent because it has varied in the course of different rounds. For instance, in the 11th, 12th and 13th rounds both one day and one week immediately preceding the day of enquiry were taken as the reference period. On the basis of both these reference periods, a person was considered to be employed if he had gainful work on that day. On this basis, a person not having gainful work would be treated as employed if he was either seeking work or belonged to the category of not seeking but available for work. Compared with this, since 14th round, the criterion of being in work has been to have worked at least one day during the reference week. Again from 16th round onwards, persons below the age of 15 or aged 60 years or above have been excluded from the figure of the unemployed even if they are actually seeking work. For further detailed and penetrating review of N.S.S. concepts please see, "Sudhir Bhatacharya, A Note on Employment and Unemployment Concepts Adopted in the National Sample Survey", in *Report of the Committee of Experts on Unemployment Estimates*, Planning Commission Government of India 1970, Appendix 1, pp. 33-38.
8. Amartya Sen (1973), "Poverty, Inequality and Unemployment: Some Conceptual Issues in Measurement", *Economic and Political Weekly*, Vol. VIII, Nos. 31-33, Special Number, August, pp. 1457-1464; and ——— (1975), *Op. Cit*, pp. 5-10 and 31-40.
9. Raj Krishna (1973), *Op. Cit.*
10. Some important studies worth mentioning in the Indian context are, Shakuntala Mehra (1966), *Op. Cit.*; I.Z. Bhatty (1973), "Unemployment: Questions of Measurement and Mitigation", *Yojana*, Vol. 17, January 26, pp. 71-80; Ashok Rudra (1973), *Op. Cit.*; S.K. Rao (1973), "Measurement of Unemployment in Rural India", *Economic and Political Weekly*, Vol. VIII, No. 39, Review of Agriculture, September, pp. A78-A90; Raj Krishna (1973), *Op. Cit.*; Kanta Ahuja (1978), *Op. Cit.;* and Yoginder K. Alagh (1979), "Indian Planning in the Eighties", *Economic and Political Weekly*, Vol. XIV, Nos. 30-32, Special Number, August, pp. 1273-1282.
11. Harbans Singh (1986), *Op. Cit.*
12. Harbans Singh (1986), *Ibid.*, p. 110.
13. Kanta Ahuja (1978), *OP. Cit.*, p. 6.

14. Manabendu Chattopadhya (1977), "Some Aspects of Employment and Unemployment in Agriculture", *Economic and Political Weekly*, Vol. X, No. 39, Review of Agriculture, September, p. A66.
15. Ashok Rudra (1973), *Op. Cit.*, p. 277.
16. Planning Commission, Government of India (1970), *Op. Cit.*, Chapter 3, pp. 14-21.

TABLE A-3.1: Number of Households in Each Expenditure Class in Punjab and Bihar

Sl. No.	Punjab		Bihar	
	Category (Per Capita Yearly Expenditure in Rs.)	Number of Households	Category (Per Capita Yearly Expenditure in Rs.)	Number of Households
1.	Below 600	18	Below 360	26
2.	600 — 640	14	360 — 380	17
3.	640 — 680	14	380 — 400	16
4.	680 — 720	21	400 — 420	17
5.	720 — 760	23	420 — 440	18
6.	760 — 800	23	440 — 460	21
7.	800 — 840	20	460 — 480	21
8.	840 — 880	21	480 — 500	19
9.	880 — 920	16	500 — 530	18
10.	920 — 960	18	530 — 560	21
11.	960 — 1020	16	560 — 590	15
12.	1020 — 1080	18	590 — 620	20
13.	1080 — 1200	17	620 — 660	16
14.	1200 — 1320	18	660 — 720	17
15.	1320 — 1500	16	720 — 800	15
16.	1500 — 1680	13	800 — 920	11
17.	1680 and Above	14	920 and Above	12

TABLE A-4.1: Labour-Use and Level of Earnings Per Acre of Gross Cropped Area in Punjab and Bihar

Sl. No.	Village/s	Labour-Une Per Acre of Gross Cropped Area			Level of Earnings Raised Per Acre of Gross Cropped Area		
		PJB	BHR	di	PJB	BHR	di
1.	V1	38.49	59.46	-35.27	383.31	353.39	8.47
2.	V2	19.25	28.11	-31.52	184.06	164.24	12.07
3.	V3	20.47	23.98	-14.64	194.20	129.74	49.68
4.	V4	19.68	37.62	-47.69	181.37	191.98	-5.53
5.	V5	27.09	9.60	182.19	253.41	52.36	383.98
6.	V6	24.08	40.92	-41.15	219.79	222.79	-1.35
7.	V7	15.65	49.69	-68.50	136.68	245.03	-44.22
8.	V8	21.88	26.50	-17.43	188.00	133.16	41.18
	All	20.99	29.52	-28.90	193.02	156.60	23.26

Note: 1. PJB = Punjab 2. BHR = Bihar 3. $di = \dfrac{PJBi - BHRi}{BHRi}$

i is the Per Capital Net Household Income of the Poor Household in *i*th village.

TABLE A-8.1: Distribution of Consumption Expenditure by Decile Groups in Punjab and Bihar

Sl. No.	Decile Group	State	% of consumers	Percentage Share of Consumption Expenditure									
				Cereals & its products	Gram and pulses	Edible oils	Milk & its products	Meat egg fish	Vegetables & fruits	Gur & sugar	Salt & spices	Processed food	Total food items
1	2	3	4	5	6	7	8	9	10	11	12	13	14
1.	First	PJB	6.82	7.28	8.26	8.54	4.96	5.81	7.57	8.13	8.48	6.43	7.08
		BHR	8.23	7.10	8.01	7.61	0.00	6.85	5.01	5.03	8.20	5.91	6.85
2.	Second	PJB	8.27	7.97	8.29	8.53	5.81	6.47	8.82	9.05	9.43	7.38	7.81
		BHR	8.58	8.27	8.74	7.96	0.50	11.03	8.59	4.95	8.45	6.85	7.91
3.	Third	PJB	8.69	7.66	7.75	8.58	6.34	6.88	9.63	9.29	9.18	9.47	7.96
		BHR	8.06	8.15	8.22	8.40	1.72	4.47	6.25	3.77	8.95	8.15	7.85
4.	Fourth	PJB	8.99	8.11	8.63	8.34	7.77	8.08	8.00	9.06	8.93	7.63	8.17
		BHR	7.71	8.30	7.91	8.30	0.29	3.88	5.72	3.72	8.46	4.84	7.70
5.	Fifth	PJB	8.81	8.43	8.81	8.87	8.86	11.47	9.61	9.18	8.75	9.70	8.82
		BHR	8.93	8.96	9.27	8.82	2.50	9.22	9.56	4.70	9.16	7.98	8.66

Contd.

TABLE A-8.1 *Contd.*

1	2	3	4	5	6	7	8	9	10	11	12	13
6. Sixth	PJB	10.20	9.22	9.22	9.40	10.65	7.19	10.15	10.06	9.72	9.93	9.69
	BHR	9.92	10.00	9.70	10.11	7.88	5.14	9.22	7.49	10.12	8.10	9.78
7. Seventh	PJB	9.35	9.54	9.86	10.17	11.42	18.20	10.41	9.85	10.64	9.25	10.07
	BHR	11.33	11.04	10.67	11.08	10.30	9.19	10.29	11.58	10.59	13.53	11.03
8. Eighth	PJB	11.83	11.94	11.44	11.52	12.78	11.93	11.12	10.57	11.04	10.91	11.74
	BHR	11.62	12.00	11.79	11.99	13.41	12.99	11.65	17.80	11.63	11.10	12.03
9. Ninth	PJB	13.16	13.08	12.45	11.50	14.52	6.96	10.97	12.19	10.71	13.65	12.90
	BHR	11.56	11.79	12.25	11.83	20.10	8.50	14.00	16.87	11.65	14.67	12.36
10. Tenth	PJB	13.88	16.78	15.29	14.55	16.89	17.01	13.72	12.62	13.13	15.65	15.76
	BHR	14.06	14.39	13.44	13.90	43.30	28.73	19.71	24.09	12.79	18.87	15.83
All	PJB	100.00	100.00	100.00	100.00	100.00	100.00	100.00	100.00	100.00	100.00	100.00
	BHR	100.00	100.00	100.00	100.00	100.00	100.00	100.00	100.00	100.00	100.00	100.00
Gini's Co-efficient	PJB		0.002	0.002	0.018	0.096	0.036	0.030	0.043	0.032	0.024	0.029
	BHR		0.015	0.003	0.007	0.531	0.144	0.109	0.253	0.019	0.111	0.041

Contd.

TABLE A-8.1 *Contd.*

Sl. No.	Decile Group	State	Percentage Share of Consumption Expenditure										
			Fuel & light	Clothing	Footwear	Education	Conveyance	Medicine & health	Durable goods	Misc. goods serv.	Non-food items	Social ceremonies	Total HH exp.
1	2	3	15	16	17	18	19	20	21	22	23	24	25
1.	First	PJB	8.30	5.46	3.90	2.97	10.88	6.93	4.30	9.85	6.90	5.37	6.91
		BHR	8.21	5.76	1.87	2.74	9.01	7.86	3.64	5.90	6.61	1.15	6.32
2.	Second	PJB	9.10	6.57	5.11	3.51	8.15	8.70	6.17	11.73	7.97	2.11	7.37
		BHR	8.79	4.11	6.77	1.57	9.76	4.47	8.43	8.09	6.31	5.59	7.50
3.	Third	PJB	9.56	5.74	3.08	3.60	7.44	9.30	5.94	10.23	7.63	2.73	7.46
		BHR	7.95	10.01	11.75	1.18	8.14	4.41	2.09	8.06	8.03	5.48	7.66
4.	Fourth	PJB	9.35	3.89	2.04	6.26	9.99	8.24	6.63	10.22	7.21	3.73	7.61
		BHR	8.31	5.58	8.64	3.13	1.17	3.97	3.47	6.07	6.10	11.35	7.81
5.	Fifth	PJB	9.79	8.93	7.15	8.34	10.19	10.80	9.52	9.90	9.50	6.92	8.79
		BHR	9.53	8.69	11.91	16.26	6.51	7.53	3.80	8.32	8.83	6.59	8.50

Contd.

TABLE A-8.1 *Contd.*

1	2	3	15	16	17	18	19	20	21	22	23	24	25
6.	Sixth	PJB	10.16	9.22	6.12	14.31	9.83	9.57	12.74	10.45	10.11	5.70	9.43
		BHR	9.19	9.94	4.51	18.22	11.52	12.29	9.86	10.56	10.19	7.68	9.65
7.	Seventh	PJB	10.06	8.66	8.22	10.30	8.15	9.63	18.70	10.63	10.13	13.30	10.35
		BHR	10.98	10.16	5.10	21.74	8.79	11.92	15.07	10.09	10.91	9.80	10.91
8.	Eighth	PJB	11.00	14.28	11.01	13.31	9.37	12.21	9.02	9.86	11.82	8.52	11.49
		BHR	10.76	11.23	12.33	12.14	12.11	15.90	17.58	14.62	12.28	14.08	12.25
9.	Ninth	PJB	11.38	12.28	22.65	22.64	12.98	10.22	10.61	8.45	12.27	26.29	13.90
		BHR	11.81	16.11	6.65	12.15	15.81	16.68	9.45	12.64	13.94	16.60	12.93
10.	Tenth	PJB	11.31	24.97	30.72	14.76	13.02	14.40	16.37	8.68	16.46	25.33	16.69
		BHR	14.47	18.41	30.47	10.87	17.18	14.97	26.61	15.65	16.80	21.68	16.47
	All	PJB	100.00	100.00	100.00	100.00	100.00	100.00	100.00	100.00	100.00	100.00	100.00
		BHR	100.00	100.00	100.00	100.00	100.00	100.00	100.00	100.00	100.00	100.00	100.00
Gini's Co-efficient		PJB	0.164	0.164	0.320	0.184	0.055	0.021	0.072	0.151	0.032	0.299	0.049
		BHR	0.003	0.116	0.148	0.131	0.067	0.129	0.232	0.063	0.079	0.197	0.060

Note: (1) PJB: Punjab (2) BHR: Bihar (3)HH: Household.

BIBLIOGRAPHY

Agarwala, B.K. and Deb, P.C. (1971), *Inter-generational Occupational Mobility in Ludhiana,* Punjab Agricultural University, Ludhiana.

Aggarwala, A.N. and Singh, S.P. ed. (1958), *The Economics of Underdevelopment,* Oxford University Press, Delhi.

Ahluwalia, Montek S. (1978), "Rural Poverty and Agricultural Performance in India", *Journal of Development Studies*, Vol. XIV, No. 3, April, pp. 298-323.

——, (1986), "Rural Poverty, Agricultural Production and Prices: A Reexamination", in Mellor, John W. and Desai, Gunvant M., (ed), "*Agricultural Change and Rural Poverty : Variations on a Theme by Dharm Narayan*", Oxford University Press, New Delhi, pp. 59-75.

Ahuja, Kanta (1978), *Idle Labour in Village India*, Manohar Publications, New Delhi.

Allen, R.G.D. and Bowley, A.L., (1935), *Family Expenditure: A Study of its Variations*, London.

Baldota, S.N. (1964), "Bias in Income Elasticity Estimates Derived from Expenditure per family Data – A Note", *Artha Vijnana*, Vol. 6, No. 1, pp. 37-43.

Bardhan, Kalpana (1973), "Factors Affecting Wage Rates for Agricultural Labour", *Economic and Political Weekly*, Vol. VIII, No. 26, Review of Agriculture, June 30, pp. A 56-A 64.

——, (1977), "Rural Employment, Wages and Labour Markets in India – A Survey of Research", *Economic and Political Weekly*, Vol. XII, No. 26-28, June 25, Review of Agriculture, July 2 and July 9, pp. A 34 - A 48, 1062-1074 and 1101-1118.

Bardhan, P.K. (1970), "Green Revolution and Agricultural Labourers in India", *Economic and Political Weekly*, Vol. V, No. 29-31, Special Number, July, pp. 1239-1246.

——, (1970), "On the Minimum Level of Living and the Rural Poor", *Indian Economic Review*, Vol. 5, (New Series), April, pp. 129-136.

——, (1970), "Green Revolution and Agricultural Labourers: A Correction", *Economic and Political Weekly*, Vol. V, November 14, p. 1861.

——, (1973), "On the Incidence of Poverty in Rural India of the Sixties", *Economic and Political Weekly*, Vol. VIII, Nos. 4-6, Annual Number, February, pp. 245-254.

——, (1973), "Variations in Agricultural Wages: A Note", *Economic and Political Weekly*, Vol. VIII, No. 21, May 26, pp. 947-950.

—— and Srinivasan, T.N. ed. (1974), *Poverty and Income Distribution in India*, Statistical Publishing House, Calcutta.

Basant, Rakesh (1984), "Attached and Casual Labour Wage Rates", *Economic and Political Weekly*, Vol. XIX, No. 9, March 3, pp. 390-396.

Bhaduri, Amit (1973), "A Study in the Agricultural Backwardness under Semi-Feudalism", *The Economic Journal*, Vol. 83, March, pp. 120-137.

Bhalla, G.S. (1974), *Changing Agrarian Structure in India-A Study of the Impact of Green Revolution in Haryana*, Meenakshi Prakashan, Meerut, Delhi.

—— and Chadha, G.K. (1983), *Green Revolution and the Small Peasant: A Study of Income Distribution among Punjab Cultivators*, Concept Publishing Company, New Delhi.

Bhalla, Sheila (1976), "New Relations of Production in Haryana Agriculture", *Economic and Political Weekly*, Vol. XI, No. 13, Review of Agriculture, March 27, pp. A 23 - A 30.

——, (1979), "Real Wage Rates of Agricultural Labourers in Punjab 1961-77: A Preliminary Analysis", *Economic and Political Weekly*, Vol XIV, No. 26, Review of Agriculture, June 30, pp. A 57-A 68.

Bhattacharya, Sudhir (1970), "A Note on Employment and Unemployment Concepts adopted in the National Sample Survey", *Report of the Committee of Experts on Unemployment Estimates*, Planning Commission, Govt. of India, Appendix 1, pp. 33-38.

Billings, Martin, H. and Singh, Arjan (1970), "Mechanisation and Rural Employment with some Implications for Rural Income Distribution", *Economic and Political Weekly*, Vol. V, No. 26, Review of Agriculture, June 27, pp. A61-A72.

——, (1972), "The Effect of Technology on Farm Employment in India", in *Comparative Experience of Agricultural Development in Developing Countries of Asia and the South-East Since World War*

II, Indian Society of Agricultural Economics, Bombay, pp. 332-342.

Box, G.E.P. and Cox, D.R. (1964), "An Analysis of Transformation", *Journal of the Royal Statistical Society*, Series B, pp. 211-243.

Byres, T.J. (1972), "The Dialects of India's Green Revolution", *South Asian Review*, Vol. 5, No. 2, January, pp. 99-116.

Chadha, G.K. (1979), *Production Gains of New Agricultural Technology*, Publication Bureau, Panjab University, Chandigarh.

——, (1986), *The State and Rural Economic Transformation: The Case of Punjab 1950-85*, Sage Publications India Pvt. Ltd., New Delhi.

Chandra, Bipin (1982), *A Study of Migrant Agricultural Labour in Punjab*, (Mimeo), Centre for Historical Studies, Jawaharlal Nehru University, New Delhi, August.

Chuta, Enyinna and Liedholm Carl (1979), *Rural Non-Farm Employment: A Review of the State of the Art*, MSU Development Paper No. 4, Department of Agricultural Economics, Michigan State University, East Lansing, Michigan.

Dandekar, V.M. and Rath, N. (1971), "Poverty in India-1: Dimensions and Trends", *Economic and Political Weekly*, Vol VI, No. 1, January 2, pp. 25-48.

——, (1971), "Poverty in India-II: Policies and Programmes", *Economic and Political Weekly*, Vol. VI No. 2, January 9, pp. 106-146.

Dantwala, M.L. (1953), "Notes on Some Aspects of Rural Employment", in *Indian Journal of Agricultural Economics 1940 - 64: Selected Readings*, Indian Society of Agricultural Economics, Bombay, 1968, pp. 2"3-286.

——, (1979), "Rural Employment: Facts and Issues", *The Indian Journal of Labour Economics*, Vol XXII, No. 1 and 2, April-July, pp. 1-24.

——, (1987), "Growth and Equity in Agriculture", *Indian Journal of Agricultural Economics*, Vol XLII, No. 2, April-June, pp. 149-159.

Dutt, R. Palme (1979 Rep), *India Today*, Manisha Granthalaya (P) Ltd., Calcutta.

Falcon, Walter P. (1972), "The Green Revolution: Generation of Problems", in *Comparative Experience of Agricultural Development in Developing Countries of Asia and the South-East Since World War II*, Indian Society of Agricultural Economics, Bombay, pp. 295-315.

Frank, Andre Gunder (1973), "Reflections on Green, Red and White Revolutions in India", *Economic and Political Weekly*, Vol. VIII, No. 3, January 20, pp. 119-124.

Frankel, Francine R. (1969), "India's New Strategy for Agricultural Development", *Journal of Asian Studies*, Vol. 28, No. 4, August, pp. 693-710.

——, (1971), *India's Green Revolution : Economics Gains and Political Costs*, Oxford University Press, Bombay.

Gough, James W. (1971), "Agricultural Wages in Punjab and Haryana: A Note", *Economic and Political Weekly*, Vol. VI, No. 13, Review of Agriculture, March 27, pp. A19-A20.

Grewal, S.S. and Bal, H.S. (1974), "Impact of Green Revolution on Agricultural Wages in Punjab", *Indian Journal of Agricultural Economics*, Vol. XXIX, No. 3, Conference Number, July-September, pp. 40-47.

Griffin, Keith and Ghose, A.K. (1979), "Institutional Structure, Technological Change and Growth in Poor Agrarian Economies: An Analysis with reference to Bengal and Punjab", *World Development*, Vol. 7, No. 4/5, pp. 385-396.

Gupta, Devender B. (1973), *Consumption Pattern in India, A Study of Inter-Regional Variations*, Tata McGraw-Hill Publishing Co. Ltd., Bombay.

Harrison, J.Q. (1972), *Agricultural Modernisation and Income Distribution*, Ph.D. Thesis, Princeton University, Princeton.

Hayami, Yujiro (1981), "Agrarian Problems in India: An East and Southeast Asian Perspective", *Economic and Political Weekly*, Vol. XVI, No. 16, Special Article, April 18, pp. 707-712.

Herdt, R.W. and Baker, E.A. (1972), "Agricultural Wages, Production and High Yielding Varieties", *Economic and Political Weekly*, Vol. VII, No. 13, Review of Agriculture, March 25, pp. A23-A30.

Houthakker, H.S. (1953), "Compensated Changes in Quantities and Qualities Consumed", *Review of Economic Studies*, Vol. XIX (3), No. 5, pp. 55-64.

—— and Prais, S.J. (1955), *The Analysis of Family Budgets*, Cambridge University Press, Cambridge.

Indian Society of Agricultural Economics (1966), *Indian Journal of Agricultural Economics (1940-64) : Selected Readings*, Bombay.

——, (1971), *Comparative Experience of Agricultural Development in Developing Countries of Asia and the South-East Since World War II*, Bombay.

International Labour Organisation (1978), *Labour Absorption in Indian Agriculture : Some Exploratory Investigations*, Bangkok.

Ishikawa, S. (1978), *Labour Absorption in Asian Agriculture*, International Labour Organisation, Bangkok.

Islam, Rizwanul (1986), "Non-Farm Employment in Rural Asia : Issues and Evidence", in Shand, R.T. (ed), *Off-farm Employment in the Development of Rural Asia*, National Centre for Development Studies, Australian National University, Canberra, Australia, pp. 153-173.

Iyenger, N. Sreenivasa (1967), "Some Estimates of Engel Elasticities Based on N.S.S. Data", *Journal of Royal Statistical Society*, Series A (General), Vol. 130, pp. 84-97.

Jha, Dayanath, (1974), "Agricultural Growth, Technology and Equity", *Indian Journal of Agricultural Economics*, Vol. XXIX, No. 3, Conference Number, July-September, pp. 207-216.

Jose, A.V. (1974), "Trends in Real Wage Rates of Agricultural Labourers", *Economic and Political Weekly*, Vol. IX, No. 13, Review of Agriculture, March 30, pp. A25-A30.

——, (1988), "Agricultural Wages in India", *Economic and Political Weekly*, Vol. XXIII, No. 26, Review of Agriculture, pp. A46-A58.

Kahlon, A.S. and Singh, Gurbachan (1973), *Social and Economic Implications of Large Scale Introduction of HYVs of Rice in Punjab with Special Reference to Gurdaspur District*, Punjab Agricultural University, Ludhiana.

Kaushal, M.P., (1969), *Mechanisation of Agriculture and Community Relations:*, Paper read at 10th All India Sociological Conference, Delhi.

Krishnaji, N. (1971), "Wages of Agricultural Labour", *Economic and Political Weekly*, Vol VI, No. 39, Review of Agriculture, September 25, pp. A148-A151.

Krishna, Raj (1973), "Unemployment in India", *Economic and Political Weekly*, Vol. VIII, No. 9, March 3, pp. 475-484.

——, (1974), "Measurement of Direct and Indirect Employment Effects of Agricultural Growth with Technical Change" in Edwards, E.O. (ed), *Employment in Developing Nations : Report on a Ford Foundation Study*, Columbia University Press.

Kundu, Amitabh (1981), "Measurement of Poverty : Some Conceptual Issues", *Anvesak*, Vol. XI, Nos. 1-2, June-December, pp. 80-96.

Kurien, C.T., (1978), "The Dynamics of Rural Transformation : A Case Study of Tamil Nadu", *Economic and Political Weekly*, Vol XV, No. 5-7, Annual Number, February, pp. 365-390.

Ladejinsky, Wolf, (1969a), "The Green Revolution in Punjab : A Field Trip", *Economic and Political Weekly*, Vol. IV, No. 26, Review of Agriculture, June 28, pp. A73-A83.

——, (1969), "Green Revolution in Bihar–The Kosi Area: A Field Trip" *Economic and Political Weekly*, Vol. IV, No. 39, *Review of Agriculture*, September 27, pp. A147-A162.

——, (1970), "Ironies of India's Green Revolution", *Foreign Affairs,* Vol. 48, No. 4, July, pp. 758-768.

Lal, Deepak (1976), "Agricultural Growth, Real Wages and Rural Poor in India", *Economic and Political Weekly*, Vol. XI, No. 26, Review of Agriculture, June 26, pp. A47-A61.

Lakdawala, D.T. (1978), "Growth, Unemployment and Poverty", *The Indian Journal of Labour Economics,* Vol. XXI, No. 1-2, April-July, pp. 1-30.

Laxminarayan, H. (1973), *The Social and Economic Implications of High Yielding Varieties of Wheat in Haryana*, Agro Economic Research Centre, Delhi, Part I and II.

——, (1977), "Changing Conditions of Agricultural Labourers", *Economic and Political Weekly*, Vol. XII, No. 43, October 22, pp. 1817-1820.

Lewis, A.W. (1954), "Economic Development with Unlimited Supplies of Labour", Reprinted in A.N. Aggarwala and S.P. Singh ed. (1958), *The Economics of Underdevelopment*, Oxford University Press, Delhi, pp. 400-449.

Lewis, John P. (1970), "Wanted in India : A Relevant Radicalism", *Economic and Political Weekly*, Vol. V, No. 29-31, Special Number, July, pp. 1211-1226.

Mahajan, B.M. and H. (1981), "Effects of Grouping of Observations on Co-efficient of Determination in Engel Curve Analysis", *Artha Vijnana*, Vol. XXIII, No. 4, pp. 352-365.

Mandal, J.C. (1983), "Share of Agricultural Labour in National Agricultural Product : An Exercise", *Economic and Political Weekly*, Vol. XVIII, No. 52-53, Review of Agriculture, December 24-31, pp. A151-A155.

Mazumdar, D. (1957), "The Marginal Productivity Theory of Wages and Disguised Unemployment", *Review of Economic Studies*, Vol. XXVI, pp. 190-197.

Mazumdar, N.A. (1970), "Intra-Sectoral Dualism and Agricultural Growth", *Economic and Political Weekly*, Vol. V, No. 13, Review of Agriculture, March 28, pp. A2-A5.

Medovoy, A.I. (1988), *The Indian Economy*, Progress Publishers, Moscow.

Mehra, Shakuntala (1966), "Surplus Labour in Indian Agriculture", *Indian Economic Journal*, Vol I (New Series), pp. 111-129.

Mellor, John W. and Desai, Gunvant M. ed. (1986), *Agricultural Change and Rural Poverty : Variations on a theme by Dharm Narayan*, Oxford University Press, New Delhi.

Mencher, J.P. (1974), "Conflicts and Contradictions in the Green Revolution", *Economic and Political Weekly*, Vol. IX, Nos. 6-8, Annual Number, February, pp. 309-323.

——, (1980), "The Lessons and Non-Lessons of Kerala: Agricultural Labourers and Poverty", *Economic and Political Weekly*, Vol. XV, Nos. 41-43, Special Number, October, pp. 1781-1802.

Minhas, B.S. (1970), "Rural Poverty, Land Redistribution and Development", *Indian Economic Review*, Vol. 5 (New Series), April, pp. 97-128.

Ministry of Labour (1954), *Report on Intensive Survey of Agricultural Labour, Employment, Underemployment, Wages and Levels of Living*, Vol. 1, Government of India, New Delhi.

——, (1960), *Report on the Second Agricultural Labour Enquiry : 1956-57*, Vol. I, Government of India, New Delhi.

Mukerjee Ramkrishna (1961), "Rural Class Structure in West Bengal", reprinted in Desai, A.R. ed. (1969), *Rural Sociology in India*, Popular Prakashan Pvt. Ltd., Bombay, pp. 281-286.

Mukhopadhyay, Swapna and Lim, Chee Peng ed. (1985), *The Rural Non-Farm Sector in Asia*, Asian and Pacific Development Centre, Kuala Lumpur, Malaysia.

National Council of Applied Economic Research (1962), *Long Term Projections of Demand and Supply of Selected Agricultural Commodities, 1960-61 to 1975-76*, New Delhi.

Ninan, K.N. (1981), "Agricultural Labourers and Poverty : A Comment", *Economic and Political Weekly*, Vol. XVI, No. 38, September, pp. 1549-1552.

Nurkse, Ragnar (1953), *Problems of Capital Formation in Underdeveloped Countries*, Oxford University Press, London.

Oberai, A.S. and Ahmed, Iftikhar (1981), "Labour Use in Dynamic Agriculture: Evidence from Punjab", *Economic and Political Weekly*, Vol. XVI, No. 13, Review of Agriculture, March, 28, pp. A2-A4.

Oshima, Harry T. (1958), "Underemployment in Backward Economies : An Empirical Comment", *Journal of Political Economy*, Vol. LXVI, No. 3, June, pp. 259-264.

Paglin, Morton (1965), "Surplus Agricultural Labour and Development : Facts and Figures", *The American Economic Review*, Vol. LV, No. 4, September, pp. 815-834.

Panikar, P.G.K. (1980), *Inter-regional Variations in Calorie Intake*, Working Paper No. 111, Centre for Development Studies, Trivandrum.

Parthasarthy, G. (1971), *Green Revolution and the Weaker Sections*, Thacker and Company, Bombay.

——, (1973), *Changes in Rice Farming and Their Social and Economic Impact : A Case Study of a Delta Village in Andhra*, (Mimeo).

——, (1979), "Inter-State Variations in Unemployment and Growth of Agriculture", *The Indian Journal of Labour Economics*, Vol. XXII, No. 1 and 2, April-July, pp. 45-50.

—— and Adiseshu K. (1982), "Real Wages of Agricultural Labourers in Andhra Pradesh : Two Decades of Stagnation", *Economic and Political Weekly*, Vol. XVII, No. 31, July 31, pp. 1245-1248.

Patnaik, Utsa (1986), "The Agrarian Question and Development of Capitalism in India", *Economic and Political Weekly*, Vol. XXI, No. 18, Special Article, May 3, pp. 781-793.

Planning Commission (1970), *Report of the Committee of Experts of Unemployment Estimates*, Government of India, New Delhi.

—— (1990), "Employment: Past Trends and Prospects for 1990s", Working Paper, Government of India, New Delhi.

Prasad, Pradhan H. (1973), "Production Relations : Achilles' Heel of Indian Planning", *Economic and Political Weekly*, Vol. VIII, No. 19, Special Article, May 12, pp. 869-872.

——, (1974), "Reactionary Role of Usurer's Capital in Rural India", *Economic and Political Weekly*, Vol. IX, Nos. 32-34, Special Number, August, pp. 1305-1308.

——, (1975), "Agrarian Unrest and Economic Change in Rural Bihar: Three Case Studies", *Economic and Political Weekly*, Vol. X, No. 24, Special Article, June 14, pp. 931-937.

——, (1976), "Poverty and Bondage", *Economic and Political Weekly*, Vol. XI, Nos. 31-33, Special Number, August, pp. 1269-1272.

——, (1980), "Rising Middle Peasantry in North India", *Economic and Political Weekly*, Vol. XV, Nos. 5-7, Annual Number, February, pp. 215-219.

——, (1985), "Poverty and Agricultural Development", *Economic and Political Weekly*, Vol. XX, No. 50, December 14, pp. 2221-2224.

——, (1987), "Agrarian Violence in Bihar", *Economic and Political Weekly*, Vol. XXII, No. 22, Special Article, May 30, pp. 847-852.

——, (1987), "Towards a Theory of Transformation of Semi-Feudal Agriculture", *Economic and Political Weekly*, Vol. XXII, No. 31, Special Article, August 1, pp. 1287-1290.

Raj, K.N. (1976), "Trends in Rural Unemployment in India: An Analysis with Reference to Conceptual and Measurement Problem", *Economic and Political Weekly*, Vol. XI, Nos. 31-33, August, pp. 1281-1293.

Radhakrishna, R. (1977), "Approximate Determination of Indifference Surface from Family Budget Data", *Artha Vijnana*, Vol. 19, No. 3, pp. 247-258.

—— and Sastry, S.A.R. (1979), "Rural Poverty : A Historical Perspective", *Productivity*, Vol. XIX, No. 4, January-March, pp. 531-543.

Rajaraman, Indira (1975), "Poverty, Inequality and Economic Growth : Rural Punjab, 1960-61 – 1970-71, *Journal of Development Studies*, Vol. XI, No. 4, July, pp. 278-290.

Rao, C.H. Hanumantha (1975), *Technological Change and Distribution of Gains in Indian Agriculture*, The Macmillan Company of India Ltd., Delhi.

——, (1977), "Agricultural Growth and Rural Poverty: Some Lessons from Past Experience", *Economic and Political Weekly*, Vol. XII, Nos. 33-34, Special Number, August, pp. 1369-1374.

Rao, V.M. (1972), "Agricultural Wages in India – A Reliability Analysis", *Indian Journal of Agricultural Economics*, Vol. XXVII, No. 3, July-September, pp. 38-57.

Rodan, P.N. Rosenstein (1957), "Disguised Unemployment and Under-development in Agriculture", *Monthly Bulletin of Agricultural Economics and Statistics*, Vol. 6, August, pp. 1-7.

Rudra, Ashok (1970), "In Search of the Capitalist Farmer", *Economic and Political Weekly*, Vol. 5, No. 25, Review of Agriculture, June 27, pp. A85-A87.

——, (1971), "Employment Patterns in Large Farms of Punjab", *Economic and Political Weekly*, Vol. VI, No. 26, Review of Agriculture, June 26, pp. A89-A94.

——, (1973), "Direct Estimation of Surplus Labour in Agriculture", *Economic and Political Weekly*, Vol. VIII, Nos. 4-6, Annual Number, February, pp. 277-280.

Saith, Ashwani (1981), "Production, Prices and Poverty in Rural India", *Journal of Development Studies*, Vol. XVII, No. 2, January, pp. 196-213.

Santra, Biswanath (1974), "Trends in Agricultural Wages: Some Indian Evidence", *Indian Journal of Agricultural Economics*, Vol. XXIX, No. 3, Conference Number, July-September, pp. 1-16.

Sastry, S.A.R. (1980), "A Survey of Literature on Poverty, Income Distribution and Development", *Artha Vijnana*, Vol. XXII, No. 1, March, pp. 62-88.

——, (1980), "Poverty, Concepts and Measurement", *The Indian Journal of Economics*, Vol. LXI, No. 241, October, pp. 241-260.

Sau, Ranjit (1973), "On the Essence and Manifestation of Capitalism in Indian Agriculture", *Economic and Political Weekly*, Vol. VIII, No. 13, Review of Agriculture, March 31, pp. A27-A30.

——, (1978), "Growth, Employment and Removal of Poverty", *Economic and Political Weekly*, Vol. XIII, Nos. 31-33, Special Number, August, pp. 1279-1284.

Schultz H., (1938), *The Theory and Measurement of Demand*, University of Chicago Press, Chicago (1972 edn.).

King, S. Seth, abridged (1971), Gunnar's Myrdal *Asian Drama: An Inquiry into the Poverty of Nations (1968)*, Allen Lane, The Penguin Press, London, Chapters 15-16, pp. 177-211.

Sen, A.K. (1973), "Poverty, Inequality and Unemployment: Some Conceptual Issues in Measurement", *Economic and Political Weekly*, Vol. VIII, Nos. 31-33, Special Number, August, pp. 1457-1464.

——, (1976), "Poverty: An Ordinal Approach to Measurement", *Econometrica*, Vol. 44, March, pp. 219-231.

Sen, B., (1970), "Opportunities in the Green Revolution", *Economic and Political Weekly*, Vol. V, No. 13, Review of Agriculture, March 28, pp. A33-A40.

Sethuraman, S.V. (1972), "Seasonal Variations in Unemployment and Wage Rate: Implications for Rural Employment Programme", *Economic and Political Weekly*, Vol. VII, No. 24, June 10, pp. 1149-1155.

Shand, R.T. ed. (1986), *Off-Farm Employment in the Development of Rural Asia*, Vol. I and II, National Centre for Development Studies, Australian National University, Canberra, Australia.

Sharma, Manmohan (1982), "Impact of Migratory Labour on the Rural Economy of Punjab State", *Man and Development*, Vol. IV, No. 3, September, pp. 66-130.

Singh Balvir (1968), *Consumption Functions in India*, Ph.D. Thesis (Unpublished), University of Delhi.

Singh, D.P. (1980), "The Impact of Green Revolution on the Poor", *Agricultural Situation in India*, Vol. 35, August, pp. 317-325.

Singh, Harbans (1986), *Employment, Income and Consumption of Rural Labour Households in a Green Revolution Region: A Case Study of Punjab and Haryana*, Ph.D. Thesis, Jawaharlal Nehru University, New Delhi.

Sinha, J.N. (1978), "Rural Employment Planning: Dimensions and Constraints", *Economic and Political Weekly*, Vol. XIII, Nos. 6-7, Annual Number, February, pp. 295-313.

——, (1981), "Full Employment and Anti-Poverty Plan: The Missing Link", *Economic and Political Weekly*, Vol. XVI, No. 50, December 12, pp. 2043-2052.

Srivastava, Uma K. et. al. (1971), "Green Revolution and Farm Income Distribution", *Economic and Political Weekly*, Vol. VI, No. 52, Review of Agriculture, December, pp. A163-A172.

Stigler, G.J. (1954), "The Early History of Empirical Studies on Consumption Behaviour", *Journal of Political Economy*, Vol. LXII, No. 2, April, pp. 95-113.

Stone, R. (1954), *The Measurement of Consumer Expenditure and Behaviour in the United Kingdom 1920-38*, Cambridge University Press, Cambridge, Vol. 1.

Sukhatme, P.V. (1978), "Assessment of Adequacy of Diets of Different Income Levels", *Economic and Political Weekly*, Vol. XIII, Nos. 31-33, Special Number, August, pp. 1373-1384.

Thorner, Daniel and Alice (1965), "Types of Employer – Labour Relationship in Indian Agriculture", in *Indian Journal of Agricultural Economics (1940-64) : Selected Readings*, The Indian Society of Agricultural Economics, Bombay, pp. 287-302.

Vaidyanathan, A. (1974), "Some Aspects of Inequalities in Living Standard in Rural India", In Bardhan, P.K. and Srinivasan T.N. (Ed.) *op. cit.*, pp. 215-241.

Verma, Ravi (1959), "Income Elasticity of Demand for Foodgrains: A Regional Approach", *Artha Vijnana*, Vol. 1, No. 4, pp. 271-281.

Viner, Jacob (1957), "Some Reflections on the Concept of Disguised Unemployment", *Indian Journal of Economics*, Vol. XXXVIII, No. 148, July, pp. 17-23.

Vyas, V.S. (1964), *Agricultural Labour in Four Indian Villages*, Sardar Patel Agro Economic Research Centre, Vallabh Vidyanagar, Sardar Patel University, Gujarat.

INDEX